178 7 8 4 2 0

ECONOMICS FOR A CIVILIZED SOCIETY

Economics for a Civilized Society

Greg Davidson

Astrophysics Program Analyst
National Aeronautics and Space Administration

Paul Davidson

J. Fred Holly Chair of Excellence in Political Economy
University of Tennessee

W. W. Norton & Company
New York   London

Library of Congress Cataloging in Publication Data.
Davidson, Greg.
Economics for a civilized society/by Greg Davidson and Paul
Davidson.—1st ed.
p.   cm.
Includes index.
1. Economics. 2. Neoclassical school of economics. I. Davidson,
Paul. II. Title.
HB171.D28   1988
330–dc19   88–12559

ISBN 0-393-02653-1

W. W. Norton & Company, Inc., 500 Fifth Avenue, New York, NY 10110.

Printed in Great Britain.

1 2 3 4 5 6 7 8 9 0

To Louise and Tamah, and the rest of our family; Diane, Robert, Cindy, and Christopher

Contents

Preface

How did we come to write *Economics for a Civilized Society*? In many ways we have been working on this book for years, in our learning, teaching and writings. In our careers as a Professor at Pennsylvania, Rutgers and Tennessee, and as a student at Swarthmore and Harvard, we have frequently seen the intellectual history of economic thought fall to waste as it is distorted to fit within the current conventional wisdom known as 'neoclassical economics'.

At one extreme of neoclassical economics is the intellectual despotism of a discipline which is more ideological than empirical. More commonly we have found intelligent and well-intentioned economists whose work is needlessly constrained and ruined by the weakness of these neoclassical conceptual foundations upon which they have built their analysis. Ours is not the cynical message that economists do not know anything – the problems we see come more from the things that economists 'know' that just are not so.

Our goal is to provide a civilized approach to the important economic policy issues that face modern societies. Unfortunately, conventional neoclassical economic thought cannot penetrate the operations of an enlightened society. Yet Western societies have invested a great deal of intellectual effort in developing the database and analytical tools of this conventional analytical analysis. Hence we have tried to salvage what can be used, if properly modified for a civilized setting, of the conventional wisdom.

We therefore provide a civilized analytical structure which can support work already done in neoclassical economics, when the latter is modified to integrate valid critiques of the conventional wisdom. In so doing we hope not only to improve our understanding of the orthodox approach, but also to probe the crucial interactions between the self-interest basis of neoclassical economics and the civic values to which the orthodox approach is blind.

An understanding of the boundaries of conventional analysis and how one can go beyond this restrictive barbaric approach is not merely of academic importance. Whether we like it or not, current economic theory has become the bedrock of our public policy decision-making process as well as the basis for our philosophy of society and its laws. Economic theory not only affects our bank accounts, but it also, in large part, determines how our society is fed and housed, and even how much we think our society can afford to defend ourselves against epidemics or enemies threatening the very viability of our population. Conventional economic theory does influence our views of right and wrong, and can thereby change the context of our lives. Our hope is to provide guidance towards a more civilized approach to all these issues.

We would like to thank the following people for their comments on aspects of this manuscript: John Kenneth Galbraith, Robert Reich, Martin Kessler, Fred Zimmerman, Stephen Benko, William Kushner, Alan Plumley, Ellen Freeberg, John Powell, and Ellie Prockop. Others who have helped us with their comments on earlier aspects of what became the basis of this book include Amatii Etzioni, James Verdier, George Brockway, Dotty Robyn, Marty Linsky, John Dunlop, Malcolm Salter, Steve Kelman, Richard Zeckhauser, David Elwood, Harvey Liebenstein, Shah Ashiqazziman, Peter Swiderski, Ken Sharpe, and Charles Gilbert. Not everyone mentioned above will agree with all of our findings but we appreciate the insights that their comments provided.

We would also like to express our appreciation to the late Sidney Weintraub who taught us, in separate economics courses almost thirty years apart, the importance of the statement of William Stanley Jevons that 'In matters of philosophy and science authority has been the great opponent of truth. A despotic calm is usually the triumph of error. In the republic of the sciences sedition and even anarchy are beneficial in the long run to the greatest happiness of the greatest number.' From Sidney Weintraub we learned much – but especially we learned that, although it is more pleasant and easy to agree than disagree, it is necessary to speak out against the fallacies which find their way into the conventional wisdom.

Finally, we wish to thank Louise and Tamah, whose contributions (editorial and other) would have earned them mention above, except that they also deserve special recognition for tolerating us as we frequently woke up at three in the morning to write down 'just one more idea'.

Washington, DC   GREG DAVIDSON
Knoxville, Tennessee   PAUL DAVIDSON

1 In Pursuit of Civilization

What's the difference between love and prostitution? If the question was posed to those whose economic philosophy has shaped American politics in the 1980s, the answer would be that prostitution is a valuable commodity, while love is worthless (you see, people are willing to pay for prostitution). This philosophy behind the recent swing to the right is known as conservative economics.

This conservative strain of economics has moved beyond the classroom as a subtle shaper of both our perception of national issues and our roles as individuals in society. Conservative economics focuses exclusively on one of the two major types of human motivation: self-interest. Unfortunately the other source of human inspiration – what we refer to as civic values – is locked out of the conservative economic framework. Consequently, when debating national policy we can compare the costs and benefits of prostitution, but are blind to the importance of love.

Nations are built on the motivating forces of both self-interest and civic values. When self-interest and civic values are combined, they reinforce each other so that a nation can enjoy both prosperity and justice. Difficulties arise when society is governed by only one of these two forces because you cannot buy justice in the marketplace, and similarly, you cannot build prosperity on civic pride alone. The art of civilized government, very simply, is to combine self-interest and civic values so that society may reap the benefits of each.

In the last twenty years we have come to view the nation's future in terms of choices between competing parts of our heritage – self-interest *or* civic values. Liberals and conservatives have each adopted a fragment of the national heritage as the centrepiece for their policies; social values for liberals and 'the bottom line' of self-interest for conservatives. Hence as the political pendulum has swung, the policy choices which the nation has been offered have, at best, provided improvements in one sphere at dreadful costs in the other. The liberalism of the Great Society programmes of the 1960s sapped the incentives behind the profit motive, just as the politics of self-interest in the 1980s have eroded and degrade civic values.

Unemployment and inflation are both evils. To deny jobs and income to those who want to work, that is, to promote unemployment in order to combat inflation, violates basic civilized values. To permit inflation, on the other hand, undermines the wealth earned by individuals acting in accordance with their own self-interest. Liberals see the civic need for a fully employed society, even if this causes inflation and thus devalues the accumulated assets held by the wealthy. Conservatives, on the other hand, demand that inflation be stopped, even if this means that some people lose their jobs and businesses as a result. The tragedy of economic policy over the last two decades is that is has been based on a false premise of conservative economics – namely that it is impossible to maintain a prosperous full employment society that is also protected from inflation.

Considerable progress in reducing the twin evils of unemployment and inflation could have been achieved, if only we were willing to go beyond the choices posed by liberal or conservative economics alone. To fight unemployment *and* inflation we must make use of both self-interest and civic values in our economic government. Until we are governed by principles which are based on both self-interest and civic values we will be doomed to political trade cycles of economic decline and social injustice interspersed with periods of relative prosperity. The transitory economic triumphs, if any, of one Presidency will merely inflame the problems of the next. In the recent past, while fleeting victories convinced first liberals and then conservatives that their hour of triumph paved the way towards a brighter future, the only constant has been the slow erosion of the resources of America and the free world.

As a result of our inconsistent government, we have witnessed decline in our civilization, both as individuals and as a nation. The right to vote, which is surely one of the most basic foundations of our democracy, was exercised in the 1986 US elections by less than 40 per cent of those who even bothered to register. The duty to pay taxes has eroded to the point where a third of the US population avoid paying their full share. In order to replace the taxes that the cheaters avoid, the taxes on honest taxpayers are more than 10 per cent higher. As a nation, we have lost the ability to cope with inflation without resorting to barbaric policies which work only if a significant portion of our population remains unemployed. We have accepted the notion that the poor not only deserve their fate, but that they are to be blamed for it (as if only a character flaw could keep a person in poverty). We have watched the break-down of one of the best accomplishments of American civilization, the post-Second

World War international economic order, without even a lingering memory of why we helped create it.

As our civic institutions erode, we lose our defences against the dangers that the passage of time may bring. History is filled with the wreckage of nations which did not realize the importance of maintaining their civilization until it was too late. The greatest danger facing any civilization is when its people forget the value of their own culture and institutions. When the Roman Empire fell to Attila in 453 AD it was the Huns who were better educated and possessed the more civilized government; the core of Roman society had already collapsed. Most great nations in history have eventually lost the spark which made their civilization great, and there is no reason to believe that America can avoid this fate – but the more we understand the importance of civic values in our own lives, the more likely we are to maintain them.

Where does this hope come from? In the twenty-five years after the Second World War the United States *did* experience unprecedented economic prosperity in concert with a vibrant and progressive civic society. The benefits of economic competition were achieved in harmony with the benefits of civic and social values, and that prosperity helped propel most nations of the world along the same path of economic growth.

Today, the conservative philosophy has captured a position of prominence, but civilized government still continues to be practised in many places. For example, Thomas Peters and Robert Waterman's *In Search of Excellence* identifies a number of corporations which have successfully mixed organizational values with the pursuit of profit. In some of our political institutions there still remains a spark of civic spirit enlightening government, as seen, for example, in Massachusetts Governor Michael Dukakis's initiative to combine social values with the incentives of self-interest in revitalizing the civic norms supporting voluntary tax-paying.

A civilized society shows compassion and caring for all members of the community. It nurtures sensitivity to the needs of others and the desire to deal honestly and openly with all. A civilized society provides the opportunity for all to earn a livelihood, while it encourages excellence in all endeavours that people undertake independent of the monetary rewards for such activities.

On the other hand, a society which requires that some members of the system be denied the sharing of economic gains and community participation in order for the economy to function is uncivilized.

Economic policies which require certain groups in society be denied employment and a livelihood in order to discipline an inflationary economy are simply barbaric. To base social prosperity on the hardship of others is a savage philosophy of government.

If a nation can thrive only on the hardships of some groups, it can not be called civilized – especially when the society is wealthy and has the capacity to produce far more goods and services than it currently does. Yet, some very influential bankers, finance writers, economists, and politicians have echoed White House spokesman Larry Speakes in declaring that unemployment is 'the price you have to pay for bringing down inflation'. David Stockman, when he was Director of the Office of Budget and Management put it more bluntly when he told the US Chamber of Commerce that unemployment is 'part of the cure, not the problem'.

We often think of either self-interest *or* civic values as the important determinant of human behaviour, but too little attention has been focused on what happens when dollars and duty interact. To discuss the design of civilized public policies, we must first examine the analytical and philosophical views of those who advocate a system based solely on self-interest as well as the views of those who attempt to enlist civic values to help achieve specific policy objectives.

We recognize that our book is not the first to call attention to the limitations of self-interest as a governing mechanism for society. But unlike many of these other attacks on conservative economic philosophy, our argument, as developed in Chapter 2, is based on a fundamental analytical distinction. Our analysis involves the conceptual difference between the external incentives of individual rewards and punishments which motivate behaviour in conservative economic analysis, and the internal incentives which motivate more complex social behaviour, such as loyalty, duty, the pursuit of excellence, love, and compassion. The concept of internal incentives permits us, in Chapter 2, to investigate in some depth the nature of civic values and how these when combined with self-interest can provide civilized principles for improving our economic environment.

Chapter 3 will provide a perspective on why economists, whose analysis rests on self-interest as the sole motivating force, tend to provide advice which rarely works and is almost always uncivilized.

The next five chapters will then develop a civilized approach to some specific major economic problems facing our nation.

As may have become clear already, we are consciously making a distinction between liberalism and conservatism with which some conservatives (as well as some liberals) may not be comfortable. Some conservatives, such as Milton Friedman, trace their philosophy back to that which went by the name of Liberalism in the eighteenth and nineteenth centuries. Thus they see themselves as the 'true' liberals, in contrast to those who have stolen the title to serve quite antithetical ends. Friedman writes that 'the intellectual movement that went under the name of Liberalism emphasized freedom as the ultimate goal and the individual as the ultimate entity in society'. Other conservatives, however, for example, columnist George Will, have accepted the conservative designation while condemning a solitary focus on free markets and self-interest. Instead conservatives such as George Will have also concerned themselves with the civic virtue of the citizenry – a topic which we identify with a liberal approach.

Nevertheless there are good grounds for making a useful distinction between an economic philosophy based solely on self-interest (which we label conservative) and one based on civic values (which we call liberal). Those who believe in self-interested individuals operating in a free market as the primary form of social organization have far more frequently considered themselves conservatives than liberals – despite the semantic games some like to play. It is clear that if a politician advocates *laissez-faire* economic policies more strongly than his/her opponent, we would not think of calling this politician's economic policies 'liberal'.

Given this distinction between conservatives and liberals based on their reliance on either self-interest or civic values, we can unambiguously trace the linkage between conservative economics and the rise of conservative governments in recent years. In so doing we will be focusing on several basic questions:

(1) *Why economics?* Why is the framework of economics suited to undertake a study of the rules for operating a civilized society?
(2) What is so bad about relying on self-interest to provide civilized policies? What are the strengths and weaknesses of this form of motivation?
(3) Why do conservatives despise and fear government? Why is the conservative view of the undesirability of government interference with individual behaviour a distorted view of the role of government in a civilized society?
(4) What are the dangers posed by organizing government around conservative ideas? How does a singular focus on self-interest

obscure important changes that have occurred in our nation and our economy? What are the dangers to which a government based on conservative principles is vulnerable? What are the attributes of a civilized society that a conservative government does not sustain?

Our discussion must take place in a political context. The United States has been dominated by conservative economic policies in the 1980s and by an over-emphasis on our business culture. Our options for tomorrow are rooted in the trends of today. How did we get here, and what must we regain in order to strike a more even balance between self-interest and civic values? Where does Ronald Reagan's philosophy and his Administration's actions fit; and why have we not heard much from liberal economists during the Reagan years?

We start our discussion at the beginnings of American civilization.

ECONOMICS AND AMERICAN GOVERNMENT

WE THE PEOPLE of the United States, in order to form a more perfect Union, establish justice, insure domestic tranquility, provide for the common defense, promote the general welfare, and secure the blessings of liberty to ourselves and our posterity, do ordain and establish this Constitution of the United States of America.

The Preamble to the Constitution identifies who are the important parties in a discussion of American government – We the People. The Preamble provides guidance as to the meaning and purpose of our government. While the words may be broad enough to encompass several interpretations, they establish basic standards during all phases of the political cycle. The aspirations of our heritage are outlined: justice, domestic harmony, defence, prosperity, and liberty. Our public debate is ultimately oriented around these goals.

We approach the major issues of public policy differently today than in the age of the founding fathers, but we face many of the same concerns. A key difference is that we speak of national policy issues in terms of economics rather than philosophy, using economic language to illuminate the problems that we face. Because of its logical structure and emphasis, conservative economics can only address issues of self-interest. Economics can be a useful guide to wise government, but it must be an economics that goes beyond the limited scope of conventional economic theory. The language of national policy must be able to support the discussion of additional resources which become available only when there is a societal emphasis on both civic values – as expressed in the spirit of the US Constitution – and self-interest.

Why cannot we keep economics separate from ideas of liberty and justice? After all, there are studies of philosophy and law that have been devoted to these areas for centuries. There are two reasons to expand economics. First, since Thomas Hobbes wrote *Leviathan* in the 1600s the ideology underlying conservative economics has been applied to political philosophy. More recently, a group of legal scholars (including Supreme Court nominees and potential nominees such as Robert Bork and Richard Posner) have begun to implement a rigid application of the textbook concepts of conservative economics in determining the nature of justice. Bringing civic values into economics merely balances the export of the science of self-interest from economics. But more importantly, government is coming more and more to depend on economics. By building on the strengths of the economics of self-interest we hope to civilize it so that the valuations behind our public debate will reflect the values of civilization.

Actually the origins of economics have a wider social scope than most economists realize. The term 'economics' comes to us from Aristotle, who in his *Œconomicos* discussed the political and social order of the basic economic unit of his time, the household estate. To Aristotle, economics was not only a matter of dollars and cents (or drachmas and obols), but also the foundation of a civilized society.

The conservative economics that has been used in our national political debate is too limited in scope to guide public policy. Of all the areas of creative human intellectual activity, only economics still clings to its nineteenth-century foundations. Great advances have been made in mathematics, the arts, and the physical and medical sciences, as these studies have continuously re-examined their foundations. As a result of this re-examination, the metaphor of the universe as a precise, clock-like machine which was common to eighteenth- and nineteenth-century intellectual endeavours has been discarded. The conservative view of economics, however, is still too often guided and rationalized by an uncivilized, mechanical nineteenth-century economic analysis that advocates Social Darwinism and the law of the jungle as guiding economic principles.

The conservative focus solely on self-interest is destructive because the civic values which conservative economics ignores are very sensitive to public attitudes. If professors make the argument that public service, patriotism, or social justice are meaningless – and this message is echoed by business and community leaders – then the importance of civic values in motivating behaviour will be weakened. This is precisely the situation we face, and it arises from the incomplete picture of the world created by conservative economics. Our conservative government has not only overlooked the erosion of civic values, it has actually contributed to that erosion. The economic policy of planned recession, practised by Presidents Ford, Carter, and Reagan in the United States, and Prime Minister Thatcher in the United Kingdom are clear examples of the barbaric policies which have been inflicted on society. Conservative economics thereby provides the framework which encourages the haemorrhaging of our civic values.

No academic discipline shapes our modern world more than economics, and yet none has weaker foundations. Conservative economics is buttressed by hundreds of years of intensive study, and yet some of the basic principles and concepts have never been demonstrated. Conservative economics examines in very rich detail a world where self-interest is the only motivation – where no one will die for their loved ones, but where everyone has his price. Duty, loyalty and love exist in name in conservative economics, but they only motivate in proportion to the pleasure they yield and the market price they bring. This characterization of civic values, however, cannot explain the extraordinary behaviour we witness during wartime, when natural disaster has struck, or even when 100 million citizens voluntarily pay their taxes despite odds which favour cheating.

Conservative economics distorts our view of the world, by focusing solely on self-interest. Self-interest can, *under certain circumstances*, inspire efforts to improve one's wealth while providing benefits to society; but our appreciation of self-interest must always be tempered with the explicit recognition that it must be constrained by civic values. Without these constraints, self-interest poses real dangers to any civilized community. Self-interest cannot inspire voluntary compliance with the law, and thus a society organized on the basis of self-interest leads inevitably to a barbaric concept of government, which in turn incites the conservative plea to 'Get government off our backs!'

How did we get so far from 'We the People'? By investigating the conservative faith in self-interest and the conservative aversion to government, we can see how the attitudes behind the conservative plea have grown to undermine traditional civic values.

THE IMPORTANCE OF SELF-INTEREST

The pursuit of self-interest is at the heart of the conservative philosophy of economics. Adam Smith, one of the forefathers of conservative economics, wrote in *The Wealth of Nations*:

> It is not from the benevolence of the butcher, the brewer, or the baker, that we expect our dinner, but from regard to their own self-interest. We address ourselves, not to their humanity but to their self-love, and never talk to them of our necessities, but of their advantage.

For Smith, human interaction boiled down to an exchange of wants; 'Give me that which I want, and you shall have this you want'. This view of motivation as being based on exchange was later expanded to include transactions which were made informally (or even unconsciously) but the basic premise remains: behaviour is shaped by the individual's calculations of the self-interest costs and benefits of undertaking any activity.

Even though the conservative philosophy focuses on individual self-interest, conservatives do believe that the community can be served by individual wants. In this famous passage, Smith explains how the combination of wants could interact in beneficial ways:

> Every individual is continually exerting himself to find out the most advantageous employment for whatever capital he can command. It is his own advantage, indeed, and not that of society which he has in view. . . . He intends only his own gain, and he is in this, as in many other cases, led by an invisible hand to promote an end which was no part of his intention. By pursuing his own interest he frequently promotes that of the society more effectually than when he really intends to promote it.

Smith's 'invisible hand' is a marketplace which effectively communicates individual wants and links them with those most able to satisfy them. Each individual is motivated to enter his most productive occupation in order to conduct more and larger transactions within the marketplace to satisfy more and more of his appetites. Thus, Smith argues, people pursuing their self-interest will strive also to be valuable to the community, leading to ever greater prosperity.

Even liberals, such as the economist John Maynard Keynes, have noted the advantages in encouraging the play of self-interest and providing for the free expression of private initiatives.

[Self-interest] is the best safeguard of personal liberty in the sense that, compared with any other system it greatly widens the field of personal choice. . . . It is also the best safeguard to the variety of life, which emerges precisely from this extended field of personal choice, and the loss of which is the greatest of all the losses of the homogeneous or totalitarian state. For this variety preserves the tradition which embody the most secure and successful choices of former generations; it colours the present with the diversification of its fancy; and, being the handmaid of experience as well as of tradition and of fancy, it is the most powerful instrument to better the future.

The conservative economic view of self-interest, however, remains fixed solely on the rosy side of self-interested behaviour. In describing behaviour in the economy, conservatives typically ignore the potential for deception and the use of brute strength to gain one's ends. In the marketplace of conservative economic theory it is assumed that businesses cannot wield any power over their competitors or customers. Individuals and businesses considering violence or deception will, according to conservative economics, calculate costs and benefits and conclude that it will not be profitable in the long run. Citizens will, it is claimed, protect themselves by ultimately withholding purchases from those who have cheated, deceived, or intimidated them.

Those who believe that cheating or deception cannot play an important role in the marketplace can not understand why, for example, the real world needs either a Consumer Protection Agency or activists such as Ralph Nader. Conservatives assert that firms would surely realize that dangerous products are unprofitable in the long run, and thus they would never put their name behind a product which threatens the public. Unfortunately, there are numerous cases where dangerous products have been marketed: Johns Manville and asbestos, GM's 'unsafe at any speed' Corvair, Ford's Pinto. Once these unsafe products have been marketed, it is in the self-interest of the business firm and its managers to deceive the public as to the inherent dangers of the product. The admission of fault due to error or deceit threatens to inflict massive costs on the producer in the form of lost reputation and legal liabilities for damages.

In our society we have a number of methods of moderating business self-interest. Members of the US nuclear industry have acknowledged that the public pressure by environmental groups made American reactors safer from accidents such as the one in Chernobyl. In the Soviet Union, without the prodding of environmental activists, the nuclear industry pursued its immediate self-interests in limiting short-run costs and in so doing ultimately exposed Soviet citizens – and others in Eastern Europe – to fatal health hazards. Although a conservative might argue that the Soviets had merely miscalculated the true risks and benefits of their industrial strategy, the safety measures which the American nuclear industry employ were chosen primarily because of public activism by concerned citizens rather than as a result of the calculations of industry managers. In the aftermath of Chernobyl, the Soviet nuclear industry did suffer the 'long-run loss of reputation' which conservatives count on to regulate business. The likelihood of this particular catastrophe reoccurring may have even been reduced. However, this after-the-fact regulation will provide little solace to the victims of the Chernobyl accident.

CONSERVATIVE GOVERNMENT

The political ramifications of conservative philosophy as expressed by its intellectual father, Thomas Hobbes, reveal the inevitable barbarism of conservative premises. Hobbes believed that only a dictator, a Leviathan, could stand up to the competing appetites of the people and enforce order and stability (if not justice). Since Hobbes believed that self-centred appetite was the only motivating force underlying human behaviour, and that this always resulted in a conflict of interests among individuals, it follows that the only viable social organization was one where a dictator places constraints upon the people. In the absence of a Leviathan, the perpetual conflict of self-interested individuals attempting to better themselves at the expense of their neighbours in Hobbes's barbaric 'state of nature' would make everyone worse off.

Conservatives have accepted Hobbes's stress on the need to impose order upon the appetites of the people, while abhorring his solution of a dictator. The conservative dilemma therefore is how to preserve the individual liberty of people who may themselves be trying to repress the liberty of others. Conservatives see the fundamental goal of society as restraining factions and individuals so that they are unable to violate the freedoms of others. From this has developed a concept of negative liberty – the idea that liberty does not mean active participation in civic life, but rather the absence of repression. Thus, the decline in voter participation is generally taken by conservatives to indicate voter satisfaction, since they are not voting *against* the status quo. From a civic perspective, however, the decline in voter turnout is a symptom of the decay in our civic values.

The free market is a very appealing concept to conservatives, because they believe that the free market can replace the Leviathan and impose order on the destructive cacophony of appetites in the economy. The freedom of the marketplace is supposed to be a freedom from oppression. However, as we shall see later, the free market *cannot* create order out of chaos. Something must restrain the self-interest of individuals or we will have Hobbes's war of all against all.

Proponents of conservative economics such as Milton Friedman, Ayn Rand, or Alan Greenspan see our society as facing only two choices for social organization: capitalist freedom or an authoritarian servitude. The capitalist society, based on the self-interested pursuit of individual appetites and achievement in accordance with the rules of the economic marketplace, is said to govern people only by their wants and their capabilities. The authoritarian society governs by decree from above, enforced by the threat of overt violence.

Looking at these two choices, conservatives assume that the benefits of liberty in a free society are only possible where there is first capitalism. We suggest that the conservative ordering is a reversal of the facts. Historically, when relatively open markets have developed, there were civilizing social and political institutions already in existence which have made this possible. Italy in the early Renaissance, and England and America in their industrial revolutions each had a very special heritage of civilized institutions which enabled them to maintain liberty, prosperity and justice in their societies for many generations.

The capitalism of conservative economics – without the moderating influence of a supportive civilized culture – is perilously unstable. If we respect people only for their capacity to produce and if we interact with others only to the degree that we can get something from them, then the existing civilized influences in our society will begin to erode. This inspires crime, violence and political revolution by those who cannot profit from existing market situations.

Karl Marx's focus on capitalist theory – as opposed to the more moderate reality of capitalism in existing societies – led him to conclude that capitalism will tend to sow the seeds of its own destruction. Marx has been proved wrong because society in its civilized practices has over time adopted policies which have moderated some of the worst shortcomings of a pure capitalist system.

The choice between pure capitalism and communism is a false one because to choose either is to have made the assumption that raw power – self-interest – is the sole pillar upon which our society rests. Civilized government, however, comes not solely from enforcing sanctions against those who violate rules, but by the government of the people working with the people to encourage voluntary compliance with standards of conduct. Civilized incentives are crucial to establishing the levels of coordination and participation necessary to run our complex modern economy efficiently.

Without civic values, we are doomed to live either in an anarchic state of nature where only the powerful thrive, or under the barbaric domination of a government which manipulates its subjects like animals. As the nineteenth-century philosopher Jeremy Bentham put it:

> Mankind is governed by pain and pleasure. . . . Pleasures and pains, then, are the instruments with which the legislator has to work.

The barbaric spirit of Hobbes and Bentham lives on. After discussing the effects of the budget deficit on congressional spending in *The Washington Post*, George Will concluded with a modern 'axiom of conservative realism: in a democracy fear does the work of reason'. Like Hobbes, Will sees human conduct as being ultimately driven by barbaric stimuli.

The public policies that emerge from the conservative mindset are not always deliberately cruel, but they are barbaric. Policies which offer both a carrot and a stick as incentives to self-interested individuals are seen as even-handed by conservatives. However, primitive appeals to appetite and fear can not establish justice or ensure domestic tranquillity. Soldiers willingly risk their lives in order to defend their families and their nation, not because they are being paid or threatened. Government based solely on policies of carrots and sticks can only lead to a domestic war of neighbour against neighbour, not the domestic tranquillity to which the Constitution aspires. Without enlisting civic virtues, we will never be able to secure the blessings of liberty. Carrot-and-stick policies are more appropriate to spur animals into action than to enlist members of a civilized society towards a common goal. Without enlisting civic values, the civilized promises of the Constitution cannot be met.

Conservative policies run into unnecessary difficulties because of their inability to enlist the support of more civilized incentives than those of naked self-interest alone. Public policies using 'carrots' often result in a flawed result known as goal displacement. For example, a city decides to rid itself of rattlesnakes in accordance with the precepts of conservative economics – a bounty is offered for every dead snake brought to city hall. Soon the poorest citizens, motivated by the bounty fee, start raising rattlesnakes! Establishing understanding of (and compliance with) the intent of rules requires common understandings. Indeed, one of the central attributes of a civilized society is the use of a shared dialect – a common language of actions and terms. Without the bonds of culture and experience it becomes increasingly difficult to conduct business or to regulate it. We must emphasize that the bonds of civic heritage are not shackles forced upon the people by governing power. Indeed, a good example of a common industrial culture is that of the Japanese, which shapes the conduct of business by maintaining a set of virtues that businessmen willingly aspire to attain. The cure for goal displacement is a society with sufficient coherence to place the self-interested incentive force of carrots into the appropriate civilized context.

From the conservative position that society should be based only on appetite or fear, it follows that any sort of welfare programme could only be harmful. In this view, the more painful it is to be poor, the more people will struggle to avoid poverty. The appetite for wealth and the fear of poverty are the only fuel for the engines that drive the conservative economy. In this hypothetical world, the work ethic cannot exist; since it is assumed that job opportunities are available for all, any unemployment must be the fault of the unemployed. This is the habitat of Ronald Reagan's welfare queens and the rest of his menagerie of cheats and wastrels. The conservative economic world is filled with malingerers, and the appropriate policy is to whip them into submission. In the real world where both hardworking and lazy people face poverty, conservative solutions inflict pain on them all.

The conservative assumptions of human behaviour shape a political sphere in which government can act only through appeals to self-interest or through police enforcement which increases the risks and penalties of violating the law. Conservative economists do not concern themselves with the development, evolution, and strengthening of civilizing institutions which support rule-abiding behaviour. Thus, the only way the conservatives can maintain public order is through the use of carrots and sticks – the 'give-aways' and the 'government interference' that they themselves deplore.

DECLINE OF INSTITUTIONS

How can we put so much faith in the potential of the people to conduct their lives in a civilized fashion? We have already made mention of the decline in the norms which support our voluntary system of taxation, the willingness to resort to barbaric unemployment policies, and the breakdown of the post-war international monetary system. Furthermore, we believe that these areas of decline are linked not only with each other, but with a larger erosion of civic norms within our society.

· Evidence of this erosion is being seen everywhere in our national institutions. For example, adversarial litigation has come to replace more civilized forms of dispute resolution on crucial public questions such as busing, abortion, and environmental protection. The explosion of formal litigation in resolving our public debates not only indicates that many of our old institutions no longer function properly, but it also raises concerns that our legal institutions will not be able to handle this overload for much longer. Professor Robert Reich writes of this threat in *The Next American Frontier*:

> There is a danger that the law itself will lose its legitimacy in the process. Legal judgments cannot create social consensus. Quite the reverse: law can resolve conflicts only through reference to shared principles.

As law loses its legitimacy (i.e.; its civic core erodes), we are left with fewer civic resources, but the same divisive issues.

Other important institutions have also been mentioned as exhibiting signs of erosion. The loyalty to one's workplace that was once common in America has been weakened by the ephemeral corporate world where both workers and executives constantly move from job to job. High level political service has frequently become little more than a ticket to punch on the way to Wall Street, where meanwhile the norms of fair trading have recently fallen suspect. Columnist William Safire noted several of these trends in the *New York Times* and concluded simply:

> We have two jobs; to make our institutions more worthy of respect; and then to respect them.

Our civilization may not yet be on the brink of collapse, but some of our institutions are. These institutions are not isolated from society at large – losing a battle for Wall Street norms in one isolated case reduces the credibility of all Wall Street traders. This corruption spills over to other areas of business, polluting the existing social norms and thus weakening them. The cynicism which evolves from such episodes saps our civic values and propels us further down the path towards barbarism.

So where do we get hope for civilization? If there is hope for a civilized society, it must lie somewhere beyond the self-interest of conservative economics. The authors of *Habits of the Heart*, a sociological inquiry into the American character, trace the roots of the American spirit of civic values back to the founding fathers:

> 'Is there no virtue among us?' asked Madison. 'If there be not, no form of government can render us secure. To suppose that any form of government will secure liberty or happiness without any virtue in the people is a chimerical idea.'

If civic values do contribute to the health of our economic and social institutions, then we are left with the surprising conclusion that the hard-headed and pragmatic approach to solving the problems of government must involve pursuit of this civic virtue among ourselves. And by civic virtue we mean nothing more ethereal than excellence in the pursuit of civic values. Even conservative George Will agrees on a definition of civic virtue as 'Good citizenship, whose principal components are moderation, social sympathy, and willingness to sacrifice private desires for public ends'.

CIVILIZED GOVERNMENT AND CIVIC VIRTUE

In the surprising resurgence of democracy in the Philippines after years of tyrannical rule under the Marcos regime, there was no image as memorable as that of the Filipino townspeople forming a human chain to protect their ballot boxes with their bodies – with their lives. The example set by these Filipino citizens will do more than protect their voice in that one crucial vote – by demonstrating civic virtue, these people have also helped to encourage such virtue in the future. This civic virtue may not be enough to guarantee the life of a civilized Philippines, but without such virtue – without civic spirit – there is little hope for any nation to rise above a barbaric past.

Civilized government enlists public co-operation by appealing to principles of justice. During the first oil shock in the autumn and winter of 1973–4, for example, long lines developed at gas stations, creating frustration and wasting scarce gasoline. Contingent rationing plans were established, nationwide speed limits set, Sunday gasoline sales were banned, and President Nixon even ordered non-essential outdoor lighting – such as Christmas trees – to be turned off. At the same time, Nixon's conservative Council of Economic Advisers unanimously advocated resolving the problem by allowing the pump price of gas to rise. Gas lines would disappear as the poor and those with less 'urgent' needs for gas were forced to conserve by the price increase. Those who could afford it would then have easy access to the available gasoline. The problem was thus not attributed to a cartel – but rather to the remaining price controls which hampered the free market.

The problem with this conservative approach of relying solely on higher pump prices to eliminate the shortage of such a basic commodity as gasoline was that it alone would not calm the panic atmosphere that beset the nation. Pricing gasoline out of some people's reach would merely have set the have-nots against the haves. It would divide the nation at a time when the economic threat came from outside the community.

Suddenly, however, an innovative solution emerged from Oregon and within a few weeks spread nationwide. The civilized system that was adopted was that cars with licence plates ending in even numbers could fill up on even days and those with odd numbers on odd days. Almost overnight the lines and much of the frustration disappeared. The erosion of the public spirit was halted. People complied with this simple odd-even rule, not because they were forced to by their pocketbooks but because it was a fair and just solution. The capacity to take action as a community to resolve a common problem not only provided for a more just solution, but for a policy which was better able to enlist the voluntary compliance needed to implement a successful resolution. If we are to harness our capacity to create just solutions to our public policy problems we must do so from a philosophical perspective which – unlike conservative economics – recognizes the worth of civic values.

THE CIVIC TRADITION OF EXCELLENCE AND LIBERTY

Before Hobbes, there existed an intellectual tradition which acknowledged the need to blend civilized aspects of human nature with self-interest in successful ventures. Its advocate, the reader might be surprised to learn was Niccolo Machiavelli – who was well aware of some of the advantages created by the pursuit of self-interest. It was he who first made the point (later echoed by Adam Smith) that competition and even conflict have beneficial applications:

> Wealth derived from agriculture as well as from trade increases more rapidly in a free country, for all men gladly increase those things and seek to acquire those goods which they believe they can enjoy once they have acquired them. Thus it comes about that men in competition with each other think about both private and public benefits, and both one and the other continue to grow miraculously.

Machiavelli's view of human nature, however, was not limited to the powerful motivation of appetite. He made distinctions between the motivations of self-interest and civic values – distinctions that are entirely absent from the writings of Hobbes and modern conservatives. For example, Machiavelli noted:

> Friendships that are acquired by a price and not by virtue are purchased but not owned, and at the proper moment they cannot be spent.

Aristotle, Machiavelli, Madison, and others in the civic tradition clearly distinguished the difference between goods which can be purchased for money, and goods which can only be obtained through other means such as virtue. (We will discuss these two sorts of goods in much greater depth in the next chapter.) The civic tradition provides us with a conception of government which is different from the negative liberty of conservatism.

What are the attributes of a good society in this civic tradition? A civilized society will work to facilitate the development of excellence in all of its members. This means that our society should maintain the personal liberty of the people *and* encourage their full employment. The central principle of civilized economics is to promote an environment in which the benefits of economic competition can be achieved in tandem with the benefits of civilization.

A civilized society recognizes virtue – that is, the pursuit of excellence for its own sake – as a fundamental motivation upon which civilization is built. 'If a thing is worth doing, it is worth doing well!' In contrast, a society where skills and characteristics are valued *only* by what can be received in exchange for them in a market will lack the civic spirit which makes organizations function effectively. A civilized society encourages the establishment of excellences – of skills which are measured not only for their value in exchange, but for the level of human capacity which they demonstrate. Included among these excellences are not only technical and artistic skills, but traits such as loyalty, bravery, and compassion.

The ideals of excellence exist only *within* a community. Whether the excellence is that of being a good secretary, a good welder, a good Christian, or a good long-distance runner, the ideal of excellence is formed among the community of practitioners. Thomas Peters and Robert Waterman write in *In Search of Excellence* how the most successful firms depend on more than the simple financial incentives of conservative economics in motivating their people:

> The top performers create a broad, uplifting, shared culture, a coherent framework within which charged-up people search for appropriate adaptations. Their ability to extract extraordinary contributions from very large numbers of people turns on the ability to create a sense of highly valued purpose.

Some proponents of conservative economics recognize the value of inspiration, but they believe that spirit can be purchased in exchange for money or goods. Money is a very flexible medium, but the only loyalty it can enlist is the servitude which the conservatives abhor. A man working only because he is given something in exchange for his labour will shirk or cut corners whenever he thinks he is not being watched. A man working at his craft – his excellence – will provide unforeseen advantages, for he works both for his employer and for himself.

A civilized society must promote *both* personal liberties and the full employment of resources. Without personal liberty, people are prevented from participating in the civic and social community in which civilized values are developed. If society excludes certain individuals or groups from participating in the public arena, then the evolving civic values will reflect this exclusion, fracturing society and raising the risks of violent protest, oppression, and other aspects of barbarism. A fractured society lacks the social coherence necessary to conduct its affairs without the intermediation of extensive and cumbersome mechanisms to force co-ordination, as Reich noted in regard to our overloaded legal system.

But personal liberty without the full employment of all of our national resources is still uncivilized. Less-than-full employment of resources is not only wasteful, but it also strikes at the heart of community values and the spirit of excellence. Jobs provide people with the basis for the practice of excellence in a very important sphere of their lives. For our society and others, occupations also play a part in creating individual roles and developing personal dignity.

If a society is organized so that it routinely violates personal liberties or operates at less than full employment, at least some of its citizenry will be at the mercy of barbaric forces. For it is barbaric to require that certain people in society be denied employment or personal liberty for the society to survive. A nation which thrives on the hardships of its members cannot be called civilized.

THE DEMISE OF LIBERAL ECONOMICS

The demise of liberalism in recent years can be traced to the liberal abandonment of the spirit of civilization. The uncivilized events of the 1960s culminating in the Vietnam quagmire under a 'liberal' Administration that preached the doctrine of the 'Great Society' eroded the credibility of those who had espoused the importance of civic values. Simultaneously, the promise of liberal economic analysis was betrayed by the erosion and near collapse in the core ideas which had supported it. Liberals lost faith in the power of civic values, and without civic values, the only resource they had left with which to shape a vision of the future was self-interest. Liberal economists attempted to rebuild their theoretical analysis on the assumption that people were, and should be, motivated solely on the basis of self-interest. Liberals adopted the analytical and philosophical axioms of conservative economics – an intellectual and ethical framework based solely on the bottom line. Having adopted the conservative starting point, all they could do was echo conservative conclusions.

The conflict between conservative logic and civilized ideals leads to a confused and bastardized version of liberal economics – and liberal policy. Liberal economics has adopted the conservative economic dogma that treats a nation as an aggregate of isolated self-interested individuals locked in perpetual struggle with each other. The monetary incentives which do shape a portion of our behaviour have been taken to represent us in our entirety. Consequently, there can be no appeal to the public interest, to the spirit of 'We the People' – all that society can amount to is many separate individuals, each looking out for Number One.

This erosion of civic virtue in liberalism could be seen in many areas. In 1961, the spirit of excellence was the foundation of President Kennedy's charge to the National Aeronautics and Space Administration (NASA) to land a man on the moon and conquer the space frontier because it was there and not because it offered untold monetary rewards. By the end of that decade, NASA was faced with the erosion of civic values which supported space exploration. The only argument remaining to promote the space programme was one based on self-interest. Thus NASA's supporters had to argue that market value of technological spin-offs from the space programme were so beneficial to the economy that they paid for the government's investment several times over.

But once a conservative economic position was adopted, it became difficult to argue for NASA funding as a means of pursuing economic self-interest (even if there is at least some evidence of the value of spin-offs). Former Office of Management and Budget Director David Stockman, a self-proclaimed 'space buff', explained how the spin-off argument does not make sense from the conservative perspective:

> The way to improve medical telemetry or anything else was to reward private inventors, entrepreneurs, and investors with lower taxes. NASA was in effect claiming that the way to build a better mousetrap was to go to Jupiter.

If we lived in the world that conservatives imagine, Stockman would be right. But in our American civilization there are values beyond the self-interest of conservative economics. The true value of the space programme for America was best seen in the afternoon and evening of 28 January 1986, after the Shuttle *Challenger* had been lost with all of her crew. As the nation listened to the news, there was something more than lost profits on the bottom line that was being mourned.

The bottom line vision of our economy has led liberals to a philosophical dead end. Once the premise was accepted that our resources would always be scarce and depletable, conflict over those limited resources was inevitable, and consequently, our society was destined to decay. Recognition of the potential abundance that a civilized society would promote was lost. A case in point is the 'limits to growth' doctrine that the Club of Rome promoted in the 1970s. Professor D. H. Meadows and his associates from the Massachusetts Institute of Technology predicted in their Project on the Predicament of Mankind that our natural resources would very shortly be depleted. Their vision was of 'a world where industrial production has sunk to zero. Where population has suffered a catastrophic decline. . . . Where civilization is a distant memory'. The 'liberal' Club of Rome suggested that programmes to accelerate economic growth should be abandoned, since the inevitable depletion of our resources doomed any such programmes. What actually failed in the 1980s were the predictions of these liberals. Supplies of oil and precious metals flooded the market. Indeed, the failure of the liberals predictions merely served to reinforce the conservative drift of liberal economics.

The loss of direction of liberal economics can be illustrated with MIT Professor Lester Thurow's book *The Zero-Sum Society*. Thurow used the example of a sporting event – where one team's gain must always be at the expense of another's loss – to demonstrate the zero-sum game concept analogy for society. The pluses for wins and minuses for losses always balance at zero. In effect, the teams are battling solely to win the game – the scoreboard is the bottom line. The moral is that just as in sports matches, there are winners and losers – some must lose so that others may gain.

Professor Thurow's zero-sum game concept does not recognize civic values as an important economic influence, and thus the analogy contains a fatal flaw; even sporting events are not necessarily zero-sum contests. The idea that 'It is not whether you win or lose, but how you play the game' is a civilized truth we tell our young. Often winning or losing is not as important as the particular excellence with which one plays the game. Kellen Winslow of the San Diego Chargers earned more respect by catching 13 passes and blocking a field goal to send the game into overtime in a 1982 playoff game with the Miami Dolphins than many players have achieved in winning any game in their entire careers, even though his team did not even reach the Super Bowl. Winslow's excellence won him a victory that was not recorded on the scoreboard. Even his statistics for that day do not capture the entirety of his accomplishment. He simply achieved an excellence which cannot be appreciated in terms of the bottom line. In sports, and in our lives as individuals and citizens, our rewards come both from the payment we receive and from the excellences we achieve.

A zero-sum society view implies that long-term prosperity for the United States depends on our capacity to endure considerable hardships for a significant period of time. This fits in with President Carter's 'crisis of confidence' address – the so-called malaise speech – but his zero-sum image failed to elicit any form of positive public response. This was not merely because President Carter offered a painful public policy while Ronald Reagan was offering a painless one, but also because recent liberal economic philosophy was shaped in the framework of conservative economics – of self-interest and not of civilization.

It is the absence of civic spirit that has turned liberal economics into a weak and strangely distorted shadow of conservative economics. Ironically, liberals like Thurow, who in earlier years had recognized the inapplicability of conservative economic doctrine to resolving real world problems, began to base their arguments for social justice on people's self-interest – and not on civic concepts such as justice.

Without civic spirit, President Carter's final 'liberal' economic policy initiatives became merely a warm-up for Reaganomics.

THE PARADOX OF REAGANOMICS

In the 1970s, after the civilized core of liberal economics had been eroded, a different economic vision arrived on the national scene. The economics of the entrepreneur, shaped by writers like George Gilder and Jude Wanniski, and promoted by Ronald Reagan, swept the political agenda clean. The national heroes of the 1980s became the garage-workshop inventor, as typified by Steven Jobs of Apple

Computer fame, and the corporate manager and deal-maker as personified by Chrysler's Lee Iacocca.

Civic virtues were presented as if they were attributes of self-interest. Gilder, in *Wealth and Poverty*, distinguishes the liberal economic doctrine of the 1970s (which he calls socialism) from his entrepreneurial creed as follows:

> [Socialism] is based on empirically calculable human power; the other on optimism and faith. . . . When faith dies, so does enterprise. It is impossible to create a system of collective regulation and safety that does not finally deaden the moral sources of the willingness to face danger and fight, that does not dampen the spontaneous flow of gifts and experiments which extend the dimensions of the world and the circles of human sympathy.

This optimistic spirit, represented by candidate Reagan as a quality of entrepreneurs, struck a chord with the American public. At a time when President Carter was peddling malaise as a justification for ineffective government, this positive vision of the virtues of human aspiration was unbeatable.

The new entrepreneurial credo that 'incentives work' was adopted by the nation as a whole, with incentives being defined as being monetary (or what we define in Chapter 2 as external incentives). To create such incentives tax rates were drastically lowered. The income tax rates of the wealthiest taxpayers plummeted from 70 to 50 per cent in 1982 and declined again to 28 per cent in 1988 – a massive change in economic and social policy. The rationale for this massive tax reduction was that the entrepreneurial spirit was to be released from regulatory restraint and high marginal tax rates, so that the ingenuity of the human spirit could create new wealth. The faith of entrepreneurs in their creative handiwork and their ability to inspire their employees would guide Americans to an ever brighter and better future.

This gospel of opportunity was the single most important idea presented by the Great Communicator himself. President Reagan has initiated a cultural change (or revitalization) by rekindling a spirit of optimism and national self-confidence. The expression of national pride heard at such public events as the 1984 Summer Olympics and the Centennial of the Statue of Liberty would have seemed artificial and insincere in the 1970s.

One of the great paradoxes of the twentieth century is that Ronald

Reagan has campaigned for office on the issues that make the United States a civilized society – the importance of family and community values in guiding our behaviour – while his Administration has governed by policies based solely on self-interest. The spirit underlying the Reagan vision is vastly different from the assumption of self-interest upon which conservative economics – and Reagan policy – is built. Love of country and community, loyalty, and other civilized values are entirely absent from conservative economics. The Reagan paradox might be traced to the pattern by which this White House has been run – those responsible for presenting President Reagan to the public and those who make Reagan Administration policy are usually different people, and none have ever been called upon to reconcile the two sets of messages which the Reagan Administration has presented.

What President Reagan has succeeded in doing is to integrate a message about the civilized virtues of human excellence with a conservative political agenda which, as it is enacted, inevitably erodes civic values. Consequently, while President Reagan's themes have helped to revitalize the aspirations of the civilized American spirit, the conservative nature of his policies have eroded the civic values which underlie his civilized promise.

This paradox explains the contrast between his vast personal popularity and the limited public support for his legislative programme and judicial appointments. The public has responded to the President's civic message, but not to his Administration's policies which have broken that civilized promise. Underneath the civilized human symbols is the same conservative economic focus on self-interest and the bottom-line. Reagan policies are still based on the premise that people cannot be governed unless forced or bribed – that everyone on welfare is secretly laughing at the rest of us, that those drawing unemployment are merely lazy, and that the poor must face their poverty without relief.

DESPERATE CHOICES OF A BARBARIC WORLD

That girls are raped, that two boys knife a third,
Were axioms to him who'd never heard
Of any world where promises were kept,
Or one could weep, because another wept.
(W. H. Auden)

History provides us with many examples of nations which have lost their civilization. Even within America there are places where our people are ruled more by hunger and fear as the result of our economic policies than the civic values of the Constitution. This grim reality not only shows how important it is to maintain the institutions which protect civilization, but also how conservative economics with its willingness to sacrifice human livelihoods to combat inflation makes us vulnerable to barbarism.

Machiavelli lived in a barbaric age, and his experience – suffering torture after his government was overthrown – made him examine the painful choices of a barbaric world. When a society's civilization has eroded, so that its institutions have lost their credibility – their virtue – then Machiavelli felt that there was no way for the people to pull themselves up by their bootstraps into a more civilized state.

> It is not enough to employ lawful means, for lawful methods are now useless; it is necessary to have recourse to extraordinary measures, such as violence or arms, and to become, before all else, prince of that city in order to be able to deal with it in one's own way.

At this desperate juncture when civilization has collapsed and barbarism rules, the only possible salvation Machiavelli sees is in one leader, in a Leviathan, who could impose order in a barbaric world. This is the nature of the world described by both Hobbes and conservative economists. If all civilized incentives no longer exist, then in fact Hobbes's belief in the need for an absolute ruler *is* correct. Machiavelli's Leviathan would dominate the barbaric world and thereby have the power to re-establish civilized customs and laws. But conservatives do not envisage any mechanism for re-establishing social order, because they do not recognize that society can collapse.

The implication for Machiavelli was very grim – once lost, civilization is not easily re-attained. In a world fallen into barbarism, the options are few and painful: remain in the rut of civil and social strife or risk the almost certain despotism of a tyrant.

'VALUE NEUTRAL' BARBARISM

It is in regard to the fundamental questions of civilization and barbarism that conservative economics leaves us unprotected. Conservative economists believe that their analysis is on firm ground because of its 'value neutrality' (i.e. the assumption that all values are merely preferences, and consequently that economics is neutral in the choice between values). Conservative economists as people have values, but in their role as practitioners of economic theory, civilized values are absent. Two authors of a text on analytic methods, Harvard professors Edith Stokey and Richard Zeckhauser provide a clear example of this value neutral perspective.

Most of the materials in this book are equally applicable to a socialist, capitalist, or mixed-enterprise society, to a democracy or dictatorship, indeed wherever hard policy choices must be made. In deciding whether a vaccine should be used to halt the spread of a threatened epidemic we need not worry about the political or economic ideology of those inoculated. Nor will the optimal scheduling for refuse trucks depend on whether it is capitalist or socialist trash that is being collected.

There is a certain truth here: an analysis of the non-civic aspects of economic efficiency can be applicable to any society. However, the context of these bottom line efficiencies can be of great importance to us. The optimal scheduling of refuse trucks that applies to both capitalist and socialist trash can be equally useful in improving the effectiveness in transporting the victims to Auschwitz or the Soviet gulags. A conservative economist is limited to saying more is better – the value of additional efficiency cannot be qualified by its contents.

Conservative economics cannot come to grips with the idea that civilization can collapse even as standard economic indicators are rising, despite the vivid example of economic growth and barbarism provided by Nazi Germany. The problem is not with the morals of conservative economists but that their paradigm cannot handle questions of civilization. Consequently, such issues tend to be ignored. But if we are to make any use of economics in governing our nation, we cannot ignore the forces which maintain our civilization.

To abandon economics would be to waste a valuable tool; to practice economics in government without consideration for civic values would be to risk the degradation of our civilization. Only when we combine an understanding of civic values with the self-interest of conservative economics will we be able to reap the benefits of our entire national heritage.

NEW DIRECTIONS FOR 1990 AND BEYOND

The real choice between civilization and barbarism was posed first
by Aristotle in examining the political economy of the polis – the
civilized states of ancient Greece:

> Any polis which is truly so called, and is not merely one in name,
> must devote itself to the end of encouraging excellence. Otherwise,
> a political association sinks into mere allegiance. . . . Otherwise,
> too, law becomes mere covenant – a guarantor of men's rights
> against each other – instead of being, as should be, a rule of life
> such as will make the members of the polis good and just.

Even in Aristotle's time, there were some who aspired to remain
true to the civic values of their nation and some who were content
with a society based on self-interest and negative liberty – a society
in which law is merely 'a guarantor of men's rights against each
other'.

The philosophical issues confronting our founding fathers were not
resolved forever with the writing of the Constitution. Every generation
must reaffirm the meanings of 'We the People' and 'the blessings of
liberty' or the civilized resources beneath the symbols will crumble.
Our nation must pursue growth in maintaining our vitality, but we
must also pursue something more. Peters and Waterman quote a
leader in one of their 'excellent' companies:

> Profit is like health. You need it, and the more the better. But it's
> not why you exist.

Just as these authors found the pursuit of excellence as the keystone
of business prosperity, so too we may find pursuit of the excellences
of civilized economics at the heart of national prosperity. We believe
it is time to stop the regression towards barbaric economics and
barbaric economic government, and to return the public agenda
towards a prosperous civilized economic system for the United States
of America and the world.

2 The Political Economy of Civilization

> My bounty is as boundless as the sea,
> My love as deep;
> The more I give to thee the more I have
> For both are infinite.
> (*Romeo and Juliet*, Act II, Scene ii)

Newtonian physics postulates that every action has an equal and opposite reaction. Similarly, it is a conservative argument that every economic benefit must exact a cost somewhere else. They view everything in the world as a trade-off, or as the current slang goes: TANSTAAFL ('there ain't no such thing as a free lunch').

The love that Shakespeare's Juliet expresses, however, defies the economic principle behind the no free lunch philosophy. The idea that there can be rewards from social interaction that benefit all is nowhere to be found in conservative economics.

For conservative economists, motivation is explained solely by a literally insatiable appetite to consume or acquire regardless of the costs imposed on others. People are said to have appetites – 'preferences' – which conservatives associate with all human values. Loyalty or love are merely appetites which may be compared and freely traded in exchange for other consumption goods.

Economists are not the only ones who follow conservative philosophy – some psychologists also focus on self-interest, attributing all motivation to mere appetite. Christopher Lasch notes in *The Culture of Narcissism* that 'when therapists speak of the need for "meaning" and "love", they define "love" and "meaning" simply as the fulfilment of the patient's emotional requirements'. What could such psychologists have to say to Juliet?

If this self-interested appetite were really the only motivation for human behaviour, then Juliet's words would have no meaning for us. Juliet's feelings, however, are neither fictional, strange, nor even unique. Love is just one of many motivations which are fundamentally different from the TANSTAAFL transactions of conservative economics. Juliet's love for Romeo improved the well-being of both

29

(despite the fact that circumstances conspired to end their romance in tragedy). Similarly, the civic values which hold our nation together can potentially inspire behaviour which yields a positive sum for society.

PREFERENCES AND MOTIVATION

Why do some people prefer bacon to sausage with their eggs for breakfast, while others prefer only toast and coffee? Why do some people participate in the local PTA, while others spend their evenings at the movies? Economists assume that each of us have our own individual set of innate and unchanging preferences, and that we can order our priorities in an unambiguous way among all possible alternatives. The assumption is that each individual's preferences are explicit (that is, everyone knows what they want and how much they want it). Consequently, no one is ever faced with a choice where they are torn by indecision – Hamlet cannot really be puzzled by the choice: 'To be, or not to be?'

In conservative economics, nothing can be said about why preferences change. Economists do not investigate changes in preferences – this is said to be outside the realm of the 'hard science' of economics. Conservative economists leave preference formation and change to the weaker 'soft sciences' such as sociology and psychology. By developing a theory void of preference formation, conservative economists have allowed an inherent weakness in their explanation of human behaviour to bias their measurement of motivation.

Economists cannot measure preferences directly. Instead, it is asserted that people respond to incentives and reveal their preferences through their market actions. For example, the public can be said to 'prefer' chocolate ice-cream over medieval mandolin music because they spend a larger share of their income on it. Economists can even explain how preferences vary: if the price of chocolate ice-cream goes up, economists will predict how this changes the demand for the mandolin music and its price. Conservative economists assert that by tracking the movement of goods, the desires which make up motivation can be measured. These market measurements, however, introduce bias (in a statistical sense) into the determination of value by exaggerating the impact of those goods which are most easily measured, and by undervaluing other goods. In other words, economics will always overvalue tangible dollars-and-cents goods as compared with intangible goods. Thus 'hard' economic data will be consistently wrong wherever civic values are important. This bias comes from the assumption that all preferences ultimately involve market transactions or exchanges, real or implicit.

Sometimes, however, goods deriving from social relations cannot be considered 'for sale' without losing their value. Imagine what would happen if a judge who was about to rule on a case attempted to auction off his decision. What legitimacy would remain to support the judge's verdict, even if neither litigant could meet his asking price, and thus no deal was consummated? Justice, the blessings of liberty, and other social goods are not easily detected by the market measurement tools of economists, and so they are systematically undervalued in conservative economic analysis. If people do not pay for something, then conservative economists must conclude that the good is worthless.

There are many things besides love and justice which cannot be valued in the marketplace without being debased; hence the conservative representation of motivation based solely on market price and preferences is incomplete. Indeed, policy shaped by conservative economics will be consistently biased in favour of motivating by self-interest. Therefore, the guidance of conservative economics is not able to lead us to the benefits of both self-interest and civic values.

INTERNAL AND EXTERNAL INCENTIVES

It is not sufficient to merely rail against the prevailing orthodoxy of a philosophy based on self-interest in order to establish the case for a more civilized approach to economics and public policy. Others before us have also noted the weakness of a conservative philosophy based on self-interest. What they have lacked, however, is a rigorous analytical foundation upon which to base their alternative approach. The following analysis is intended to provide the structure necessary to encapsulate previous critiques (as well as our own) in a form which can challenge the conservative approach.

In everyday human behaviour we recognize that people are motivated by many different incentives which reflect either self-interest or civic values. When the incentive for an action comes solely from a source external to the performance of that action, as might be the case with a wage payment to perform an unpleasant job, the payment is an external incentive. Only self-interest is reflected in the transactions of external incentives.

When an incentive comes solely from the performance of an action *per se* (and not in exchange for something else), as with craftsmanship for its own sake, then the reward in internalized within the craftsman, and is thus defined as an internal incentive. The internal incentive of civic values comes from performing an action, not in exchange for something else.

When we speak of internal incentives we are *not* referring to social pressure in the form of the threat: 'Do this or the community will shun you' (Nor do internal incentives motivate an action in exchange for a future reward or reprieve.) The plea 'Do this and I will love you' is an external incentive. Not only will social and emotional threats fail to enlist internal incentives, but the very process of treating civic values as external incentives will degrade and corrupt the existing internal values. Instead, internal incentives work by communicating pre-existing rules of behaviour so that self-interest need not be called into play.

Traditionally, economists treat all incentives as if they were external. These external incentives are easier to measure, since they are based on transactions which are often documented in the form of contracts or market prices. External incentives are what underlie conservative economic preferences – motivations based on an actual or implicit calculation of costs and benefits from the viewpoint of self-interest. Internal incentives are something quite different from these preferences; love, duty, honour, and excellence shape our lives with an influence which is more than simple appetite. Internal incentives are harder to measure, since they depend more on social context. When all incentives are treated as if they were external, internal incentives tend to be undervalued or ignored.

Internal incentives have some special advantages that external incentives lack. Civic values do not necessarily wear out with use, and they can prove mutually reinforcing ('The more I give to thee the more I have' proclaims Juliet). The honour and esteem a community of peers awards for professional excellence does not exact a cost somewhere else – often, this respect will ennoble both those who are honoured as well as those extending the honour.

Self-interest cannot explain many human choices. What possible market price could make a rational economic man decide to die for his country? Conservative economic theory implies that external incentives – market prices – are not only a feasible method of enlisting soldiers, but in fact the best way to maintain an army. This view provided the basis for Professor Milton Friedman's argument that we should enlist as soldiers only those who choose to work in the army for the prevailing wage. In wartime, however, a system built on self-interest cannot maintain civic spirit. During the Civil War, for example, citizens in the North who were drafted for military service could hire someone to serve in the army for them. This policy of allowing wealthy citizens to discharge civic duties through the payment of external incentives did not work – the result was draft riots in the streets of New York, and a degrading of patriotic motivation.

The conservative view that a mercenary army is always best is in stark contrast to Machiavelli's strong concern that a free and civilized people take military duties on themselves, a concern taken by the founding fathers and put into the Constitutional right to bear arms. Machiavelli doubted the viability of a society which depended on the hired poor to defend the possessions of its wealthy members. Values beyond self-interest will be necessary to motivate an army which will bravely face death in defending the nation.

Conservative economists may argue that we have misrepresented their views, and that theirs is not merely a science of self-interest. They often assert that love, loyalty, craftsmanship, and patriotism are integrated into their analysis as individual *preferences*. What they mean by these words, however, is something entirely different from the reality of these values in a civilized society. Take the value of loyalty, for example. For conservatives to say that one has a preference for loyalty means nothing more than that one is loyal only in proportion to the pleasure it yields. Although conservative economists may claim that this surrogate sentiment accurately represents the reality, we conclude that true virtues have characteristics which can not be purchased in the conservative free market. An analysis based solely on external incentives inevitably boils down to the Hobbesian world of self-interest.

The inability of conservative economics to account for behaviour based on community and loved ones as motivating forces fundamentally distorts its view of how society operates. A conservative approach obscures vital issues of public policy because it discards the most crucial motivations: the incentives that can hold society together or tear it apart.

THE POLIS

> External goods, like all other instruments, have a necessary limit
> of size. Indeed all things of [external] utility are of this character;
> and any excessive amount of such things must either cause its
> possessor some injury, or, at any rate, bring him no benefit. [It is
> the opposite with goods of the soul.] The greater the amount of
> each of the goods of the soul, the greater is its utility.
>
> (Aristotle, *Politics*)

It was Aristotle who first recognized the distinction between
internal and external incentives. His remarks in regard to external
incentives are consistent with the position of conservative economics
as to preferences and the law of diminishing returns.

But Aristotle also describes another form of motivation which
exhibits different characteristics. Writing for the political leadership
of his time, Aristotle was also attuned to the motivation of Juliet –
'The more I give to thee, the more I have.'

Aristotle uses the term 'the goods of the soul' to refer to internal
incentives. He is not referring to the Christian 'soul' in this passage,
but rather to the essence of man 'the political animal' (or literally,
'an animal intended to live in a polis'). Internal incentives are rooted
in what has been called organizational culture, or more broadly,
social norms. These norms are centred around a social hub, which
may be a nation, a family, a profession, or an organization. Aristotle
makes explicit the connection between internal incentives and civic
values. The Greeks referred to the social hub as the *polis*, and they
saw it as the heart of their civilization. Where a polis exists, shared
values within an organizational or social tradition produce internal
goods which the members of the polis enjoy. In our social and
professional lives we participate in many poleis (plural of polis).

This conception of community does not exist in conservative
economics, hence it is also absent from public policy discussions
which are based on this economic paradigm. Professor Mancur Olson
of the University of Maryland views a community as a collection of
individuals who are constantly calculating the individual benefits of
their membership, and comparing them with the benefits they would
receive if they left the community. This representation of the polis is
misleading because it attempts to slice incentives which are entirely
based on community into individual choices. Where there is a strong
sense of community, abandonment is not even considered as an

option – as those who have given their lives for their country have demonstrated. While Professor Olson's view may provide an insight into the behaviour of political coalitions, we must be careful not to extend it to groups or organizations where civic values play a strong bonding role. The power of a polis, as with the Amish in Pennsylvania, or among members of the Civil Rights movement in the 1960s, is never achieved by many individuals separately weighing the benefits from membership. The legend of the rugged individual exists more in American mythology and Hollywood westerns than in American history. The Constitution begins 'We the People' and not 'Each of Us'.

DIALECT

> Dialect: the form of variety of a spoken language particular to a region, community, social group, occupational group, etc.
> *(Webster's New World Dictionary)*

Every polis has its particular dialect, that is, its own interpretation of words, phrases, and concepts. Dialects include everything from shop talk to in-jokes, from regional dialect to the language of meanings established by religious teachings. The particular dialect of a polis can reveal much about its strengths, weaknesses, character, and membership. Just as language defines nationhood in the international realm, so does a shared dialect indicate the existence of a polis among or within nations.

The dialect established by a polis can reinforce values by providing guidance as to what is expected of polis members. Even one word can provide the context that makes a polis thrive. Peters and Waterman attribute the excellence of Bell Telephone to:

> Theodore Vail's seventy-five year old insistence that the company was not a telephone company but a 'service' company.

A shared language reinforces the feeling of membership in a polis and also provides signals as to what that membership means. Lee Iacocca writes:

> It's important to talk to people in their own language. If you do it well, they'll say 'God, he said exactly what I was thinking.' And

when they begin to respect you, they'll follow you to the death. The *reason* they're following you is not because you're providing some mysterious leadership. It's because you are following them.

Civic values are continually iterated and modified through the development of dialect which comes about as a result of social and personal interaction.

In an economy that works well, the dialect of one polis will tie into the dialects of other groups so that all of the separate dialects form a compatible whole. Former Secretary of Labor John Dunlop writes:

> Each of the actors in an industrial relations system – managerial hierarchy, worker hierarchy, and specialized public agencies – may be said to have its own ideology. An industrial relations system requires that these ideologies be sufficiently compatible and consistent so as to permit a common set of ideas which recognize an acceptable role for each actor.

The norms and expectations of those within an industry can be discovered in the meanings of the words with which the groups communicate.

Our standard industrial practices do not work unless all parties have a shared language of definitions and rules of the game. The self-interest of an employee or sub-contractor is always in opposition to the interest of his employer, since the former want to do the job with as little effort as possible and the employer wants the best job regardless of effort. Without common understanding, they will both expend a great deal of effort in arguing over every decision to be made in carrying out the project. Frequently, the development of a professional code of ethics, and/or long-term personal relationships between parties is necessary for them to mutually develop and adopt a common language of meanings.

The development of a shared dialect is not limited to parties with similar or mutual interests. Even adversaries not bound in a common enterprise may develop understandings as to the meanings of the slightest nuance of each other's behaviour. Even during warfare, the common understandings of enemies still benefits each by establishing the parameters by which the conflict may be pursued. Any level of trust brings the risk of betrayal, but co-operation also holds the potential for producing additional rewards for all. Even in a Darwinian environment it is often the co-operative species which prosper.

If dialect is essential to understanding, then the dialect adopted in discussing specific policy problems in this book and elsewhere will also be important. We must be aware of what our words really signify. Although our discussion must be abstract to be generally applicable, to be useful it must deal in particulars. It is important to keep this distinction in mind; no one ever dies for an 'internal incentive' *per se*. Where people give their life, it is for particular reasons intricately wound up in the interstices of their personal role in their own community or family.

We discussed in Chapter 1 the difficulties in pinning down the labels 'liberal' and 'conservative' in even a general sense. We have taken on an even greater challenge in referring to civilization and virtue. When we describe something as being civilized, we hope to be saying more than merely that we approve of it. When we use the adjective 'civilized', we are making reference to a harmonious combination of self-interest and civic values as established in the ideals and institutions of a society. When we write of virtue, we mean the pursuit of excellence (or internal incentives) in the context of previously established social roles and ideals.

Conservative economics is supported by its own dialect: 'the free market', '*laissez-faire*', and 'the bottom line' in common usage, and concepts such as 'marginal cost' and 'optimal allocation' for economists. In order to challenge the paradigm of conservative economics it is necessary to establish a vocabulary for those aspects of economic and social behaviour which conservative economics does not address. Thus we are attempting to create a dialect through the terms 'internal incentive', 'the polis', and even 'dialect' itself. In this we are following Hobbes, who in the first eleven chapters of *Leviathan* expounded the basic premises of conservatism in the form of definition of a multitude of terms, from 'Good' ('the object of any man's appetite or desire'), to 'Reason' ('nothing but reckoning – that is, adding and subtracting'), to 'Compassion' (grief arising in an individual 'from the imagination that the like calamity may befall himself'). Our analytical dialect is much less comprehensive than that of Hobbes, but we believe that it provides the basic structure needed to construct an alternative analytical paradigm to that of Hobbes and the conservatives.

The crux of public issues is often revealed in the dialect of both sides. In *What Price Incentives?* Professor Steve Kelman of Harvard's

Kennedy School of Government highlights how paradigmatic
interpretations of the world leave economists and environmentalists
'talking beyond each other'. Environmentalists may oppose pollution
taxes even if they acknowledge their economic efficiency and (external) incentive effect, because such taxes help to legitimize the role
of polluters and their right to outbid others who wish to maintain a
clean environment. Any step in the direction of pollution taxes
contradicts the environmentalist vision of norms and roles, and
thus weakens their polis. Consequently, even if environmentalists
completely understand the benefits of economic efficiency, they will
still be motivated to reject pollution taxes and maintain faith with
their community (and to continue to enjoy the internal incentives
that their membership provides).

In the 1984 Democratic Presidential Primary campaign, Senator
Gary Hart advocated the conservative economic policy of making
corporations have to pay for the water, land, and air into which they
dumped their pollutants. It was interesting (but not surprising) that
this idea was not advanced as an argument for economic efficiency;
rather it was phrased in liberal dialect as a way of placing an additional
burden on socially undesirables: 'Why not a tax on polluters?' The
dialect available to Hart to communicate with the public about
pollution had a negative tone. If the external incentive benefits of
pollution taxes are ever to become politically feasible, it will be
necessary to influence the values of the polis of the environmentally-
concerned public so that they agree with the conservative notion that
a certain amount of pollution is acceptable.

Dialect can also be the means through which a new community is
created. Three million Israelis and millions of other Jews worldwide
share the common bond of Hebrew – a language which existed only
in the context of religious ceremony until Ben-Yehuda, a Lithuanian
scholar, emigrated to Jerusalem in the late nineteenth century and
began to revive the language single-handedly. Other societies are
working to repeat Ben-Yehuda's success, with Gaelic in Ireland and
with Catalan and Basque in Spain. From boot camp to college
orientations, the introduction of a new dialect can be a powerful tool
in establishing a new polis.

Finally, dialect can provide the means with which to combine
several poleis, and thus enlist a wide range of civic values in the
service of a single ideal. The authors of *Habits of the Heart* rightly
note the genius of Martin Luther King, Jr in shaping the polis of the
civil rights movement:

Juxtaposing the poetry of the scriptural prophets – "I have a dream that every valley shall be exalted, every hill and mountain shall be made low" – with the lyrics of patriotic anthems – "This will be the day when all of God's children will be able to sing with new meaning, 'My country 'tis of thee, sweet land of liberty, of thee I sing'" – King's oration reappropriated that classic strand of the American tradition that understands the true meaning of freedom to lie in the affirmation of responsibility for uniting all of the diverse members of society into a just social order.

King's words remind us not merely of the power of civic values, but also the value of their content. For King, freedom was not the negative liberty of conservatives, but rather something which combined the values expounded in the scripture with the values of the American civic heritage. The essence of King's idea of civilization was a free community rich in the 'blessings of liberty':

> When we let freedom ring, when we let it ring from every village and hamlet, from every state and every city, we will be able to speed up the day when all of God's children, black men and white men, Jews and Gentiles, Protestants and Catholics, will be able to join hands and sing the words of that old Negro spiritual. 'Free at last! Free at last! Thank God almighty, we are free at last!'

THE STRATEGIC IMPORTANCE OF DIALECT

Words can be weapons in the conflict over public policy. The following quotation comes from a business publication rallying opposition against the establishment of the Occupational Safety and Health Act (OSHA). It demonstrates the strategic corruption of language in industrial relations:

> Imagine yourself sitting in your office, a few months from today. A young man barges in. You recognize him as a man you once refused to hire. He had no education and no potential talent you could use. His main experience consisted of cashing welfare checks.
> But he shows you he's now a representative of the federal government – an "inspector" with the Department of Labor. And he threatens to have you fined $1,000 a day if you don't do as he says.

The young man – who knows nothing about your business – then tramps through your plant, without a warrant, ordering you to take costly steps to improve "safety and health."

Such scenes could be duplicated throughout the country should a new proposal being deliberated on Capitol Hill be signed into law.

The hidden agenda of *Nation's Business* was to promote the idea that government will only hire incompetents, and that there could not possibly be anything wrong with the plants to be inspected. The meaning of 'inspector' and 'safety and health' (quotation marks in the original text) to *Nation's Business* and the constituency to which it was appealing is clearly different from that intended by those who established OSHA. *Nation's Business* was trying to establish a negative connotation for these terms in the minds of its constituents. There is one polis for *Nation's Business* and its constituents and a different one for OSHA framers and their supporters. These poleis do not form a compatible whole. Instead, they come into conflict in an environment of uncertainty and shifting rules, roles, and norms.

Nation's Business was fighting a very real war of words in this article, and one of the first casualties is the dialect of common understandings that might have helped both sides. When dialect becomes suspect, the resources dedicated to purely antagonistic conflict will have to be increased, as a more uncertain environment necessitates greater efforts to protect against a larger number of potential threats. Thus additional costs are imposed on both adversaries, and on society as a whole. Imagine a war where neither side knew the word for 'surrender' in the language of the other – the loser would not be able to capitulate, thus dragging the fight on at a cost to both until one side was annihilated.

Dialect can be more important than 'pure economic facts'. Unions sometimes reject a wage offer if it is understood to be a concession, whereas the exact same wage offer may be approved if it is seen as a 'new package'. However, unions cannot be paid merely in the coin of flowery rhetoric. Over time, experience will establish new meanings for the words of management and unions, and these meanings will shape the course of labour negotiations as much as will concerns of dollars and cents.

A political example of how the meaning of words can change over time was provided when the Democratic National Committee concluded in November 1985 that when the term 'fairness' was used by Democratic candidates, it had a very different meaning for the voters than what was intended. Frank O'Brien, director of the DNC direct-mail programme admitted that 'When party leaders talk about fairness, middle-class voters see it as a code word for giveaway'. As a result, 'fairness' was abandoned (as a word, if not an ideal) in favour of 'compassion', at least until the current stigma regarding fairness wears off.

The presence of a shared dialect indicates the existence of an extended community and thus the existence of mutually generated internal goods. But when one party takes advantage of the other by changing the meanings of previously shared terms, that party betrays the mutual trust and weakens the shared polis. Not only do they no longer share the meaning of the disputed term, but also in the future the meanings of every word of the betraying party are also cast into doubt.

Dialect is a very special human institution that exists wherever man does. A shared language is a valuable asset which benefits all parties by reducing transaction costs and by being part of the process of generating the internal goods that the polis produces. Also, the strength of the industry-wide polis (indicated by shared language) is a critical variable in determining economic outcomes.

THE VOLATILE INTERACTION OF INTERNAL AND EXTERNAL INCENTIVES

A successful society will reap the benefits of both self-interest and civic values. Both internal and external incentives must be enlisted, but the values of self-interest do not easily combine with the values of a polis. Entrepreneurs who place an order with friends or relatives may be voluntarily sacrificing some of their own profit (in terms of external incentives) if they buy second rate or over-priced goods because of the internal incentive of family. If they buy the lower quality merchandise, they reduce the economic efficiency of the sectors from which they buy and sell. In this situation, although a market with sellers and buyers *still appears to exist*, the special efficiencies that conservative economists associate with free markets will not.

Similarly, the introduction of external incentives can sometimes diminish the effectiveness of already existing internal incentives. Psychologist Barry Schwartz of Swarthmore College provides the example of some elementary school students who were given tokens as a reward for reading books. Although the number of books read in school increased, the books they chose to read became shorter, the level of comprehension declined, and reading outside class decreased.

The fact of the matter is that the market philosophy in which everyone has his price implies certain norms and roles that may infringe on an existing polis. In certain instances, even the offer of a market transaction can contribute to the erosion of a polis. If Romeo had offered Juliet gold ducats to sleep with him, something of immense internal value would have been lost. The difference between love and prostitution is vast, but if we are to use the market measurement tools of conservative economics, then the difference which will be measured is that prostitution is valuable (people demonstrate a 'willingness-to-pay') and love is worthless.

When government policy is based only on self-interest, it can degrade the civic values of its citizens by treating their civic concerns as if they were solely financial. Professors Philip J. Borque and Robert Haney Scott of the University of Washington in Seattle suggested that there was a 'simple way' to resolve the controversial issue of nuclear waste disposal by allowing the free market process to work:

> Open, competitive bidding by states on government contracts [to store hazardous waste] would resemble a market process. Providers of the site would be compensated for their perceived social costs.

In other words, these economists advocate telling concerned citizens something like this:

> We recognize your concerns that nuclear waste disposal may increase the risk of cancer for you and your children. How much do we have to pay you to forget about all that?

The answer for a civilized society is not in dollars. Even if citizens of a town made a deal for a million dollars each, what would happen as cancer cases began to develop? Even if the cancers are not related to the nuclear waste site, imagine the tensions between those struck with the tragedy and those spared to enjoy their new wealth with impunity. How would parents feel, having accepted a million dollars, if their child was born with severe birth defects?

This conservative economic solution was actually proposed in a March 1987 Senate bill put forth by Bennett Johnston of Louisiana and James McLure of Idaho. $100 million was offered to any state or Indian tribe willing to accept a high-level nuclear waste dump. The offer was immediately denounced as a bribe, and Nevada Governor Richard Bryan went so far as to refer to it as 'nuclear blackmail'.

The most humane *and* efficient way to handle serious controversies is not to try to buy our way out, but to go through the messy and difficult political process, so that the relevant citizens themselves may participate in coming to a just solution. That eventual solution may involve payment to the community, but only as part of a process which enlists the civic resources of the community as well. The purpose would not be to reach a solution merely by adding up the individual preferences of the citizens, but rather to have them shape a solution as a community. External and internal incentives must be combined with great care if we are not to waste either.

INSTITUTIONS

I am not an advocate for frequent changes in laws and constitutions, but laws and institutions must go hand in hand with the progress of the human mind. As that becomes more developed, more enlightened, as new discoveries are made, new truths discovered and manners and opinions change, with the change of circumstances, institutions must also advance to keep pace with the times. We might as well require a man to wear still the coat which fitted him when he was a boy as a civilized society to remain ever under the regimen of their barbaric ancestors.

(The Jefferson Memorial, Washington DC)

We live in a world of change in which the external and internal incentives that motivate human behaviour are constantly evolving. The environment is continually reshaped by developing technology, the ebb and flow of natural resources, and evolution of the values of the polis. Government is a process by which we manage our affairs during this social and economic evolution. As the world evolves, new problems are always emerging.

Societies sustain a productive harmony between internal and

external incentives through the development of institutions – that is, pre-established laws, customs, practices, or formal mechanisms which simultaneously distribute internal incentives and protect the polis from the erosion of values over time and from the corrupting influence of external incentives. For example, the institution of a dowry helped to provide an effective mechanism for capital formation and wealth distribution while protecting the social and emotional integrity of marriage from the potentially corrupting influence of external incentives. But the dowry also illustrates how an effective institution for one period in a society's evolution can become undesirable as the society's values and economic environment change.

One example of a public institution which has evolved to resolve an everyday problem is the regulation of driving. For millennia there was no need for rules to determine traffic lanes. But with the development of carriages, and later automobiles, the ensuing congestion made it inconvenient (and dangerous) to permit each individual to exercise his choice as to which side of the road to ride on, or which side to pass a slower traveller. And so gradually 'rules of the road' were developed which spelled out proper procedures for use of roads. Although these rules were simple, they eliminated some real problems and made transportation significantly more efficient.

As the economy developed, the needs of travellers evolved and were met by frequent elaborations and additions to the original rules of the road. In the 1920s a black inventor named Garrett A. Morgan developed and sold the idea for traffic lights to General Electric. Traffic lights effectively utilize internal and external incentives through the combination of a clear and fair determination of the right-of-way with the self-enforcement carried by the dangers of running a red light.

The introduction of traffic lights brough enormous efficiencies, but also led to further evolution of our driving institutions. In borderline cases, some people broke the new rules of the road, and thus it was necessary to change the role of police in our society (to the point where the main contact many people have with police is in regard to driving). Other more complex concerns have also evolved as a result of the technological and civic changes in driving. Our driving institutions and technology have become so effective that hundreds of thousands of vehicles can be co-ordinated within a single city. This very efficiency increased the usefulness of cars until their number in certain cities has grown beyond the capacity that the existing institutions and infrastructure can handle. Other problems have emerged and been resolved – remember the gas lines during the Energy Crisis, and the adoption of the odd–even rationing scheme. The perpetual process of evolution, adaption, and further evolution continues.

A well developed institution will support the basic values of the polis and enhance economic productivity. For example, a competition which recognizes excellence for its own sake is an institution which goes back at least as far as the first Olympiad in 776 BC. The shared pursuit of excellence strengthens the polis. The shared experience can not only encourage a striving for excellence along traditional routes, but it can also increase productivity by encouraging innovative ideas. The display of these innovative approaches leads to their transmission throughout society. Thus the enjoyment of the civic values of Olympic competition were successfully combined with the external incentives of enhanced productivity.

However, as with the evolution of species, there can be evolutionary dead ends for institutions as well as advances. For example, after the development of the 360 computer, IBM Chairman Thomas Watson, Sr asked vice-president Frank Cary to design a new research and development system to prevent a repeat of the chaos that occurred during the development of the 360 computer. Unfortunately, the institution Cary designed did more than eliminate chaos – it also stifled creativity. As Peters and Waterman recount:

> Cary did what he was told. Years later, when he became chairman himself, one of his first acts was to get rid of the laborious product development structure that he had created for Watson. 'Mr. Watson was right,' he conceded. 'It [the product development structure] will prevent a repeat of the 360 development turmoil. Unfortunately, it will also ensure that we don't ever invent another product like the 360.'

Cary was fortunate in having the opportunity to correct his earlier error. Society will eventually abandon mistaken efforts to develop new institutions – the challenge is to identify the institutions which are not working and remove them before they further erode.

The internal incentives of the institution can be a powerful force, but without effective guidance the values can evolve in unhealthy ways. Sometimes a polis will develop counterproductive values from which come internal incentives that promote neither external efficiency nor the vitality of the polis, as Peters and Waterman add:

Poorer performing companies often have strong cultures, too, but dysfunctional ones. They usually focus on internal politics rather than the customer, or they focus on "the numbers" rather than on the product and the people who make and sell it.

Internal incentives are not always beneficial (either to individuals or the people as a whole). Hatred and prejudice can come from an uncivilized polis which degenerates to the point where these sentiments take on the appearance of central virtues.

THE TIPPING MODEL OF EROSION

Professor Thomas Schelling of Harvard has developed a 'tipping model' which can be used to examine one way in which the erosion of norms can occur. Schelling's model describes how a small number of individuals possesing different preferences from the rest of the polis can take a certain action, thereby changing the polis environment so that others in the group find it in their interest to take the same action, further changing the environment, until the entire group takes the action originally preferred by but a few.

An example is the game of poker, an institution which is often represented as a zero-sum game in economic terms (where the gains of the winners are exactly offset by the losses of the losers). But if this is a friendly game of poker among members of a strong social group, then at the end of the evening both winners and losers will have benefited from playing. It is only when a few of the players abandon the principles of the poker polis and start to cheat that the environment turns sour and they are left with a zero-sum competition. The cheaters, in effect, degrade the existing polis and in so doing establish a new regime in which it is likely that more of the players will begin to cheat (since the incentive to win money becomes proportionately more important as the internal incentives from playing by the rules are diminished). The warning of the tipping model is that a small erosion may sometimes trigger an avalanche.

An important attribute of the polis (and a measure of its long-run viability) is its ability to keep self-interest in check and maintain the discipline needed to prevent cheating. It is our experience that poker games are generally honest not because there exists adequate surveillance and credible sanctions, but because the norms of behaviour are that you simply do not cheat in a friendly game of poker.

Similarly, the vitality of a civilization lies in its capacity to maintain the strength of its institutions so that self-interest cannot begin to tip the nation towards barbarism.

EROSION OF A NATIONAL POLIS

Civilization can be weakened when (1) internal incentives are eroded as individuals devote themselves to the sole pursuit of self-interest, or (2) the values of the group are corrupted, in that the rewards for the group come only at the expense of others. In this latter case we can say that the polis has developed uncivilized or corrupt values. Nevertheless, the internal incentives of such uncivilized poleis can encourage behaviour to further their barbaric ends. Khomeini's Iran, Nazi Germany, and the Ku Klux Klan all drew upon internal incentives to motivate their followers towards acts of violence.

The internal incentives of such barbaric regimes do not reflect civilized virtue, as the rewards came only at the expense of others – in violation of our positive-sum premise for civilized societies.

In this sense, therefore, if one can discern a polis evolving around the ideology of conservative economics, its incentive scheme cannot be labelled virtuous. Since conservatives conceive of systems of zero-sum games, any definition of excellence that they may develop implies that the winners have beaten 'the losers'. The ideal figure in the conservative cosmology is shrewd, hard-working and innovative, but he may also be amoral, manipulative, and deceitful when circumstances require it.

Just as all barbaric regimes require particular victims in order to justify the shortcomings of their social order, the conservative economic polis requires an underclass of lazy and undeserving in order to explain the existence of the unemployed and poor.

Positive action must be taken to maintain and invigorate a civilized polis – otherwise, there is a tendency either for it to erode or to become corrupt. Once this occurs, society finds it difficult to restore and revitalize its civilization. As Professor Benjamin Barber puts it:

> Communities that do not grow and evolve become brittle and frail – become something other than communities. To be genuinely free, a community must be just; to be sustainable, justice must be embedded in community.

Corrupt societies tend to sow the seed of their own destruction, because they silence the new ideas that might bring new life, and they set into motion the desire for revenge which will motivate their victims. However, this tendency may take years, or even generations to manifest, providing very little consolation to those who live and die under the oppression of a corrupt society.

During the early stages of erosion, it is still possible to attempt reforms and revitalize civilized behaviour. It is, however, necessary to behave within the existing set of norms. Appeals to ethical ideals cannot be used as motivation to re-establish the very same values that have been lost in the first place. For example, the advertising campaign for military recruitment which was begun during the Carter Administration initially did not try to appeal to American youth on the basis of patriotism, but rather in terms of self-interest. 'Be all that you can be!' was the slogan as the emphasis was on the career development advantages of military service ('It's a great place to start!'). As the counter-culture of the Vietnam era faded and a new patriotism developed, the Armed Services have been able to expand their advertising campaign to include appeals based more on military virtues ('It's not just a job – it's an adventure'). Over a period of years – and in synchronization with changes in the national polis – the Armed Services succeeded in transforming the earlier message of career advancement into one which could revitalize military virtues in our society.

People in an eroded polis frequently will not recognize any difference between the current norms and the original ones; indeed, the greatest problem with the polis erosion is that it is not readily seen by polis members. For example, our voting participation has declined, as the democratic process has come to be regarded as either a battleground for special interests or a horse-race between candidates ruled by their media consultants. As a people we have allowed ourselves to accept the notion that our votes really do not matter. At no point have we recognized that an important civic value was being lost. While we recognize that voter participation is at the lowest level in decades, we do not see this as an important change in the way we govern ourselves. In other words, the institution has remained outwardly the same, but the inner meanings have changed.

THE STRENGTH OF AMERICAN CIVILIZATION

We have been fortunate in our history that America has always had abundant civilized resources. The unique American experiment in civic democracy was made possible by the inherited norms and principles which allowed our founding fathers to collectively create a new nation. As Professor Benjamin Barber of Princeton writes:

> Our greatest asset is our spirit: the spirit of political liberty and civic activism evident in the towns Tocqueville toured on his journey across America in the early 1830's; the spirit of adventure that once opened up the West; the spirit of giving by which Americans have always shown themselves prepared to help their neighbors and participate in voluntary associations without calculating the return on their altruism; the spirit of tolerance that permitted the victims of a hundred worldly persecutions to find sanctuary here, and that made America a nation that saw equality as a function of will rather than birth; the spirit of patriotism that inspired the young to serve their country without the promise of a free ticket to college; the spirit of democracy that made liberty not merely a private matter but a matter of respect for the dignity of others.

The civic heritage established by our Founding Fathers, and elaborated upon by the American people during the growth of our nation, has guided the development of the American polis.

Even when the harsh external incentive force of the Great Depression struck America, we did not turn to the fascist solutions of Germany, Italy, Japan and Spain. The members of the German and Italian ethnic communities in the United States saw themselves as Americans first. They were not moved by appeals from their European kinsmen. Even the Japanese Americans, interred in camps for much of the war, served with great distinction in the US Armed Forces. Our civilized resources were sufficient to pull us through without resorting to such drastic – and almost inevitable fatal – measures.

CIVIC VIRTUE

In a productive and civilized economy, every member of society plays a role in maintaining the viability of our institutions, even as we participate in their evolution. Machiavelli's term for pursuit of excellence in this civic role was virtù – or virtue. In economics for a civilized society, virtue is the practice of actions which generate and reproduce internal incentives, or more broadly, a virtue is an action that strengthens the polis. An act of kindness which inspires others to achieve the same standard of conduct is an act of virtue. A healthy marriage conveys credibility to the conception of marriage in the polis, thus reinforcing polis values.

A society which strives continuously for full employment enhances the value of belonging to the community, while a society that justifies unemployment and loss of income as the necessary and inevitable cost of a comfortable survival for the rest of the community erodes the very basis of its civilization.

Civic virtues require full participation of all members in the process by which social values change and evolve. These processes involve formal political mechanisms such as voting and jury duty, and economic activity such as workplace interaction, customer–business relations, and government institutions handling economic dislocations.

Civic virtue includes being a good team player – but this team role also includes the responsibilities to develop new ideas, to promote civilized behaviour, and to work against the erosion of existing civilized values. By practising ones' excellence – in a profession, as a parent, or in athletic endeavours – a person may set an example that promotes the civilized values that he or she is pursuing.

There is also the form of leadership by which one establishes a new polis from the start, thus creating a new set of guiding principles under which to organize a co-operative effort. The birth of a new polis for a business or agency is a very special event, a combination of politics and poetry. In the realm of corporate kingdoms, inside our larger society-wide polis, often it is an individual leader who creates the polis and virtues of his or her own organization, as described in *In Search of Excellence*:

All the companies we interviewed, from Boeing to McDonald's, were quite simply rich tapestries of anecdote, myth, and fairy tale. And we do mean fairy tale. The vast majority of people who tell stories today about T. J. Watson of IBM have never met the man or had direct experience of the more mundane reality. . . . These days, people like Watson and A. P. Giannini at Bank of America take on roles of mythic proportions that real persons would have been hard pressed to fill. Nevertheless, in an organizational sense, these stories, myths, and legends appear to be very important, because they convey the organization's shared values, or culture.

This individual leadership is entirely absent from conservative economics, even though this type of leadership is commonplace in the business world. In conservative economics a good manager merely chooses the optimal combination of available inputs to produce maximum profits. Civilized leadership, however, is composed by more than the computer-like choice of optimal combinations imagined in conservative economics.

Citizenship and leadership are both civilized virtues which we can practice in our families, our jobs, our neighbourhoods, and in our national governance. Through enlisting civic virtues our public policies can work more efficiently and can help to establish a more just society. The Preamble of the Constitution guides us towards the meaning of our government and our purpose as a people. Without civic values in economics – our chief tool of government – we will never be able to achieve justice, domestic tranquility, a secure national defence, prosperity, or the blessings of liberty.

3 What's Wrong with Economists?

THE TUNNEL VISION APPROACH OF CONSERVATIVE ECONOMICS

Most economists analyse the world using a set of notions known as the neoclassical model. Economic problems are viewed strictly from the perspective of business self-interest; civic values are ignored. Consequently traditional conservative economic policies have a major flaw; they fail to provide civilized solutions to our pressing economic ills.

BUSINESS AND GOVERNMENT IN AMERICA: PARTNERS OR ADVERSARIES?

The belief that developed countries must choose between either an unfettered private enterprise system or a completely governmentally regulated economy is false. As Harvard Professor Robert Reich observes:

> Americans tend to divide the dimensions of our national life into two broad realms. . . . Our civic culture embodies a vision of community, premised upon citizenship. Its concern with democratic participation and the sharing of wealth stems from a conviction that such commitments enrich life and affirm the interdependency of individual lives. . . . The business culture embodies a moral vision of its own – one of individual responsibility and freedom. According to this vision, the market offers a superior organizing principle for society because it promotes the common good while preserving individual autonomy.

In reality, both civic and business attributes are integral parts of all our private and public institutions. As Peters and Waterman note in their book, *In Search of Excellence*, the most profitable companies are characterized by the possession of a particularly strong *esprit de corps*.

In recent years, emphasis on the business view approach has been freely used by politicians, civil servants, and financial media writers in public discourse despite its limitations. This tropistic application of a severely limited view to resolving important problems of our society by people in high places is not new. Walter Bagehot, the pragmatic nineteenth-century editor of *The Economist*, complained that the policy makers of his day did not attempt to determine whether the theoretical principles underlying their decisions were appropriate for developing financial policies and practices. Bagehot wrote about these policy makers:

> They could not be expected themselves to discover such principles. The abstract thinking of the world is never to be expected from persons in high places; the administration of first-rate current transactions is a most engrossing business, and those charged with them are usually little inclined to think on points of theory, even when such thinking most nearly concerns those transactions.

Those responsible for policy development rarely have either the time, or the inclination, to think seriously about points of abstract theory. It is not surprising, therefore, that their perspective has led to rationalizing policies that either completely fail to meet their objectives (e.g., the 1981 'supply-side' tax cut was supposed to eliminate government deficits by 1984), or, even if they do succeed in one area, they do so by invoking uncivilized solutions which create or exacerbate problems elsewhere in the system, for example, the Federal Reserve's taming of the inflation problem by increasing unemployment and bankruptcies.

Policies founded solely on the conservative view of how the economy operates often not only distort the civic values which hold society together, but often produce results which are counterproductive to the economy. For example, the conservative notion that it is essential to balance the federal budget in order to ward off future inflation leads to current demands for raising taxes and/or reducing government expenditures. Raising taxes to pay for ongoing projects creates unemployment, recession and an unprofitable business climate.

Cutting government spending on ongoing programmes, on the other hand, not only causes additional unemployment but it can also be damaging to the future productive growth of the economy. For example, cutting back on government projects to improve mass transportation, highways, harbour, and airport facilities will increase delays, accidents, and raise the future cost of transporting goods to market, thereby requiring higher prices. Reductions in spending on environmental clean-up projects (e.g. sewerage treatment facilities under the Clean Water Act) increases exposure to future health hazards which eventually exact a cost in terms of lost work days, health care, and even lives. Attempts to balance the budget by reducing unemployment benefits, welfare programmes (e.g. aid for dependent children, school lunch programmes), or federal revenue sharing policies can result in a less healthy future population, or the lack of local facilities necessary to promote productive economic activity in impoverished sections of our nation. In all these cases, the long-term results of a short-sighted conservative vision of the desire to avoid deficits will be to burden the economy with higher costs and more inflation in the future.

Yet despite the shallow logical foundations upon which conservative dogma are based, conservative dogma is deeply ingrained into the public perception of economic problems. Accordingly, in order to open the public discussion to a civilized economic analysis, it is necessary to demonstrate the specific ways in which the predominant conservative ideology impedes the way we examine the 'facts' in public forums.

WHO CARES IF NEOCLASSICAL THEORY DOES NOT REFLECT THE REAL WORLD?

Institutions and the economic system

Humans have elevated themselves from the 'law of the jungle' to a civilized state by designing institutions to provide innovative responses to unforeseeable changes in the economic environment. Even among humans, the spectrum of economic development from primitive tribes to complex, economic democracies is closely related to the degree that the various human communities have developed socio-economic institutions to interact with, adapt to, and even regulate the economic environment to serve the needs of mankind.

This power to control the economic situation is a double-edged sword. Used well, as it was during the decades following the Second

World War, it provided enormous increases in prosperity and in living standards. Used poorly, as it has been since the early 1970s, it can result in a stagnating economy in which the current generation is unable to achieve, much less surpass, the average living standard of the previous generation. And if the institutions are abused there is the potential to create real economic misery and havoc (as in the Great Depression).

Thus, economic analysis of real world systems cannot ignore the institutional setting in which economic activity takes place. Yet practitioners of neoclassical economics believe one of the primary virtues of their analytical system is that it is devoid of any institutional content and hence equally applicable to *all* the economic problems of *all* living creatures. Believing they are 'hard' scientists, neoclassical economists have attempted to establish the existence of immutable economic 'laws' which all living creatures must obey, in the same way that the law of gravity must be obeyed not only by humans in developed economies, but by primitive tribes, all animal and plant life, and even inanimate objects.

In the world we inhabit, however, there are no universal economic laws. Instead, economic behaviour is altered by civilizing institutions, so that economic principles are neither timeless nor independent of the civic setting and the prevailing institutions. The neoclassical model cannot provide the universal solution for all our economic maladies, for all times, despite claims to the contrary by many economists.

Do the facts fit neoclassical theory?

When confronted with real world economic observations, neoclassical economics normally fails. For example, conservative economists assert that the rate of inflation is directly related to the excessive rate of growth in the money supply. The facts, however, show that between 1977 and 1981 in the United States the money supply grew by approximately 32 per cent while the price level rose by 40 per cent. Between mid-1982 and mid-1986, on the other hand, the money suply rose by over 40 per cent, while the price level only increased 12 per cent. (For comparison, the annual federal deficit increased from $45 billion to $58 billion – approximately 2 per cent of the GNP – in the earlier period and from $112 billion to $167 billion – approximately 5 per cent of the GNP – in the later period.) Yet, this conspicuous failure of the conservative model to predict the decline in the rate of inflation since 1982, despite the higher rate of growth of the money supply (and larger government deficits) has not undermined its powerful standing in the profession. Nor has it discouraged conservatives from insisting that the only way to fight inflation is to limit the money supply growth to 3 per cent a year and to eliminate the federal deficit.

Contradictory facts and incorrect forecasts are explained away by conservative economists with the claim that predicted consequences will occur 'in the long run' with a 'long and variable' lag over time. Hence if events appear to be incompatible with the theory, it is simply because the full impact of any action has not yet occurred. In the long run, after a long (but unspecified) time lag for things to work their way out, it is claimed, the prediction will ultimately come true. Counterfactual empirical evidence can always be dismissed since we are not yet in the long run!

THE 'HARD SCIENCE' APPROACH TO ECONOMICS

Outcomes are inevitable in neoclassical economics

In 1968, MIT Professor Paul Samuelson wrote that in their quest to provide a scientific basis for their discipline, modern economists must believe in a 'unique long run equilibrium [i.e., an inevitable outcome for the economy] independent of the initial conditions'. Underlying this creed is the presumption that the economic system operates under what Samuelson called 'the ergodic hypothesis'.

The word 'ergodic' does not often come up in ordinary discourse except among mathematicians and some physical scientists. In using this ergodic terminology, Samuelson is, as he readily admits, drawing an analogy with nineteenth-century statistical mechanics where the ultimate long-run 'equilibrium' outcome of a system is independent of the initial conditions. For example, the ergodic presumption permits physicists to predict that an unhindered pendulum will always come to the same (long-run equilibrium) point of rest at the bottom of its path no matter where in the swing we start it off from. In economics, the 'ergodic' analogy of the swinging pendulum is that an unhindered economy will always come to the same long-run position of rest (at full employment), no matter where in the business cycle swing the system starts from.

It is this belief in an ergodic economics that permits conservative economists to postulate the existence of unique, inevitable outcomes and therefore makes economics a *hard* science – on a par with nineteenth-century physics. This seemingly innocuous presumption of the existence of unalterable long-run economic equilibrium outcomes implies that there are natural laws which govern the operation of the economic system propelling it towards a stable, desirable (often termed 'efficient') solution, just as the natural law of gravity propels a swinging pendulum towards the midpoint of its swinging arc. Consequently, if ergodicity is postulated for economics, then all the predictions of neoclassical economics can be expected to occur here on earth *in the long run* – if only we trust the invisible hand of natural laws to operate in the absence of government interference.

Keynes's reaction to the usefulness of such long-run equilibrium concepts as the basis of policy was clear:

> But this long run is a misleading guide to current affairs. In the long run we are all dead. Economists set themselves too easy, too useless a task if in tempestuous seasons they can only tell us that when the storm is long past the ocean is flat again.

To believe in the inevitability of economic outcomes is to deny that humans can have any control over their economic destiny. Accordingly, a considerable amount of mischief can be rationalized under the rubric that economics is an ergodic science. If one accepts the view that the economic pendulum is always swinging towards a full employment prosperity, then any attempt of the government to improve the current situation can only hinder the long-run ability of the economy to right itself.

Samuelson provides an interesting example of how this presumption of a unique equilibrium position can influence our view of the economic scene. Because of the ergodic hypothesis, neoclassical economists believe in a long-run market-determined distribution of income independent of the initial income distribution (just as the pendulum's equilibrium is always at the bottom of the swing independent of how far from this position we start the swing from).

Suppose that the equilibrium distribution of income leads to the rich living in huge mansions while the poor sleep in the streets of the cities. A government (not under the influence of neoclassical dogma) might try to redistribute income towards the poor so that they can at least obtain some shelter from the elements. In a long-run neoclassical world of economic science, however, the unique equilibrium solution would prevail. As Samuelson puts it, 'if the state redivided income each morning, by night the rich would again be sleeping in their comfortable beds and the poor under the bridges'. Accordingly, the conservative 'hard science' view of economics justifies the existing income distribution – no matter how inequitable – as part of the normal working out of the natural laws of economics.

The dominance of neoclassical economics

The 'hard science' claim of neoclassical economics recommends itself to the self-interest ideology of the powerful, for it rationalizes the existing distribution of income, wealth, and power as the *natural* outcome of some immutable law of nature.

Of course, money can not buy friendships but it can secure alliances. The financial requirements of higher education in recent decades have made the academic profession vulnerable to the temptations posed by grants, provided by the rich and powerful – including recent conservative governments – for economic research. To be a continuing recipient of such grants, one must be able to provide still another 'proof' of the desirability and inevitability of the free market outcome.

In an earlier day, before research grants were an important aspect in university budgets, diverse academic views and discussions were tolerated and even encouraged on campus. Nowadays, as both private and public universities are run by Administrators with an eye on the business culture focus on the bottom line, alternative lines of investigation which may enrich intellectual stimulation and development but which do not bring in significant outside research money tend not to be encouraged. Under such a system, conservative economic theory, with its implicit justification of the existing distribution of income and wealth, tends to dominate professional discussions as 'successful' economists follow the 'invisible hand'.

ECONOMIC OUTCOMES ARE NOT INEVITABLE

To repeat, ergodicity asserts that economics, like Newtonian mechanics, involves 'timeless' laws which control the behaviour of all subjects within the scientific discipline. Thus, just as Newtonian physicists believe that the dinosaurs, and all other living creatures past and present (and future), have always obeyed (and will obey) the law of gravity on the planet Earth, so do neoclassical economists assert that all past, present, and future living creatures obey the same 'timeless' laws of economics as they engage in the processes of production and trade. Governmental laws, rules, etc. which attempt to alter the long-run 'natural' outcome of ergodic economic processes are as useless as a government edict that would outlaw the law of gravity in order to make Earth the centre of the solar system.

Those who believe that economics is an ergodic science, therefore, eschew any hard thinking about the vexatious problems we face. Nature, guided by immutable economic laws, will provide the inevitable outcome – without government's help.

The truth, however, is that unlike the world of the physical sciences where all living creatures obey unchanging natural laws (such as the law of gravity), there are no universal economic 'laws' which govern all animal behaviour in economic affairs, or even all human behaviour.[1] Thus economic principles are not ergodic even among species – much less over time within the human species. Since economics is a soft science, then what is essential is to think hard and long about our economic processes which are responsive to civilizing influences. Humans can work together to mould their economic destiny.

WHAT HAVE ECONOMISTS DONE FOR US LATELY?

Lincoln once said that God must have loved the poor, he made so many of them. To which, one might facetiously add, that conservative economists are only doing God's work by providing a rationalization for recent policies which have created more poor in our midst. Since the late 1960s, conservative economics has generated a rationalization for reversing a forty-year movement towards policies which promote full employment and a more equitable income distribution.

President Roosevelt's New Deal supplemented by Keynesian policies had in fact moved the world closer to a full employment environment and a much more equitable distribution of the nation's economic bounty. The statistics on unemployment and the distribution of income in the United States show that for a quarter of a century since the Great Depression progress was made towards eliminating unemployment as a major economic problem and simultaneously reducing the percentage of the poor in the US. Lower income households received a proportionately larger share of the growing economic pie.

When by the later 1960s the problem of inflation became substantial, these objectives were jettisoned. Since then deliberate policy decisions have unleashed economic forces which reversed progress towards becoming a more civilized economy. Unemployment has again become a chronic problem, even in the prosperity swing of the business cycle. Simultaneously, the distribution of income has become more unequal. For example, between 1947 and 1967 the poorest 20 per cent of the population of the United States saw their share of the total income of the economy increase from 5 to 5.6 per cent. By 1986, it had declined to 4.6 per cent. For middle America, the increase between 1947 and 1967 was from 52 to 54 per cent; it has now slipped back to 51.6 per cent. The richest fifth of the American population, on the other hand, witnessed their share of income fall from 43 to 40.4 per cent between 1947 and 1967, but under recent policies it has climbed back to 43.7 per cent. Twenty years of progress in promoting a more equitable distribution of income has been reversed in the subsequent two decades.

At the same time, the proportion of the population living in poverty has grown. In the prosperity of the Reagan Eighties, the poor have gotten poorer, and the very rich, richer.

This growing inequality in income is not only economically unhealthy for an economy which depends on mass production and mass consumption for its prosperity but it also contributes to the erosion of the polis. The creation of classes of losers and winners can only weaken the fabric that holds a civilized community together.

The generation of people entering the work-place after the Second World War were able to look forward to a higher standard of living than their parents – thanks in large measure to the civilizing New Deal and Keynesian policies designed to deal with the problems of that era. Since the end of the 1960s, the likelihood of earning a higher standard of living than one's parents did has significantly diminished – as barbaric policies rationalized by neoclassical analysis were hammered out to deal with the new economic problems.

ORTHODOXY, CIVILIZED ECONOMICS, AND OUR MAJOR ECONOMIC PROBLEMS

The major problems in economics are divided into two categories: microeconomics and macroeconomics. *Microeconomics deals with the difficulties inherent in a single market* or small group of markets, for example, the market for chain-saws, or petroleum products, etc. *Macroeconomics*, on the other hand, *deals with the difficulties inherent in the total national or global economy*; for example, with questions of inflation, employment, etc. Although there is an obvious relationship between a tree and a forest, nevertheless the microbiology of a tree is different from the macrobiology of forests. Similarly, the microeconomics of individual markets is related to but different from the macroeconomics of the nation.

Ultimately, however, it is the macroeconomic problems which have an indelible impact on our lives. Inflation or severe unemployment tend to threaten the stability and the sense of community among members of a society. Traditional methods of coping with these problems often exacerbate one while attempting to solve the other. In the resulting maelstrom, the benefits of living in a civilized society are often jeopardized. Accordingly, the rest of the chapters in this book will be spent discussing macroeconomic issues – and civilized solutions. For if we can get our macroeconomic house in order, we may find it easier to resolve our microeconomic problems.

Nevertheless we would be remiss if we did not at least suggest that even at the microeconomic level, a single-minded emphasis on the importance of self-interest in a free market environment may produce undesirable micro-solutions. When government does not look for civilized solutions to the fundamental microeconomic problems of our highly interdependent society, the results can be barbaric. As the following example demonstrates, 'deregulation' which unleashes self-interest in a free market is not always a good thing.

IS DEREGULATION A UNIVERSAL MICRO-SOLUTION?

In recent years, especially in the United States, there has been a movement towards 'deregulation' of all industries in the expectation that unregulated markets and a pricing system unconstrained by any government rules will provide better services for the public.

In a more academic tome than this one we might delve deeply into the fallacy of accepting a conservative microtheory which presumes that unless proved otherwise, micro-markets perform efficiently in providing the greatest amount of benefits for the lowest costs. The discussion would show that failure of free micro-markets to perform 'efficiently' is an almost ubiquitous phenomenon; and hence we can not simply rely on the invisible hand of free markets to achieve the efficient solution that economists daydream about.

There are no simplistic and universal solutions to achieving good market performance. Each market must be studied on a case-by-case basis. Performance criteria that are acceptable in our society must explicitly be developed and checked for compatibility not only with business standards but with civic goals as well. Then clear rules and regulations can be developed which prescribe acceptable economic behaviour within a civilized system.

In the limited space remaining in this chapter, we will take three cases to illustrate why 'free markets' need not provide desirable results. These three illustrations are: networking, congestion, and the development of UHF television transmission facilities.

NETWORKING

What do we, as a civilized society, want from the transportation and communications networks that binds our geographically dispersed population together as a nation? The feeling of belonging and participation in a polis is maintained by the ability to easily move around and/or communicate with the other members of our national community. In an earlier era the explicit policy of public utility regulation of transportation and communication enterprises was to provide universal service. All should have easy access to the networks of our 'common carriers'. This simple principle permitted the United States to sustain our view of ourselves as 'One Nation, indivisible'. Despite a widely scattered population coming from a multitude of ethnic backgrounds, we could communicate and travel easily in a gigantic 'from sea to shining sea' melting pot. The American polis was strengthened by this provision of inexpensive access to a great transportation network of railroads (before the Second World War), air transport (in more recent years) and telephone and postal communications.

To make sure that all communities had a minimum level of access to these networks at roughly comparable prices, public policy encouraged cross-subsidization. People who lived in high density areas (where access costs per person were very low) paid more than the cost of providing their service in order to ensure that other members of the polis in far-flung regions (where costs of extending the network were higher) could be linked-in at affordable costs. The result was truly a national network which strengthened the sense of community.

In recent years, however, a conservative movement for common carrier deregulation began. It sets groups of citizens against each other by encouraging, under the mantle of economic efficiency, the dismantling of significant outlying portions of the service networks which had promoted the American polis. Those persons in high density (i.e. urban) areas were told they were chumps for 'wastefully' cross-subsidizing the members in the hinterlands. If the citizens in the outlying areas could not, or would not, pay their higher costs for access to the network, then they should not be provided with such service. Making each person pay for the cost of providing services to his location, it was argued, would be efficient compared with a system of public utility regulation which promotes cross-subsidization in order to pay for as wide a network as possible to serve all the people. Never mind that the universal service principle helped generate a feeling of belonging to the American polis.

In a healthy community, individuals do not continually measure the benefits of exiting *vis-à-vis* the costs of remaining part of the group. Exiting merely to avoid the costs of maintaining the network was not considered socially acceptable – and hence the polis retains its viability and strength.

The reader might recognize that a similar argument underlies the need for all to participate in the financing of public education whether they have children in the public schools or desire to provide a private education for their offspring. Only if all the members of the polis recognize that they can not opt out of the public educational system, can a literate polis be maintained and strengthened.

The neoclassical argument that deregulation is desirable does not recognize (1) the effects of violating community values by denying adequate service to all, while maintaining preferential access to service in high density areas, (2) the costs of the decline in regional economic vitality in the hinterlands due to the lack of network facilities, or (3) the cost of additional congestion due to the increase in traffic on the heavily used routes where costs are low. Indeed, unrestrained competition on the heavily used routes might so seriously weaken the 'common carriers' that firms which initially provided 'low cost' operations (e.g. Frontier airlines, Peoples Express, SBS Skyline, etc.) would ultimately fail leaving the consumers' fate in the hands of a remaining cartel.

We have not yet experienced all the results of deregulation of our transportation and communication network, yet it should be clear that 'deregulation' has not provided the Utopia promised by its advocates. There is a growing fear that the deregulation movement has gone too far. Unfortunately, we can not know whether the fear is justified for we have not developed benchmark criteria to compare what the society wants from these sectors to compare with actual performance. At least in the days of public utilities 'regulation', society's goals of providing every area with access to networks was being achieved. Today, in our era of deregulation, the only criterion is a metaphysical one, whatever the market does provide must be what we desire!

Accordingly, despite deregulation of the telephone industry, one can not logically demonstrate whether the consumers of telephone services are either better off than they would be if telephone services was organized as a public utility. Some consumers of telephone services have improved their economic situation because of deregulation, while others have suffered a degradation in service and significant increases in the cost of maintaining telephone service in their homes. It is not at all clear that deregulation of the telephone system has been a universal good – or that it is better for society than what could have been developed under a regulated system which encompassed both the business and civic values. We must, therefore, be able to discuss the issues of regulation in the realm of civic values – it is not enough to dismiss regulatory rules with the argument that the free market knows best.

The trend in the 1970s and 1980s away from regulation of specific industries in the public interest (e.g. airlines, utilities, banks, etc.) was typically rationalized on the basis that deregulation *per se* would improve market performance. There is no doubt that this deregulation movement altered the pre-existing market situation, creating winners as well as losers. There is no evidence indicating that the resulting market situation meets the economists' yardstick of achieving an efficient solution where all market participants have improved their economic situation. Of course, the previous regulatory system was not perfect, nor did regulatory agencies always make decisions that were in the public interest. But just as eternal vigilance is the price of liberty, so watchfulness is a necessary condition to make sure economic institutions continue to adapt to new environmental conditions in order to fulfil the public service roles that they were designed for.

CONGESTION

The overuse of public facilities can cause congestion and lead to traffic delays. Everyone who uses a bridge, public park, train, airline, or any other shared facility may contribute to congestion and the degradation in the quality of service during periods of peak use. Those who use the facilities thereby impose a burden on other users. The conservative solution for the congestion problem is for those who can pay the most for the use of the facilities to outbid the others for exclusive use of the facility. Thus, for example, if more people wished to use a bridge than the bridge could hold, the priority in the sequence of crossing would go to those who were willing to pay the most for the use rather than wait. (As in most 'efficient' conservative solutions, the poor are most likely to be at the end of the line.) Under this market solution, for example, ambulances would not be able to obtain the traffic right of way to cross the bridge by using their siren; instead, the efficient business culture solution would be for the ambulance driver to pay every road user a sum sufficient to bribe him/her to move out of the way!

The civilized view, on the other hand, is that the victim in the ambulance must have priority in order to save precious seconds – regardless of whether the victim is rich enough to afford to bribe others to get out of the way. Most readers would think this solution is proper; but, conservative economic logic suggests that the 'siren solution' is inefficient and thus not beneficial. According to conservative philosophy, this is a clear example where government interference (by enforcing the rule that emergency vehicles have the right of way) is deleterious! Here then is an obvious case where a society, because it wishes to be civilized, has ignored the conservative solution.

Conservatives may argue that the siren solution is a special case. This is fine by us as long as conservatives are willing to admit the existence of 'special cases'. Our discussion of external versus internal incentives attempts to identify what makes such special cases prevalent, and therefore how to derive general principles which identify 'special cases' in all modes of economic life.

Even in non-life threatening situations, most civilized societies choose to resolve the congestion problem via the first-come-first-serve principle, rather than by the free market solution of going to the highest bidder. Most readers would want reservations honoured when they go to a hotel or restaurant even if there are more people wanting to use the facilities than can be accommodated. Bribing the head waiter or the reservation clerk to cut ahead of reservation holders may provide an efficient solution, but it is one which most of us would find to be uncivilized, unpleasant, and undesirable. Similarly, in inclement weather, the civilized solution to the congestion problem is to queue up in taxi stands, not to push people aside or outbid them for cab service. Ultimately it is this civilized behaviour that moderates our individual self-interest and allows businesses to survive and thrive in any highly evolved economy.

THE DEVELOPMENT OF UHF TRANSMISSION FACILITIES

Several years ago, VHF spectrum space for television transmission was completely filled, while UHF space was completely empty. The conservative solution to this congestion problem on VHF was to auction space to the highest bidders. The reasoning was that when the price for VHF space was raised sufficiently, broadcasters would find the cheaper UHF space an excellent substitute for their transmissions. The only problem was that because no one was transmitting on UHF, television sets were not built to receive UHF signals. The consumer could, of course, pay extra to have a UHF receiver custom built into the TV – but since there were no programmes on that part of the spectrum, it was not in the buyer's self-interest to do this. Since UHF transmission could not be received by TV in American homes, it was not in the self-interest of any broadcaster (or advertiser) to use that part of the spectrum. Here then we had a variant of the chicken–egg dilemma. If only UHF transmission was widely available, consumers would want TV's with UHF receivers, and if only consumers had such TV sets in their homes, broadcasters and advertisers would be willing to use this part of the spectrum. The free market could never resolve the dilemma.

The United States government – recognizing the desirability of expanding broadcasting transmission to all the nation, solved the problem simply mandating that all newly produced TVs had to contain UHF receivers. The mass production economies of providing UHF reception on every set, allowed UHF reception to be built in at a minimal increase in the purchase price of a TV. In a very short period of time, as households bought second TVs for their homes, or replaced old ones, the entire nation was receptive to UHF broadcasting. It was now in the self-interest of entrepreneurs to use

UHF channels if VHF ones were not available. The VHF congestion problem was resolved, simply and in a civilized manner without conflict and haggling in the marketplace.

CONCLUSIONS

The real lesson to be derived from these illustrations is that businesses are not compelled to compete in accordance with natural market laws beyond humans' capacity to alter. Every market must have some set of 'rules of the game'. In a civilized society, social institutions play an essential moderating role on the law-of-the-jungle behaviour in pursuit of external incentives.

Since the dawn of recorded history human progress has been associated with the development of community rules and institutions to resolve conflict without violence. The common understandings of the rules of the game – as specified in the interpretation of law and in the establishment of customs – plays a decisive role in constraining behaviour and helping to determine outcomes.

There is no monolithic government, just as there is no faceless abstract market. There are specific people who often recognize that they are interacting in the pursuit of their own self-interest. Often the same people play influential roles in both governmental agencies and private industries. The rules under which we operate the economic system are in a constant state of flux, and the economically powerful can often have a significant say in how things change. Assuming away the importance of the interaction between the laws of our society and the people who shape and mould our social as well as political mores, is to deny the human condition.

A civilized society itself is a public good. Civilization would not have been purchased by individuals acting alone and calculating costs and benefits of their civilized actions. Unless a certain critical mass of a population simultaneously and collectively adopt civilized standards of behaviour, the full rewards of civilization can not be enjoyed by anyone. Once adopted they are enjoyed by all – even those who do not toil to create the civilizing environment.

Moreover, civilization is not something which can easily be purchased on a piecemeal or incremental basis. Consider the concept of justice for all – a keystone for any civilized society. If a society permits justice to be metered out solely in each case as to whether the benefits of the decision outweigh the costs of this specific decision, then the integrity of the principle of justice to all will soon be eroded. For example, in a civilized society, the judicial system may have to provide a specific decision which in its own context is not popular because it does not provide specific benefits to the current population. Nevertheless this decision may be necessary in order to promulgate the principles of a civilized society.

Note

1. A major implication of the fact that we do not obey any immutable economic law in our economic behaviour is that the economic future, unlike the astronomical future, is uncertain. Hence economists cannot reliably forecast where the economy will be even a few weeks or months from now, or even the stock market's value tomorrow. Astronomers, on the other hand, using the unchanging law of gravity and previous observations of the positions of the heavenly bodies can confidently predict the position of the planets days, weeks, years, and even centuries into the future.

   Because economics involves non-ergodic phenomena, all economic prediction is an art form, not a science. Like any art form, some practitioners are much better at it than others. The use of expensive and impressive computer hardware and software in formulating economic predictions does not guarantee excellent forecasts any more than the use of the most expensive paints and canvas ensure one will produce an art masterpiece.

4 Why Taxpayers Pay their Taxes

Armed with the information shown in Figure 4.1 drawn on a paper napkin and fortified with accompanying drinks, economist Arthur Laffer initiated the reshaping of American society with White House Chief of Staff Richard Cheney in 1974. The history which was made by Arthur Laffer's napkin reveals some of the inadequacies of the conservative view of human nature, but its story also demonstrates the overwhelming influence that economic ideas can have on the nation.

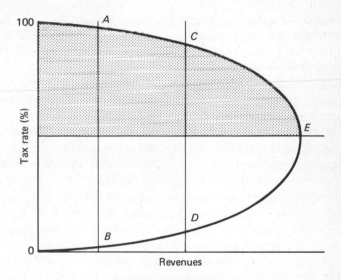

Figure 4.1

For conservatives, the problem with taxes is their disincentive effect on workers and businesses. Consequently, conservative solutions will focus on cutting tax rates to reduce disincentives. From our perspective, the important issue surrounding taxes is the need to support the institutions which will maintain voluntary taxpaying in a civilized society. Our approach to tax reform is in the context of the civilized sphere where civic duties and cold cash interact. An oft-forgotten aspect of the tax protests of the American Revolution was that they were not directed at taxes *per se*. The battle cry was 'No taxation without representation!' – that is, without civic justice. Civilized tax reform will be organized around a co-ordinated application of external and internal incentives to earn credibility, change attitudes, and to build institutions which will maintain the norms which underlie this important duty of citizenship.

We will first focus on the conservative conclusions in regard to taxes and the motivation to work – conclusions which have been tested and proved false under the Reagan Administration. Next, we will examine how conservative economists account for tax compliance, and contrast that with an approach which combines self-interest with civic values. Finally, we will outline a number of civilized policies which address the public policy concerns with taxes and taxpayers which we have identified.

Supply-side economics, which traces its lineage back to Arthur Laffer's cocktail napkin, came as a backlash against the excesses of the eroded liberalism of the 1970s. Supply-siders were a group of conservative economists who believed that prosperity resulted from the activity of daring entrepreneurs who (when unhindered by high taxes and government regulation) would create a flood of new and productive businesses. This virtuous creation of a new supply of goods was contrasted with the image of a ponderous 'liberal' bureaucracy managing the economy through demand-side interventions. Six years after meeting with President Ford's Chief of Staff, the ideas of Arthur Laffer were to guide the government of the USA.

In the intervening years the Laffer curve was drawn on many other cocktail napkins to make the simple point that tax rates, especially on the wealthy, were too high. The explanation of the graph was that 'there are always two tax rates that yield the same revenues'. For example, at a tax rate of 0 per cent no revenues will be raised. At a tax rate of 100 per cent no one would keep anything they earn, so there would be no incentive to work. If no income is earned then revenues will be zero.

Laffer argued that people's work effort was inversely correlated with the tax rate; as taxes rose, people worked less. Laffer defined point 'E' on his curve shown in Figure 4.1 as the tax rate at which government revenues would be the greatest. He claimed that the US was at point A, and since this was above point E on the Laffer curve, the existing tax rates were encouraging people to avoid taxes by working less. Reducing taxes therefore would encourage people to work harder, and therefore earn more income on which taxes could be collected.

Other supply-side economists expanded Laffer's message by arguing that high tax rates encouraged cheating by encouraging taxpayers to under-report income and to engage in transactions which were not easily traceable by the IRS. As long as tax rates were 'high', supply-siders argued, the payoff for cheating or non-compliance in terms of unpaid taxes would exceed the costs of getting caught. If, however, tax rates were lowered, then the profit from cheating would be reduced, thereby encouraging more people to comply with the tax laws.

Finally, it was noted that high tax rates encouraged people to invest in unproductive but legal tax shelters. Lower rates would make such sheltered investments less profitable, encouraging investors to switch to other productive – but taxable – investment. (Of course, if the tax shelters were truly non-productive, then they should have been removed from the tax laws entirely – but this latter point was not made by the supply-siders.)

In sum, given the 'high' tax rates existing in 1980, supply-side economists argued that any reduction in rates would raise tax revenues by increasing work effort, reducing non-compliance, and by moving investment from tax sheltered to taxable projects. In 1981, supply-siders predicted that a 25 per cent across-the-board reduction in tax rates would lead to a balanced budget by 1984.

Supply-side economics took the nation by storm. Supply-siders were seen as economic Santa Clauses giving every tax payer a permanent Christmas present – lower taxes. As a predictive theory, however, supply-side economics was responsible for the largest economic miscalculation in history. Instead of the balanced budget confidently predicted to occur by 1984, the national debt almost doubled from $900 billion in 1980 to $1.6 trillion in 1984.

The enormity of this forecasting error had led some to believe that supply-side economics was merely a red-herring designed to detract attention from a hidden agenda; namely (1) to reverse the trend towards a more equitable distribution of income begun by Roosevelt after the Great Crash in 1929, and (2) to run such enormous deficits as to precipitate a public outcry to reduce the size of big government. This hypothesis gains some support from David Stockman's confession in his autobiography *The Triumph of Politics* that two months before the 1980 election he recognized that Reagan's proposed tax cuts would not lead to balanced budgets. Instead, he expected deficits on the order of $100 billion by 1985 – an optimistic estimate, as it turned out. Stockman perceived annual deficits of this magnitude 'more as an opportunity than as a roadblock' in an attempt to carry out the conservative agenda of reducing the size of government. Stockman's confession of this ulterior motive is a particularly damaging comment as to the substance of supply-side ideology. Stockman was not only one of supply-sider Jude Wanniski's strongest converts, but he had provided 'incisive criticisms and cogent amendments' for the first edition of *Wealth and Poverty* (according to author George Gilder).

Close examination of supply-side economics indicates why there was such a failure to predict real world outcomes. No evidence was provided to demonstrate that the US was above point E on the Laffer curve – it was merely assumed that we were. If, on the other hand, the nation was below point E, lower tax rates would just reduce total revenue. The latter situation turned out to be what actually occurred. Even though supply-side economics never met the promises of its advocates, we still find our public policy directed at the supply-side goal of reducing 'high' tax rates. It is therefore necessary to take a more careful look at taxpayers' behaviour to see where Laffer and our national policy went wrong during the Reagan years.

There is a lesson in this supply-side episode: economics and economic ideas can make a difference in our legislation, and in our economic and social lives. The way we look at the economic world will inevitably shape the way our economic world looks. Despite the obvious failure of supply-side economics, in 1986 the United States continued to pursue supply-side goals of reducing tax rates, this time not to balance the budget, but rather under the guise of 'tax simplification'. Tax rates were again reduced, with the top rate falling from 50 to 28 per cent. Despite its loss of empirical credibility, the conservative philosophy of supply-side economics apparently lingers to shape our national government.

SUPPLY-SIDE ECONOMICS AND TAX COMPLIANCE

The most important economic policy undertaken by the Reagan Administration has involved concentrated efforts to relieve the burden of taxpaying. Reagan tax policy was promoted not only as a way of improving the economy, but also as a means of eliminating 'unfair' (high) tax rates and thus improve tax compliance. The fairness of the Reagan policies, however, has been based on the conservative view that the motivation for tax-paying depends only on the external incentives created by the tax rates to be paid and the risks of punishment for non-compliance.

Conservative proponents of tax reform and simplification have attributed the growth in non-compliance to the fact that inflation pushed most Americans into significantly higher tax brackets during the 1970s without any increase in real income. Although people's money income and hence their tax bracket rose during this decade, inflation significantly eroded this gain in income. People found themselves earning more money but paying significantly more in taxes. Faced with higher prices because of inflation, people's after-tax income bought little more than they could have purchased with less money in the 1960s. Thus conservatives concluded that taxpayers' incentives for tax compliance and working hard were being eroded by the progressive tax brackets inherited from the liberal legislation of the 1940s to the 1960s.

Hence in the 1980s, conservative economic ideology implied that the lower (and less progressive) tax rates were not only a panacea for boosting economic growth, but for encouraging tax compliance as well. The forces determining employment and economic progress will be dealt with later; in this chapter we will examine tax compliance and see how the supply-side solution misses the core of the tax non-compliance problem.

WHY TAXPAYERS PAY THEIR TAXES

Conservative economics has a great deal to say about taxes, but it does not really face up to the simple question of why people pay their taxes. What motivates some people to pay their taxes and others to cheat? Wanniski labels the point 'E' on the Laffer curve as 'the point at which the electorate desires to be taxed'. In mathematical terms, point E is the tax rate that produces maximum revenue, *if* we assume that taxpaying behaviour is shaped solely by the tax rates that people face. What does this mean in terms of the people who make up this 'electorate'?

In a civilized society, civic and social values and not simply calculations of after-tax income gains play a significant role in determining how hard people work and whether they pay their taxes. Under a civilized progressive tax system, citizens are asked to pay taxes based on their ability to pay rather than their need for government services.

In contrast, conservative philosophy asserts that efforts to earn income are necessarily unpleasant and undesirable. People will, therefore, work less if they receive less after-tax pay; or they will cheat more if they face high tax rates so that their pay for the unpleasantness of working is high enough to compensate them for their exertion. Rational self-interested individuals, by definition, do not care about the civic values of tax compliance; self-interested individuals will only pay taxes if motivated by the external incentives of low tax rates and strong enforcement with severe penalties. Conservatives cannot explain the 'non-rational' behaviour of people who see a civic duty in paying taxes. The concept of duty defies the foundations of their philosophy.

In Wanniski's conservative cosmology, there cannot be a monolithic 'electorate' – there are only individuals striving to improve their own welfare. An individual's decision to cheat on her taxes has an insignificant effect on total government revenues and thus the services which that individual can expect to receive. If tax-paying is viewed as a collective purchase of government services, then the price each self-interested individual would be willing to pay, under their conservative philosophy, should be close to nothing, because each citizen receives virtually the same government services whether she pays taxes or not.

Conservatives believe that most individuals pay their taxes because of the fear of getting caught if they try to cheat. For only calculations of external incentives (such as the risk of capture and the pain caused by the potential penalties) can motivate compliance, according to conservatives. As *Forbes* magazine puts it, 'People pay taxes largely because they perceive revenue collectors as vicious ogres without souls'. This conservative proposition carries with it some perverse political ramifications – *Forbes* goes on to state that any deviations from this barbaric role for tax collectors will only impede the functioning of the tax system.

Conservatives also argue that the taxes paid and the effort of record-keeping paperwork associated with taxes create a burden (or 'tax wedge'). This wedge reduces the volume of goods that people can afford; hence there are fewer goods and services to inspire workers to work.

According to Wanniski, the tax wedge therefore forces transactions out of the 'money' economy and into the 'private' underground economy (where the tax collector cannot see the transaction). Wanniski's underground economy is one where neighbours Smith and Jones swap their own labour rather than hiring each other for money payments to produce the things each wants. Government cannot tax swapped chores as easily as it can tax cash transactions, argues Wanniski. But are the well-paid executives who face the highest tax rates going to be raking their neighbours leaves merely to avoid taxes? Moreover, the difficulty of finding a neighbour with the exact skills *and* needs to conduct a swap (surgical podiatry for computer hardware manufacture?) makes barter at most an occasional phenomenon. More likely, the incentive effect of tax rates – if they are 'too' high – will be to avoid paying taxes by using 'off the books' cash transactions wherever the odds of not being discovered are larger.

As tax rates decrease (i.e. as the wedge gets smaller), the conservative argument holds that people are more willing to report their wages and pay for goods rather than swap chores. President Reagan's Economic Recovery Tax Act (ERTA) gained support in Congress partly because the reduced tax rates it established were expected to increase compliance and reduce incentives to search for tax shelters and loopholes. According to the IRS 1986 Trend Analysis compliance did increase between 1979 and 1982 for taxpayers in four of twelve groups, including those with the highest non-farm business income, the highest business partnership income, and the highest salary income. The powerful change in external incentives associated with the 20 per cent tax cut for those in the highest tax brackets *did* make cheating a less profitable activity for some. However, non-compliance continued to grow among those in the other eight categories whose tax cut was not as large. Unfortunately, even as Congress has passed another 20 per cent cut in the highest tax brackets, we must recognize that continuously cutting taxes on a massive scale is not a viable way to slow the national decline in voluntary tax compliance. If we are trying to buy our way to tax compliance through low tax rates, we are paying too much for what we receive.

After the 1982 ERTA bill reducing all tax brackets was enacted into law, *Business Week* magazine reported massive increases in the use of dubious and illegal tax shelters. The IRS Trend Analysis reported that non-reporting of business income among all taxpayers significantly increased between 1979 and 1982, reducing the amount of taxes paid by $6 billion. They suggested that this loss was linked to the proliferation of tax shelters.

Conservatives cannot explain why reduced tax rates increased the demand for tax shelters in 1982. If the risks of being caught remain the same and the benefits of non-compliance with lower rates are smaller, then self-interested individuals will find non-compliance to be less attractive than it was previously. Hence the demand for tax shelters should be inversely correlated with tax rates. If individuals were only calculating individual costs and benefits, when they face lower tax rates they should not choose to increase their non-compliance and use of tax shelters.

The conservative position is that people will not comply with tax laws unless the price is right – that is, people must be rewarded individually to obey the law. The acceptance of this philosophy sends a signal to the population which will directly influence the existing norms of the taxpayers. If the process of weighing the individual costs and benefits of tax compliance is given legitimacy by community leaders espousing conservative philosophy, then a damaging blow is struck against civic values involving duties and social responsibilities which will reverberate for years to come. The civic spirit of a democratic tax system can be vitiated by allowing non-compliance to proliferate unheeded, and by excusing its growth by claiming tax rates are so high that self-interested members of society have reason to avoid taxes. The result will be to steadily erode the credibility upon which the remaining voluntary compliance of the system is based.

NON-COMPLIANCE: RECENT HISTORY AND THE SEARCH FOR CAUSES

When Ronald Reagan was elected President, tax compliance at the federal and state levels had been falling for fifteen years. The IRS reported that between 1973 and 1981 the amount of revenue lost each year from non-compliance with federal tax law increased by 58 per cent (after adjustment for inflation). The IRS concluded that such losses would continue to grow. According to the intentionally conservative estimate of the IRS, $90 billion in revenue was lost to federal income tax non-compliance in 1982 alone. That enormous sum of money exceeds the amount that the federal government spent that year on Justice, Education, Commerce, the State Department, Housing and Urban Development, Transportation, the Environmental Protection Agency, NASA, and the operations of the House and Senate, the Federal Judiciary, and the White House, all combined.

The IRS divides its measurements of types of non-compliance into five categories: under-reporting income, misusing deductions and credits, not filing the forms, non-payment of existing recognized tax liabilities, and all forms of non-compliance due to crime. Table 4.1 shows that in 1982, understatement of income represented the largest drain on IRS receipts from non-compliance.

Table 4.1

Under-reported income	$52.0 billion *(58% of total)*
Overstated expenses, deductions, credits	13.0 billion *(14%)*
Non-filers	3.0 billion *(3%)*
Delinquency	7.0 billion (approx.) *(8%)*
Crime	9.0 billion (approx.) *(10%)*
Corporate non-compliance	6.0 billion *(7%)*
Total	90.0 billion

The $90 billion total shown in Table 4.1 represents an increase of 58 per cent in the estimated loss of annual tax receipts due to non-compliance since 1973.

To identify *the causes* of non-compliance, however, it is necessary to go beyond these figures and examine as directly as possible what drives tax-paying behaviour. The December 1984 Internal Revenue Service's *Taxpayers Attitudes Study* used a variety of techniques to elicit truthful answers about tax-paying behaviour. Some non-compliance is accidental, and can be attributed mostly to errors with tax forms, but the IRS study focused on intentional non-compliance. The responses of taxpayers were studied in order to find a pattern of similar characteristics among non-compliant taxpayers. The only variables substantially correlated with non-compliance were those associated with the social values held by taxpayers. Those who agreed that cheating was acceptable behaviour and those who thought that most other people cheated were those most likely to cheat on their own taxes.

The IRS found no evidence to suggest that actual tax cheating was related to individual perceptions of the costs and benefits of compliance. An individual's analysis of the risks of being caught for tax evasion was unrelated to whether he cheated. Those who believed that the risks of being caught cheating were very small were no more likely to cheat than those who felt the risks were large.

The assertion that high tax rates are responsible for low compliance is contradicted by comparing the evidence in Sweden with that in the United States. In Sweden in the early 1980s tax rates were very high (55 per cent for a worker earning $10 800) while in the United States the combined rates of federal, state, and social security taxes for a similar worker would be around 15 per cent. Nevertheless, according to figures reported by the IRS and the Swedish National Central Bureau of Statistics, roughly the same proportion of taxpayers cheat in each country. Other countries, such as Italy, have even lower tax rates and yet experience even higher rates of non-compliance. Moreover, a 1969 survey by Professor Burkhard Strumpel of the University of Cologne compared several European nations and concluded that absolute levels of tax rates do not determine compliance. All of these studies show that attributes of different national cultures, which are unrelated to the existing external incentives of marginal tax rates, can shape the level of income tax compliance. The cultural and political history of each national polis plays an important role in tax compliance. Even different regions of the United States historically demonstrate significantly different levels of tax compliance, as Figure 4.2 from the IRS's Trend Analysis demonstrates.

Most of the remaining studies of why people cheat on taxes indicate the importance of social and cultural history. A consistent finding in non-compliance studies over the last twenty years is that the younger that taxpayers are, the more cynical they are about the integrity of their fellow citizens, the more willing they are to engage in questionable behaviour and to falsify the amount of income they have earned, and the more critical they are of government in general. A study in Sweden in 1974 notes that since the young generation showed a greater propensity for tax evasion, the problem might get worse in the future – the young cohort will carry their weak tax norms and attitudes with them as they enter the higher paying jobs which come with middle age.

Paralleling these findings are indications that the current level of tax-paying norms is not strong. In a study in Oregon in 1981, for example, tax cheating was considered to be slightly worse than driving without a licence and far less serious than shoplifting. In another survey, respondents from North Carolina in 1975 ranked tax evasion as slightly more serious than stealing a bicycle.

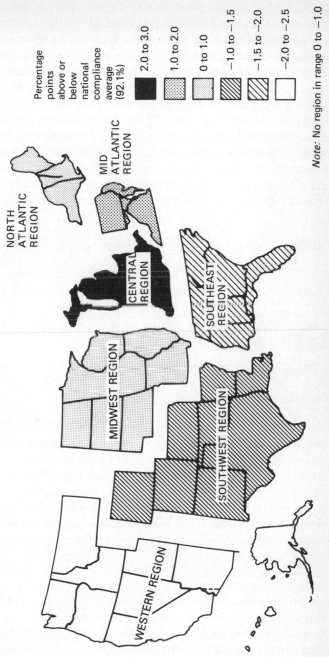

79

Compliance level by region, 1965–82

Percentage points above or below national compliance average (92.1%)

- 2.0 to 3.0
- 1.0 to 2.0
- 0 to 1.0
- −1.0 to −1.5
- −1.5 to −2.0
- −2.0 to −2.5

NORTH ATLANTIC REGION

MID ATLANTIC REGION

CENTRAL REGION

SOUTHEAST REGION

MIDWEST REGION

SOUTHWEST REGION

WESTERN REGION

Note: No region in range 0 to −1.0

Figure 4.2

Clearly a realistic appraisal of why citizens pay (or do not pay) taxes must consider both the internal incentives of social norms as well as external incentives. In contrast to the conservative view of tax-paying, the empirical evidence is that non-compliance has strong correlations with the erosion of civilized norms. Furthermore, the IRS's study of tax behaviour indicates that calculations of costs and benefits are frequently not an important determinant of whether or not a taxpayer will pay his taxes. To devise policies to encourage tax compliance therefore we must examine both the calculating behaviour that conservative economists see, as well as the internally motivated behaviour of the polis. Finally, we must pay particularly close attention to the volatile interaction of these internal and external motivations.

INTERNAL AND EXTERNAL INCENTIVES, AND TAX-PAYING

In conservative economics the primary reason why people pay taxes is that they are afraid of the economic penalties of getting caught if they cheat. In his classic work *The Logic of Collective Action* Professor Mancur Olson asserts that

> no major state in modern history has been able to support itself through voluntary dues or contributions. . . . Taxes, compulsory payments by definition, are needed.

The weakness in this argument – that the fear of sanctions accounts for tax compliance – is that, based on the evidence available, any reasonable calculation by self-interested taxpayers of the probability of getting caught and the relevant penalties involved would motivate greater non-compliance than has been experienced historically. Despite a reluctance on practical grounds to admit that tax cheating is a crime that pays, there is a general consensus among tax officials that their powers of enforcement are not sufficient to account for the high level of compliance that does occur. Former Commissioner of the IRS Jerome Kurtz has argued:

> Our system works best when it works automatically and unobtrusively . . . enforcement activity alone cannot achieve acceptable levels of compliance. Ours is, after all, a voluntary compliance system supplemented by enforcement.

Moreover, Professor Mark Moore of Harvard suggests that increased enforcement can actually *reduce* voluntary compliance, a conclusion which is logically inconsistent with the philosophy of neoclassical economics:

> [I]f enforcement alone is expanded, the existing norms supporting compliant taxpaying may deteriorate even more quickly. For the expansion of enforcement actions communicates an idea of what is expected of people as well as what is desirable. And if the system is set up on the basis that people will not pay taxes unless forced to do so, taxpayers are granted a license to adopt this attitude for themselves.

This is not to imply that enforcement never plays a role in tax compliance. The recent decline in compliance has come at a time when enforcement activity also has fallen. The risk of even being audited has always been low, and dropped from 2.59 per cent in 1976 to 1.55 per cent in 1982. The risk of being audited has fallen even more drastically for the wealthiest taxpayers (those with income over $50 000). Even if caught, the prosecution arm of the IRS poses a very limited threat. Of the roughly 25 million cases of tax non-compliance estimated for 1982, less than 2000 were actually prosecuted and only half of these individuals were sentenced to gaol. Most cases were settled by payment of interest or penalties.

Internal and external incentives both have a role to play in determining tax compliance. Tax scholar Clara Penniman expresses the relationship between the need for solid enforcement and the development of the civic ethic of voluntary compliance with the tax system:

> [F]eeble administration converts honesty into dishonesty. Unless the income recipient feels (1) that others in a like position are made to discharge their tax liabilities and (2) that the tax-administering agency is making some effort to protect the state's interests by independently checking his income, he will consider it no great misdeed to underreport his income and adopt a 'come and get me' attitude.

Internal and external incentives should be woven together for a successful tax compliance policy. The Franchise Tax Board of California notes in describing their Fair Share programme that enforcement is one important aspect of shaping both current and future norms:

> [E]nforcement programs do have an important role to play, both in terms of providing short-term, limited corrective actions, and in terms of building long-term confidence in the viability of the tax system.

Thus, a viable tax system comes from the effective use of both internal and external incentives.

Enforcement not only plays a large role in directly determining the revenue raised in a given year, but it also shapes the values of the polis – an influence which will be felt in future years. The effect of enforcement on the polis can be either reinforcing or corrosive. Indeed, the primary example that we will discuss – Massachusetts' 1983 Revenue Enforcement and Protection Program (REAP) initiative – was a success largely because the limited enforcement capability that was available was used in effective co-ordination with norm-setting actions. The problem of selecting the appropriate use of enforcement to maintain and strengthen the polis is the same question we have raised earlier as to setting the proper co-ordination of internal and external incentives. As we explained in Chapter 2, a choice of this type will depend on the particular traditions and beliefs which are currently held by American taxpayers.

The actions of a few non-compliers can erode the taxpaying polis, shifting the balance so that others begin to cheat, eventually leading to actions as a group which were originally preferred by only a few, as reported in Sweden in the 1970s:

> The amount of tax evasion and the compensating additional taxes needed have reached a critical point, and the resultant pressure on honest taxpayers creates a strong tendency to tax evasion even among . . . those originally satisfied with the tax system.

Conservatives refuse to recognize that the civic values supporting taxpaying norms can collapse – non-compliance can become, in the conclusion of a 1974 study by East Carolina University Professors Song and Yarborough, 'a favorite sport which taxpayers play unabashedly against their government'. In such a situation the erosion of norms follows the example provided by Professor Schelling's tipping model which we discussed in Chapter 2.

The contagious nature of non-compliance was noted in a study of Ohio residents in 1976 which concluded that 'the more tax evaders a taxpayer knows, the more likely he is to evade taxes himself'. As long as the belief in the integrity of ones' fellow taxpayers is still strong, compliance is voluntary and cheating is simply not considered as an option by most of the population. However, when taxpaying norms decline, compliance becomes more and more based on calculations of the risks and payoffs from cheating.

The task of government in encouraging voluntary compliance is to strengthen the civic community from which tax-paying norms originate – to strengthen the polis. To change social norms it is necessary to operate in the context of the current norms while simultaneously laying the groundwork for a new set of norms. A government cannot appeal to a sense of moral duty if current morals are weak or in disrepute. As Penniman suggests, it is here that strict enforcement can be used to strengthen the legitimacy of the reforming government agency, and to prod individuals out of their current habits towards the new tax-paying regime.

Once social norms have eroded and their influence diminished, we do see a greater applicability of conservative economics. This points to a larger truth regarding conservatism: their paradigm is most applicable where social values are weak, where civilized behaviour has disappeared, and where therefore the external incentives of appetite and fear play a greater role.

The final word on the relationship between enforcement and social norms was made almost 500 years ago by Machiavelli:

> Just as good customs require good laws in order to be maintained, so laws require good customs for them to be observed.

When civic institutions and formal enforcement mechanisms are employed in concert, the combination increases the efficiency of both civic values and self-interest.

REVITALIZING THE TAX-PAYING POLIS

There have been a number of discrete initiatives to increase voluntary compliance, as well as several co-ordinated campaigns, including one in Massachusetts which we will examine in some detail. These programmes have both increased enforcement *and* simultaneously attempted to revitalize social norms in order to increase future voluntary compliance.

Actions to strengthen enforcement, taken in isolation, can of course help to maintain and strengthen tax-paying norms – if the tax agency can select those enforcement measures which are perceived to be fair applications of force (i.e., in line with current norms). For example, the State of Minnesota pursues 'flashy livers' – boat owners and those with expensive cars and special licence plates – in order to benefit from public support for such 'sting the rich' enforcement.

Norm-setting actions alone can also have a positive effect on compliance if other existing norms can be *refocused* on the non-compliance problem. For example, tax collectors in Massachusetts have worked to redirect the values behind the current activism against drunk driving to encompass tax cheating by using similar language and advertising to frame the problem. It has been suggested that the methods and sentiments of anti-smoking activism might be similarly shifted onto the problem of tax cheating.

The most effective policies come from combining the external incentive of increasing risks via more stringent enforcement with the internal incentive pressures from the polis. Civic values ease the pain of government intervention, while enforcement gives credibility to the revitalized norms. Recent actions of the Commonwealth of Massachusetts illustrate such a process, in four stages.

(1) *Framing the issue*. The state developed alternative tax-paying norms by building on selected elements existing within current values. In order to establish the attitude that tax evasion is not a victimless crime, the Massachusetts legislature and the media were informed that tax evasion totalled $640 million (although later estimates indicate that the figure for 1983 may have been in excess of $1 billion). After publishing lists of major tax delinquents and identifying uncollected tax bills of $300 million, it was stressed that if non-compliance were eliminated, taxes could be lowered by 10 per cent. Non-compliance was therefore not merely cheating on an abstract 'government', but taking money away from neighbours (which was less acceptable than cheating on an impersonal government). Finally, the state worked to 'emphasize the service aspects [of] a department that cares' in order to establish the theme that enforcement was protecting the honest taxpayer from paying more because of the tax cheats.

(2) *Establishing credibility*. Massachusetts applied an enforcement 'shock' to get people's attention. A carefully orchestrated seizure drive began in May of 1983 to convey the threat of enforcement.

This enforcement drive by itself collected $128.8 million – a 70 per cent increase over the previous year. The state also set out to establish *continuing* media coverage of department enforcement through a series of seizures and other enforcement actions. However, despite these actions, state officials admit privately that this enforcement was too little to change significantly the odds against the tax cheater, instead making more of a real contribution as a means of communicating that the state was getting tough.

(3) *Institutionalize the new order.* The state established institutional foundations to provide for future maintenance of the new customs being established and to reinforce the perception that a change was occurring.

A major legislative initiative in June 1983 instituted major new powers:

(i) Tax evasion was made a felony, punishable by up to five years in prison and fines up to $100 000 for individuals.
(ii) Revocation of state and local licences and contracts of non-complying individuals and businesses.
(iii) Contracting with private collection agencies (as the federal government already did).

At the same time, the Taxpayer Assistance Bureau was strengthened, a Problem Resolution Office was created, tax forms were simplified, and efforts were made to hasten the refund process – all of these actions supported the view of a fair and socially just tax system for a civilized community.

(4) *Transition.* A transitional mechanism was needed to avoid the injustice of treating past behaviour under the new normative standards, and to allow taxpayers to change their norms while saving face. As Massachusetts Tax Commissioner Jackson relates, 'With the beefing up of Departmental resources and the tough new tools and ground rules under the REAP law, I felt strongly that a *transitional* mechanism was appropriate, in fact essential'.

A three-month amnesty programme from November 1983 to January 1984 allowed tax delinquents, non-filers, and outright evaders to pay their accumulated debt without prosecution. The state undertook an ambitious public relations campaign to make clear that 'Amnesty was a one-time, last chance offer' after which it would be 'No more Mr Nice Guy'.

Massachusetts received immediate increases in revenues from the amnesty (although such increases were not strictly voluntary – they were received in response to a direct state intervention). Fifty thousand individuals and corporations took advantage of the amnesty programme, adding $80 million to tax revenues as of January 1985. Over four years, Massachusetts estimates that increases in total voluntary compliance brought in $1.7 billion. This is in addition to the $3.3 billion in revenues brought in by seizures and revenues from the improved economy. Current estimates are that non-compliance has been cut by 25–30 per cent.

The success is not limited to one year's tax returns. Those who acknowledged their previous non-compliance during the amnesty period will remain on the tax rolls in the years to come. From a broader perspective, the re-establishment of the norms surrounding the important public duty of tax-paying may have benefits in other spheres of civic life. Increased voluntary compliance with tax-paying responsibilities will help prevent the erosion of legitimacy of government and law that comes with the 'sport which taxpayers play unabashedly against their government'. The positive example set by a tax system which achieves a high level of compliance may even have some influence on other parts of our lives where voluntary compliance is important (such as driving).

Conservatives misinterpreted what was going on in Massachusetts, even after the successful amnesty. *Forbes* described the amnesty with the analogy of child-rearing: 'When you let a bad kid get away without punishment once, how do you ever convince him again that you mean what you say?' Note how the conservative view of human nature leads them towards treating the public like children as opposed to responsible adults. Since the public, like children, are assumed to lack any moral character, it is unsurprising that improvements in compliance cannot be attributed to civic values. Thus, the *Forbes* article concludes that any increase in compliance must be due entirely to enforcement – a claim which even Massachusetts' own tax officials do not make.

Tax Commissioner Jackson's view of the programme in Massachusetts summarizes three essential elements in changing taxpayer attitudes:

> Why did Amnesty work in Massachusetts? I like to think that for those who took the offer it was a combination of *fear*, *guilt*, and *gratitude*: *fear* of what would happen if they did not settle up, *guilt* about their past mistakes and *gratitude* that we were giving them one last chance to square things away.

Massachusetts' success cannot be explained by conservative economics alone. Fear came from the state's enforcement efforts, which conservative economics does recognize. Guilt represents the conflict in values of the polis when lax tax-paying norms were confronted by the state's framing of the tax cheating issue. Gratitude lays the motivational basis for a shift of attitudes about tax cheating, and the establishment of allegiance to the norms of a renovated tax-paying polis. Conservative forces had a role in events, but in this example they were not central.

EVOLUTION OF AN INSTITUTION: TAX AMNESTY

A public policy initiative such as a tax amnesty programme is a fledgling institution – that is a new mechanism which is partially built on existing law and custom, and partially created by the interactions between the politicians and the people. The meaning which people initially attach to this new political initiative is very important – their understanding of the new policy in their dialect will be the base upon which all future implementation efforts will be grounded.

A particular public policy programme such as tax amnesty will earn its reputation based on experiences reported from where it has been attempted. The initial meaning of any tax amnesty programme may be different after it has already been implemented elsewhere, because the recent experience of the earlier programme influences perceptions. Even if successive amnesty initiatives in two very similar states have identical provisions, if the first initiative failed (due to a political scandal or some other event unrelated to taxes), then the second attempt starts off handicapped merely by the negative association with the first effort.

Between 1982 and 1986, nineteen states completed tax amnesty programmes. The appetites of tax officials across the nation has been whetted by the thought of an immediate windfall of new revenues from taxpayers 'coming clean' during the amnesty period. California reaped $144 million, Illinois $154 million, and Massachusetts $80 million. However, if government officials view tax amnesty solely as a quick revenue-raiser, they may miss the important role which tax amnesties can play in helping shape long-range tax-paying behaviour. The opportunity to perpetuate improved tax compliance – and the higher future revenues which this ensures – is lost.

Although Massachusetts and California both mobilized comprehensive campaigns to improve tax compliance norms in co-ordination with their amnesty programmes, other states have been content to take the money and run, with no concern for longer run impacts on social values. Thus the meaning of a tax amnesty – its reputation as a policy tool – can become tainted, as evidenced in the writing of *Washington Post* columnist Hobart Rowan:

> First the slogan was 'privatization' – the sale of government assets. Now it is 'tax amnesty'. An era of oppressive federal deficits always produces innovative gimmickry designed to avoid more painful ways, such as tax increases, to stem the flow of red ink.

If tax amnesties (or other policy initiatives) are used only to attain the limited external incentive benefits that conservative economics identifies, the possibility of more civilized use of those programmes is diminished.

Once the importance of civic values in maintaining and strengthening tax compliance is acknowledged, then the non-compliance problem can be addressed by taking advantage of these tax-paying values and by protecting these values from potentially corrupting influences. We can illustrate both of these options with a brief outline of policies which have been proposed to improve compliance in the real world where tax-paying norms are important. These policies are valuable not only in addressing non-compliance, but also in demonstrating how far we have come from the simple view of tax-paying behaviour in conservative economics.

THE DIALECT OF TAX FORMS

Tax forms can influence the public context of tax-paying. One of the most publicized goals of the tax reform movement has been to simplify the tax form itself. This desire may seem anomalous in view of the fact that three-quarters of all taxpayers already use simplified 'short' forms. As University of Wisconsin Professor Clara Penniman points out, however, mechanical simplicity is not the same as comprehension. The important question is not whether taxpayers can complete the forms, but whether they understand the law and its purposes.

The process of sitting down and staring at the tax form itself is the primary contact taxpayers have with the tax process. Their interpretation of taxes – the meaning of taxes in the public dialect – is drawn from a history of annual rituals: clearing the kitchen table, sharpening pencils, assembling documents, trying to comprehend strange terms, adding and subtracting numbers, and – increasingly – seeing the bulky forms and immediately handing them to a professional tax consultant. Public perception of the 1986 Rostenkowski–Packwood tax reform bill was established less by the Congressional debate and the successful September 1986 vote, than the W-4 form for tax withholding which the IRS sent out to all American workers. Tax 'simplification' arrived in the guise of four highly complex pages that baffled even the employees of the IRS as they filled out their own forms.

In recent years several states have modified their tax forms not only by making them clear and attractive, but also by providing such information as how the state spends the revenues it collects. Massachusetts has been praised by its citizens for recently including a message of thanks to the citizens for having paid their taxes. Such changes, however, are not enough. Despite the improvements we have seen, most tax forms are still strongly reminiscent of a grade school work-book, carrying with them the connotations of the student–teacher relationship, not the civic relationship between the taxpayer and her government.

A tax form can be changed to facilitate the development and maintenance of the tax-paying polis by institutionalizing concern with the duties of tax-paying. For example, some small towns such as Dover, Vermont send out a list of all known tax delinquents to their residents, thus identifying those who are violating tax-paying norms, as well as (by omissions to the list) providing a clean bill of health to all others. It is not hard to imagine what happens the day the tax form arrives in the mail – everybody immediately goes to the list to see if there is anyone on the list that they know. Massachusetts has already put the names of tax-evading businesses in the newspaper. These simple institutions shape an environment in which the issue of compliance is raised in a regular fashion that can support the development of tax-paying in the polis.

NEW INSTITUTIONS FOR A NEW POLIS

There is a thin line between the attitude that tax cheating is acceptable and the actions of that part of the tax return industry whose 'business is to sell "tax savings" to the taxpayers'. As California's Franchise Tax Board notes, 'demand for abusive tax shelters and illegal protest schemes have spawned a tax evasion industry'. Currently, the tax advice industry is organized around the principle of finding the biggest breaks possible for their clients. But it may be possible to change the institutional essence of this industry – to shape its polis so that tax advisers promote compliance rather than evasion.

Harvard Professor Mark Moore advocates the licensing of tax advisers, drawing the comparison between tax advisers and electricians, plumbers, and tavern owners (all of whom are licensed), because all are in businesses which have important implications for public safety and order. The intent of licensing is to change the 'business' of the tax return industry into compliance. Third-party regulators have been used effectively in the past – in the 1930s the Securities and Exchange Commission began licensing accountants, and thereby enlisted them to serve public goals of accurate and honest presentation of information. Professor Thomas McCraw of the Harvard Business School attributes the SEC's success to the fact that the existence of the institution of Certified Public Accountants (CPAs) benefited all investors by guaranteeing that every accountant's reports would follow honest and uniform standards and practices. The accountants benefited as their profession became more financially rewarding (since by limiting entry into the field they were able to raise their standard salaries). Furthermore, the licensing led to an increase in the status for the profession of those who had passed this hurdle. Professor McCraw summed up the success of the SEC in creating a new profession as 'the model of public manipulation of private incentives' in creating a self-perpetuating form of business regulation. In a similar way, it may be possible to convert tax advising into a new profession.

By licensing tax advisers, we can co-opt those who are currently driven to degrade these tax-paying norms in their unregulated pursuit of external incentives. Tax advisers are ultimately bound within legal constraints, but without clear and unambiguous laws (which depend in part on a common national dialect) the profit motive will encourage tax advisers to chip away at the margins of the law. The process of co-opting is through licensing, which is precedented in the cases of electricians, plumbers, and bar owners, so the government action has some standing within existing norms. Government can follow established precedent in providing a role for tax advisers in the creation of a new tax compliance institution.

TAX CODE REFORM IN THE 1980s

Tax reform proposals have blossomed annually on Capitol Hill in the 1980s, promising fairness and simplicity as well as increased compliance. The offerings have included everything from Texas Congressman Ron Paul's uncompromising flat 10 per cent (based on the historic practice of church titheings) to the approach proposed by Senator Bill Bradley and Congressman Richard Gephardt which formed the basis of the bill passed into law in October 1986. This approach was not a simple flat tax, but rather a convoluted plan with several 'bumps' (different tax rates), which threaded its way through numerous political compromises in an attempt to bring together a political constituency.

The Rostenkowski–Packwood compromise which became law in September 1986 may represent a significant simplification in terms of conservative economics in that it reduces the number of marginal tax brackets, but it still is largely incomprehensible to those who do not speak the language of tax law. At most, the tax bill is slightly clearer than previous law. Rostenkowski–Packwood, Bradley–Gephardt, and the 1985 Reagan Administration tax simplification proposal (dubbed Treasury I in its virgin form) have not maintained the initial level of public enthusiasm because the sentiments underlying public attitudes towards tax-paying are not based on economic concepts such as the marginal burden of complex taxes. No self-interested person likes paying taxes – whether there is one tax bracket or twenty! Tax-paying is a public duty which few tax-payers can entirely understand in its current form, and so consequently they find it difficult both to gauge whether they are appropriately fulfilling their role, and to determine whether others are paying their fair share. The problem with these attempts at tax reform is that they have only addressed issues of conservative economic efficiency – they have not been directed at the public alienation and scepticism that eats away at the values which support tax-paying.

Recent polls have shown that a large majority of Americans believe that politically influential groups and the wealthy get special tax advantages. Moreover, a *Washington Post* poll in 1985 reported that 80 per cent of the population said that they would not complain about the amount they pay in taxes if they thought that the rich were paying their fair share. This mistrust of the rich, however, does not carry over into support for raising upper income tax rates. Instead, the brunt of the animosity against the rich falls on their ability to evade their share of taxes via loopholes uncovered by an army of tax consultants.

The IRS's 1984 survey of taxpayer attitudes indicates that the public consistently overestimates the actual level of tax non-compliance, often by more than double. The emphasis in public attitudes upon loopholes for deductions (as opposed to under-reported income, for example, which is four times as great a drain on revenues) indicates how particular forms of non-compliance are suspected far more than their actual incidence merits. According to the IRS, methods of non-compliance which are more available to wealthier taxpayers – such as false deductions and credits, and writing of personal expenses as business costs – were four times more prevalent in public perceptions than in reality.

The political popularity of the idea of broadening the tax base – that is, to eliminate the myriad of deductions and exemptions – comes in part from the belief that the current tax burden is *not* fairly distributed. The problem is mobilizing a broad constituency in favour of an alternative distribution of after-tax income is the same problem which is present in undertaking the establishment of any new institution. Machiavelli writes:

> There is nothing more difficult to execute, nor more dubious of success, nor more dangerous to administer than to introduce a new system of things: for he who introduces it has all those who profit from the old system as his enemies, and he has only lukewarm allies in all those who might profit from the new system.

A successful coalition for tax simplification and reform must be motivated, therefore, by more than the goal of receiving a more favourable redistribution of external incentives. This is because redistributions of external incentives are frequently understood to be zero-sum games, leading to the difficult situation that Machiavelli anticipated. Additionally, it is almost impossible to hold together a coalition comprised of individuals who can only calculate their external costs and benefits from their participation. Unifying internal incentives must also be available to hold the coalition support for tax simplification and reform.

The problem with tax reform on Capitol Hill is that what is touted as 'simplification' still remains so complex and inaccessible to almost all taxpayers that their sentiments for fairness and simplicity seem to be ignored by the legislative debate. Issues in the tax debate have not been argued in the dialect of a civic polis, but rather in the language of economics and accounting. Arguments are made not on the basis of duty, but on the bottom line for each individual taxpayer – how each person's after-tax income will be affected by the changes in the tax burdens. In other words, the tax reform we have seen is the tax reform of conservative economics – it can at best achieve only those benefits which come from removing irrational and counter-productive external incentives of the current tax system. Again, this brings to mind the débâcle of the W-4 withholding forms – in order to increase the precision of paycheck withholdings, the IRS produced a good form in terms of conservative economics which, in practice, merely added to taxpayer frustration and alienation.

Unfortunately, conservative tax reform can not meet the promises claimed by political advocates of tax reform. There can be no windfall benefit for all citizens merely from redistributing external incentives: if we are to raise the same amount of revenue, savings to one group of taxpayers must be paid by a heavier burden on others. Tax reform in 1986 was confined within the limits of a zero-sum game. Not only will the Rostenkowski–Packwood reform fail to reverse the erosion of the tax-paying polis in the USA, but also by raising false hopes of simplicity and fairness, the 1986 reforms reduce the credibility of any future reform effort.

For tax reform to be viable it must clearly be different from the current system. If the primary issues is who gains and who loses (i.e., external incentives only), then Machiavelli's dictum rings true, and the hope of potential beneficiaries will be weaker than the fear of the potential losers. Incremental changes cannot signal a new order of things – they tell taxpayers that the game is the same and that only the distribution of rewards are being changed. Only a reform movement aimed at changing underlying social attitudes will allow the possibility that new rewards of a different sort will be reaped.

The virtue that lies behind the public appeal of tax simplification is not merely the desire to reduce the burden of filling out the tax form – three-quarters of the population already use the simple form. The appeal of simplicity is that it permits people to understand the principles on which one of their primary social duties is based. Furthermore, a byzantine tax system makes all those who do not understand its ways feel like outsiders. Since money has the capacity to purchase a reduction in one's duty as a citizen (through the services of tax consultants and lawyers), the internal incentives of tax compliance are particularly vulnerable to erosion. The taxpayer may easily become suspicious that he is being made a fool by his own honest compliance when others profit by legal and illegal loopholes. Simplicity (i.e., ease of comprehension) is a necessary first step towards tax code reform that will support improved tax-paying norms.

THE CONSERVATIVE DIALECT OF TAX REFORM

The dialect of conservatism can actually forestall serious consideration of tax reforms which might work through the use of civic values. The dominance of the dialect of self-interest in our public debate ensures that the first reaction to any new tax proposal is to calculate the taxes one owes, and determine whether this tax plan makes one a 'winner' or a 'loser'. 'What this policy means to you' will be seen by the news media, the politicians, the the public in terms of what is the bottom line for each taxpayer.

The next conservative comparison to assess the impact of the new plan on the nation is to compare how well others are doing, and to see if the rich and the poor are being treated in accordance with one's preferences for social equity. Eventually, we would even start to look for a way to compare this initiative within the existing political framework – we would consider the reputation of previous tax reform initiatives which had similar external incentive effects to this plan (i.e., help the rich, burden families, create disincentives for enterpreneurs, etc.). But by thinking about tax reform from the perspective of conservative economics, civic values somehow get lost.

The most important discussion is the one that does not naturally occur. What are the principles of a fair tax system? If I pay taxes in accordance with this plan, can I be confident that my fellow citizens are also participating? Are the requirements of this tax-paying duty in line with the beliefs and principles I hold as an American citizen?

In *The Silver Blaze*, it is the dog which does not bark that provides Sherlock Holmes with his key clue to solve a murder. In our public debate on tax reform, it is the questions which are not asked which explain why public sentiment for fair and simple taxation is not being inspired by the plans which have been proposed. In the debate over fair taxation, has anyone yet defined fairness in terms of values and not dollars? The first step in starting real tax reform is to re-establish the dialect of civic responsibility in regard to tax-paying in the sphere of public debate.

The most dangerous aspect of the philosophy of conservative

economics is that it encourages us to overlook the civic values which are of crucial importance not only to the vitality of our civilization, but also to the effective operations of our institutions. In looking to our self-interest first, we can miss the choices that benefit ourselves both individually and as a nation.

5 The Basic Problem of an Entrepreneurial System – Unemployment

We live in an entrepreneurial economic system. Entrepreneurs – the managers of business and government enterprises – are people who make the day-to-day decisions on production schedules, employment hiring, trading activities and investment spending.

The difference between business and government enterprises is that the former are owned by individuals rather than the community at large. Business managers respond to opportunities for profit to employ workers and create income in the private sector. Managers of government enterprises (e.g. The Tennessee Valley Authority, public schools systems, the London Underground, etc.) are civil servants who provide employment and generate income in response to the legislative mandates given to them.

It is the decisions of entrepreneurs which determine whether our economy will suffer from unemployment, or whether we will achieve a state of economic bliss where all who want to work can.

Conservatives argue that if only the government would get out of the way – get off the entrepreneur's back – the mere existence of the resulting *laissez-faire* free enterprise economy will guarantee, at least in the long run, prosperity and full employment. Free enterprise economies, however, have had a rather checkered history as they have suffered severe, and sometimes lengthy, periods of unemployment. The conservative retort to this historical record is that in the short run, unemployment is the necessary price we have to pay to achieve the long-run goal of prosperity. As the economics news editor of the *Wall Street Journal*, Alfred Malabre, stated in his book *Beyond Our Means* 'slumps act to cleanse the economy of strains and distortions that normally mark a peak of the business cycle', thereby drawing an implicit and distasteful analogy to the necessity of taking a laxative to purge the digestive system of the excesses of eating three square meals a day.

But the prosperity peak of a business cycle is the only time that a free enterprise system even comes close to providing full employment and economic well-being for all its citizens. Surely that is a condition to be nurtured rather than purged. A civilized view suggests that the unemployment of business slumps inflicts unnecessary costs on workers and their employers alike. Moreover, even if this price is paid, there is no guarantee that prosperity will inevitably follow the slump. Instead there is a perverse sort of Humpty Dumpty economics here – conservatives hope that if they can make the patient sick enough, he is bound to get better. However, as the Great Depression clearly demonstrated, it may be terribly difficult to recover from the economic malady of unemployment.

To more clearly comprehend why a *laissez-faire* enterprise economy does not guarantee full employment in the long run and why slumps are neither desirable nor inevitable in the short run we must analyse and understand the role entrepreneurs play in our economic system.

HOW THE PRIVATE SECTOR OPERATES

How does the private sector of the economy generate jobs, products, and market prices? Why cannot the private sector deliver the full employment promised by conservative economics? We hope to answer these questions and in so doing show how the shortcomings of the private sector can be rectified by governmental fiscal and monetary policy acting as a balancing wheel to make up any deficiency that would otherwise occur in private sector employment.[1]

Business managers are sometimes motivated to expand production by 'non-economic' reasons such as the desire for personal grandeur or civic responsibility. We will concentrate, however, on the conservative argument that self-interested managers aim solely to produce goods which are expected to sell for more than what they cost to produce. We will assume that entrepreneurs in the private sector are primarily interested in their cash-flow position. Managers will increase production and hiring if they *expect* future sales revenues to exceed the additional cash outlays involved in increasing production. They will reduce employment if they *expect* cash outlays to exceed sales revenues. Hence, business optimism regarding the profitability of expected future sales sparks the economic activity that generate the fires of prosperity. In a civilized society it is the responsibility of the government to make sure these sparks are continuously generated.

The advantages and flaws of the entrepreneurial system

A half-century ago, Keynes reminded us that the 'outstanding faults of the economic society in which we live are its failure to provide for full employment and its arbitrary and inequitable distribution of income'. To cure society's failure to provide full employment, Keynes advocated a programme of systematically maintaining healthy entrepreneurial expectations. This could be accomplished by either having government directly increase its purchases from the private sector whenever business expectations were grim and a slump was expected, or to cut taxes to encourage private spending, or for the authorities to reduce interest rates to stimulate additional investment spending. The resulting additional demand would generate more optimistic sales expectations of managers and thereby encourage business expansion. As the unemployment problem was cured and we entered an era devoid of business cycle slumps, Keynes believed the distribution of income would naturally become more equitable.

In the twenty-five years following the Second World War, Keynes's policies were not only effective in winning the battle against high unemployment, but as a side-effect, they also led to a much more equitable and less arbitrary income distribution. In recent years, however, the record shows that industrial societies have regressed in their efforts to alleviate these major flaws of modern economics. Since the mid-1970s, unemployment has grown to post-Second World War highs for even the more successful economies such as Japan and West Germany; while in recent years the income distribution has become more inequitable.

This backsliding from the civilized solutions already achieved may have led many radicals to condemn our system and set off on a search for a more Utopian (socialist?) solution. Our entrepreneurial system, however, should not be cast off so lightly, for it does possess some significant advantages over traditional socialist schemes. The decentralized decision-making by individuals in our economy who expect to be rewarded for 'correct' decisions often makes for better planning and production in line with consumer desires than centrally run economies. In an economic world where the future is uncertain and can not be statistically predicted, a decentralized entrepreneurial system is continually seeking to discover what consumers will want to pay for in the future, often before consumers themselves know what they will desire. Diversity and the opportunity to exercise personal choice are among the greatest civilized assets of a decentralized entrepreneurial system.

It should be the goal of civilized economies to design policies that eliminate, or at least reduce the existing flaw of unemployment in our economy, while simultaneously striving to maintain the advantages of decentralized decision making. The resulting economic environment would promote personal liberty and freedom of choice without invoking discipline through the fear of unemployment. A revitalized and improved economy where unemployment and unnecessary income loss is no longer a perpetual threat can provide the basis for the most powerful economic system yet devised on the face of the Earth.

HOW THE PRIVATE SECTOR GENERATES JOB OPPORTUNITIES

Expected future spending creates today's jobs

The production of goods and services takes time – and often considerable time – between the day that workers are hired and the day when there is a product to sell. This means that entrepreneurs have no choice but to be guided in today's production and hiring decisions by the expectations they form regarding what buyers will purchase at some future date.

For example, manufacturers of fashion clothing may have to begin the production of their winter line in March in order to have sufficient quantities in inventory at the start of the autumn shopping season. Yet, at the beginning of Spring, most consumers will not have the slightest idea of what clothing they will be purchasing six months hence. Managers, therefore, have no choice but to be guided by the best expectations that one can 'guesstimate' as to what the consumers will be prepared to pay for when they are ready to buy clothes for the following winter.

Money contracts and cash flows

All market-oriented production and trade activities are controlled and limited by contractual arrangements. Once managers are confident enough with their sales expectations, they start production by negotiating contracts for hiring the workers and ordering the materials necessary to complete the job. Signing these hire-purchase contracts at fixed money prices puts the enterprise at risk by requiring specified cash payments at specific future dates. Nevertheless these contracts are desirable because they enable management to obtain cost controls over lengthy and complex production processes. In the absence of these fixed contracts, managers of firms that produce goods with long gestation periods would never be able to calculate the total cost of their production operations *before* they start up the process. And without the cost control estimates that contracts provide, how could entrepreneurs try to guess whether buyers will pay an amount sufficient to cover the production costs and make the operation worthwhile?

A producer of chocolate bunnies for Easter, for example, will enter into contracts for the purchase of cocoa beans and the hiring of labour in the middle of Winter. On the basis of these contractual arrangements, the manager can estimate the cost of producing chocolate rabbits. She can then decide how many Easter bunnies the market will buy at prices which will cover these costs and provide a sufficient profit margin.

Without the institution of contracts, entrepreneurial hiring and purchase decisions would be impossible and market oriented economic activity would cease. With these contracts, managers can estimate costs and their cash flow obligations over time.

Contracts and civilized behaviour

A basic requisite of any civilized society is that behaviour is limited by well established laws, shared norms, and commonly understood traditions. Civilized economic behaviour assumes people will honour their contractual commitments under the civil law of contracts. Contracts are an essential institution for maintaining civilized behaviour in the production and trading process of the entrepreneurial system.

Contracts are legal documents which commit the seller to make delivery and the buyer to make a monetary payment at a specific time (either today or at a future date). Under the civil law, the State assures that both parties to a contract comply with its terms – and if either party reneges, the state will determine, and enforce, the punitive *monetary* damages to be paid to the aggrieved party by the defaulting party. The State, therefore, acts as a guarantor of contract performance and assures the aggrieved party of 'fair' monetary compensation if the other side fails to meet its commitment. Thus, for example, if the cocoa bean seller was unable or unwilling to meet his contractual commitment to the chocolate bunny producer, the latter could sue the seller and receive a monetary reward equal to the damages suffered because the productive plan for producing chocolate bunnies was interrupted.

Only non-market production and exchange processes, such as those done within a family, monastery, nunnery, kibbutz, etc. can be organized without any money contractual basis. In these cases, the civic-cultural group spirit is so overwhelming that all members of the group 'know' that the others will carry out their assigned tasks. In any system where the civic culture is significantly altered by the business view of individuals motivated solely by self-interest, however, enforceable contracts are necessary to provide assurance to each that others will perform as they say they will.

Cash flow is the 'blood circulation' of enterprise. Sales contracts assure cash inflows to the firm, while hire-purchase contracts indicate the forthcoming cash outflows. When cash inflows exceed cash outflows, i.e. sales exceeds cost, the firm can grow and develop. If, however, cash outflows exceed inflows, costs are exceeding revenues, the firm is being bled white and is on the way to the moribund state of bankruptcy. In this latter case, only a blood transfusion, what people on Wall Street call an infusion of funds, can prevent the inevitable demise of any private sector enterprise. Thus, the maintenance of liquidity, i.e., the ability of the enterprise to meet cash outflows as they come due is essential to its viability.

Contractual orders, revenue estimates, and employment

Some firms hire workers and produce output only after they have received customers' orders. These firms are known to produce 'custom-made' products. They produce only 'to contract'; tomorrow's sales depends entirely on today's orders. Employment hiring for such firms varies directly with the received commitments (legal promises) of buyers to purchase.[2]

Alternatively, some firms, especially at the retail level, produce without first receiving sales orders. They produce 'to market' or 'on speculation'. Managers in these firms set today's production schedule solely on their expectations of future sales without having commitments from buyers.

The managers of firms that produce to market can never precisely predict what sales will be. The best they can do is to make an educated guess ('speculate') as to what consumers will be prepared to pay after a lengthy production period. Labour hiring, for these firms, is therefore entirely dependent on managerial belief that demand will be sufficient to buy the output at profitable prices when the goods are ready to be brought to market.

In sum, then, employment in the private sector depends on entrepreneurial *expectations* of future sales. These expectations are based on (a) existing and expected forthcoming orders of buyers and/or (b) the managers' guesses as to what future buyers will want. Whenever expectations of future sales fall, managers reduce production schedules and employment decreases.

If, for example, retailers fear a forthcoming slump in sales, then they will not only reduce their current labour hiring but they will also reduce their orders from suppliers. This change in retail sales expectations will thereby quickly filter back to wholesalers, manufacturers, and subcontractors, causing employment and production to decline in the supplying industries that produce to contract. The resulting increase in unemployment and lost wages feeds back into a further decline in retail sales as the unemployed are forced to curtail their retail expenditures. This can induce further cut-backs in orders and employment resulting in recession or depression.[3]

In an entrepreneurial economy only the expectation of spending can create jobs today; a penny spent by a buyer is a penny earned by a seller and/or his suppliers. If these pennies are not spent on the products of industry, the result will be lost jobs and profit opportunities, so that 'A penny saved (and therefore not spent) is a penny not earned'.

Contracts, jobs, and an uncertain future

Managers know, however, that 'to err is human' and that their sales expectations may be wrong in both the short run and the long run. In our uncertain world, if human nature did not experience the temptation to take a chance, then entrepreneurial activities would quickly wither away. The managerial virtue of having the courage to meet a challenge when the possibility of success is not as statistically predictable as tossing a coin is why we admire the 'entrepreneur' more than the actuary.

But only a fool would rush in to challenge the unknown without some strategy to protect oneself against unforeseeable and unpredictable deleterious outcomes. The successful entrepreneur is not a fool and therefore does not take on the unknown without some defence in case of disappointment. Long duration money contracts specifying fixed cash obligations limit the downside risks facing an entrepreneur to those she believes her liquidity position can survive. With potential losses limited, the allure of potential success (and the possibility of a huge windfall in sales revenue if the market is better than expected) is more appealing. For firms that produce to market the possibility of a virtually unlimited gain more than offsets the possible downside loss limitation set by hire and purchase contracts.

In the neoclassical model, on the other hand, the entrepreneur is a robot decision-maker who acts on the basis of 'rational expectations' based solely on a computer probability analysis of past data to statistically predict future sales correctly. The robot entrepreneur can never make an incorrect decision. In the real world, on the other hand, as Keynes noted:

> Businessmen play a mixed game of skill and chance, the average result of which to the players are not known to those who take a hand. If human nature felt no temptation to take a chance, no satisfaction (profit apart) in constructing a factory, a railway, a mine or a farm, there might not be much investment merely as the result of cold calculation . . . our decisions to do something positive, the full consequences of which will be drawn out over many days to come, can only be taken as a result of animal spirits – of a spontaneous urge to action rather than inaction, and not as the outcome of a weighted average of quantitative benefits multiplied by quantitative probabilities.

Keynes's view of entrepreneurial action is antithetical to the rational manager of a neoclassical world and hence his civilized policy proposals are diametrically opposite to the *laissez-faire* programme advocated by conservatives.

It is these conflicting views of the entrepreneurial decision-making process which lead to different conclusions regarding the likelihood of free markets to automatically generate job opportunities for all, i.e. for full employment. The robot entrepreneurial decision-maker of a neoclassical world is presumed to 'know' with actuarial certainty that all output can *always* be profitably sold just as apples on a tree 'know' they will *always* fall to the ground under the inevitable law of gravity as soon as they release themselves from the branches of the apple tree. Consequently conservative economists who assume entrepreneurs have rational expectations about future sales conclude that there is no role for government in providing full employment. The authorities can not fool entrepreneurs into hiring more workers than they would already be doing in a *laissez-faire* environment.

In a world where the probability of sales revenues cannot be as reliably predicted as a coin toss, that is, in a world where the future is uncertain (i.e. non-ergodic), the 'robot' manager of the neoclassical model simply could not function. In a non-ergodic world – our world – it is Keynes's 'businessmen' who reign supreme. In this world, sales expectations depends on a spirit of entrepreneurship in the community – a spirit which depends in large measure on the cultural and economic environment generated by the values of the community. Keynes referred to this entrepreneurial mood as 'animal spirits' in order to distinguish it from the mechanical robot decision-maker programmed to maximize profits on the basis of statistical evidence obtained from past outcomes.

The animal spirited business manager is the prime mover of the entrepreneurial economic system. In an uncertain world managers' decisions regarding productive activities are geared towards a mixture of external incentives (the desire for income) and internal incentives (the desire to accomplish something noteworthy, challenging, and respected by the community). The community, via its cultural and civic values, provides the setting for determining the importance of the various elements in the mix of goals entrepreneurs strive for. The use of expansionary governmental fiscal and monetary policy can create additional profit opportunities which in a society where expansive entrepreneurial action is honoured can generate a full employment.

The prosperity of any entrepreneurial economic system depends on maintaining an ebullient spirit among managers. Expected increases in demand are necessary to induce managers to hire more workers. On the other hand, pessimistic expectations will cause managers to reduce hiring opportunities. If, at any moment of time, realized sales are just meeting entrepreneurial expectations and if managers project current market conditions into the future, employment will remain virtually unchanged. Everything is precariously hinged on the psychology of the business decision-maker.

Government therefore can and must take action to influence that psychology. If managers become pessimistic (perhaps because they are disappointed in current market performance), then government has the ability, through its taxation, expenditure and monetary policies, to stimulate additional demand which will wake entrepreneurs out of their lethargy and encourage economic activity. As long as there are idle workers and unused capacity, the entrepreneurial system is not delivering the goods! It is wasting available resources which could, if employed, improve the well-being of all the citizens of society.

The necessary conditions for generating full employment are that managers must (a) expect sales revenue to be sufficient to profitably cover all the production costs associated with a fully employed system, and (b) expect future demand will continue to grow as rapidly as capacity and labour force grows. Neoclassical theory *assumes* that these two conditions will always prevail because of a hypothetical immutable economic principle known as Say's Law. The assumption of Say's Law assures that Adam Smith's 'invisible hand' of free markets can always bring about full employment. Keynes, on the other hand, argued that in an entrepreneurial system there is no invisible hand mechanism, no Say's Law, to ensure a balanced growth between demand and supply.

Consequently, only government is strategically located within the entrepreneurial system to take action when necessary to ensure that demand keeps up with supply. Consequently, to understand the debate between Keynesians on the appropriateness of stimulative fiscal policies (even if these require continuing deficits) and conservatives who mindlessly demand a balanced budget and, like Chicken Little, always proclaim that the sky is falling whenever government deficits occur, one must obtain some understanding of the relevance of a Say's Law assumption to policy analysis.

SAY'S IMMUTABLE SCIENTIFIC LAW AND THE GREAT DEPRESSION

Do people work only to consume? The basis of Say's Law

Most economists assert that humans fundamentally dislike working for a living. People bear this gruelling burden of work only because they believe they will earn sufficient income to buy the products of industry necessary to cover the basic necessities of life and, hopefully, some luxuries to make life more enjoyable.

In an entrepreneurial society, in general, the fact that one must work to earn income, and therefore survive (and thrive) is true and obvious. Neoclassical economists, however, carry the argument one small – but significant – step further. They insist that the *only* reason why people are willing to work is that they *always* want more and more products of industry. Accordingly, anytime people earn income, conservatives assume that these people instantly spend their *entire* income on the current products of industry. (Borrowing from banks to spend in excess of one's current income is grudgingly admitted as a possibility. Borrowing, however, is not permitted to alter the generality of the system which requires one to not only earn income today to buy goods today, but insists that as a community we always spend our entire income, not more or less, on the products of industry.)

The nineteenth-century French economist, Jean Baptiste Say, had argued that since all income was earned by producing things, therefore the production of goods (supply) always created income which, in turn, was always used to buy (demand) all that industry produced. According to Say's Law 'Supply creates its own Demand'. In other words, since production generated enough income to buy everything that was produced *and since all income was spent*, full employment was assured. Everyone who wanted to work would be a potential buyer of everything that could be produced; managers could therefore always expect to profitably sell all they could produce.

In an earlier century, when most workers were barely able to survive on their wages, the view that people worked to earn income in order to spend it *all – immediately*, on current output, led to the widespread acceptance by economists of Say's Law – where supply creates its own demand.

Say's Law is still held to be a fundamental principle underlying today's neoclassical model in explaining the behaviour of consumers. Students are still taught that buyers have insatiable appetites for products; buyers are constrained in the volume of their purchases only by the size of their income. It follows that whenever one's income rises, the budget constraint is raised and one spends all of this increment in income on more goods.

This budget constraint concept implies that buyers in general can not, and do not, ever plan to spend more *or* less than their income on the products of industry. Consequently, neoclassical economists can depend on the operation of the immutable Say's Law to guarantee that demand will grow in tandem with the capacity of industry to produce. It therefore follows that in a Say's Law world, managers will never be disappointed by poor sales performance. They can always profitably sell anything they can produce and hence it always pays them to hire all who are willing to work.

Expert opinion and Say's Law

Given the inevitable outcome predicted by Say's Law, conservative economists in the early 1930s could not explain the persistence of the 'Great Depression'. The fact that firms found that their production flows merely glutted the market and that they were unable to sell what they were producing was logically inconsistent with conservative theory. That firms would therefore dismiss workers increasing unemployment and inducing a further drop in sales was theoretically impossible and therefore unthinkable. The facts of the Great Depression just did not fit the theory. Massive permanent unemployment is impossible under Say's Law.

The conservative economic experts of the 1930s did grudgingly admit that temporary departures from the full employment that Say's Law promised was possible, just as the swinging pendulum might temporarily move away from its equilibrium position of rest. But the economy like the free-swinging pendulum would, if left alone, quickly right itself. President Hoover, listening to the conservative economic 'experts', whose theories were based on Say's Law, was paralysed into inaction. He could only promise that if the government remained neutral, 'prosperity was right around the corner' as the economy, like the free-swinging pendulum, would soon right itself.

Keynes's rebuff of Say's Law

Keynes attempted to persuade his fellow economists that Say's Law was not a long-run immutable principle applicable to entrepreneurial economics. Keynes felt it was necessary to dislodge Say's Law from the minds of economic experts and economics textbooks in order to ultimately influence policy makers to take positive actions rather than for them to wait upon the 'long-run' free market forces to swing toward a full employment equilibrium.

In a monetary economy people are never required to, nor do they necessarily, spend their entire income to purchase currently produced goods. Income earners may wish to protect themselves against what they know is an unpredictable future. People 'know' that it is always possible to find oneself without a job or income in an entrepreneurial economy where things can turn hostile without warning. Whenever people become more fearful of the uncertain future, this increased anxiety causes buyers to reduce their purchases out of current income and to use these savings to increase their holdings of liquid assets such as cash and other liquid assets readily resalable for cash.

Say's Law and Liquidity

To be liquid means that one has the ability to meet one's contractual obligations as they come due. In an entrepreneurial system, contractual commitments of buyers whether they are entrepreneurs or householders results in a stream of cash outflows. All buyers therefore require the liquidity of cash to meet these obligations. As Chapter 6 explains, money is that thing which by delivery can always discharge a contractual obligation in an entrepreneurial economy, and therefore the possession of money provides liquidity.[4]

Whenever people's fear of the unknown economic future increases, they will rush to build up liquidity rather than spending as much of their income as before on the purchase of goods. As people reduce spending, entrepreneurs will find sales receipts falling. This decline in demand makes managers pessimistic regarding future sales. They will reduce production schedules, hiring, and orders from suppliers, thereby causing the latter to further reduce employment. The economy can therefore collapse into a stagnant state of high unemployment unless, and until, something happens to significantly stimulate total spending. If spending can be revived, then as entrepreneurs realize there is an upswing in demand, they will rehire workers to meet the growing market. In a *laissez-faire* system in which Say's Law is not applicable, however, there is no 'invisible hand' which automatically ensures the revival of demand. Only the visible hand of the government can provide a recovery of demand when the private sector stops buying.

It is therefore the responsibility of a civilized government to use its powers to make sure total market demand neither declines nor stagnates. Increased government purchases and/or tax cuts to increase people's after-tax income and their spending can always pump up total market demand, encouraging managers to expand their production and employ idle machinery and workers.

HISTORICAL PARALLELS – ROOSEVELT AND REAGAN

The economic events of the period 1929–33 in the USA were dreadful. Between 1929 and 1933, the Gross National Product (GNP), a measure of the total output of industry, declined by almost 50 per cent. GNP reached its low point in 1933 when almost 25 per cent of the labour force was unemployed. The economy seemed unable to turn the proverbial corner. Roosevelt's 'brain trust' of advisers looked for any new approach to solve the unemployment problem. Unless some drastic action was undertaken, the existing economic system was unlikely to survive. Keynes's policy suggestions provided some rationalization for the large public work programmes that pragmatists recognized had to be undertaken if people's income was to be sustained and increased, thereby reviving the moribund expectations of entrepreneurs.

President Roosevelt instituted his New Deal legislative programme – a plethora of bills attempting to improve the economic situation. Most of this legislation deliberately stimulated the demand for goods by incurring what was considered at the time huge government deficits (approximately $2 to $6 billion dollars a year – a sum equal to 2–5 per cent of the GNP). Throughout the period, however, Roosevelt's programme was constrained by fears that the large deficits of Roosevelt's New Deal were 'fiscally irresponsible'; if the deficits continued for any number of years the long-run result would be disaster and national bankruptcy. Although the resulting expansion from 1933 to 1940 was, by historical standards, very robust, the fear of an unmanageable National Debt constrained Roosevelt's willingness to further expand the economy. Consequently, by 1940, after seven years of the New Deal, the GNP was no greater in real terms (that is adjusted for price level changes) than it had been in 1929. In the intervening decade, the population had grown substantially. Hence, the real income per capita in 1940 was still below what it had been in 1929.

During the Second World War, fears of an escalating National Debt were thrown to the winds. The important thing, as in all wars, was to defeat the enemy and not to limit the National Debt. Annual federal budget deficits of between $20 and $55 billion were incurred (equal to 14 to 33 per cent of GNP), while the GNP jumped from $125 to $212 billion. By the end of the war, the National Debt *exceeded* the GNP by 27 per cent. (For comparison, despite the tremendous dollar deficits of the Reagan Administration which have doubled the total national debt in less than six years, the total national debt was, in 1986, only about half the size of the GNP in that year while the annual deficits between 1982 and 1986 varied between 2.6 and 6.3 per cent of GNP.) It took the great deficits of the Second World War to defeat the Axis powers and to re-establish true prosperity to the United States. Keynes's policy of deliberate government spending, regardless of the size of the national debt, had made full employment an achievable objective for a civilized US economy. Once fears of the size of the debt were put aside, sufficient demand could be generated to bring prosperity to the system. Unfortunately it took a war to prove the effectiveness of Keynes's civilized policy.

A philosopher once noted that those who do not study history are destined to repeat its errors. The historical economic record of the Roosevelt recovery from 1933 to 1945 does have a lesson to teach us. Especially interesting is the fact that despite the overall progress achieved by the New Deal there was a single brief but sharp fall in the GNP during the first year of Roosevelt's second term in office.

From 1933 to the beginning of the Second World War, with the exception of 1937, the federal government pursued a policy of increasing government spending to raise the level of economic activity. In the last year of Roosevelt's first term, the annual federal deficit exceeded 5 per cent of the GNP. By 1936, the total National Debt was approximately equal to 42 per cent of the annual GNP and many conservative economic experts were warning of imminent economic disaster, if the government did not end deficit spending and take positive action towards a balanced budget.

In the election year of 1936, Roosevelt, bending to warnings that the horrendous deficits of the federal government could not continue, did go along with Congressional attempts to reduce the deficit by curtailing government spending in 1937. The result was a halving of the deficit from $4.4 billion to $2 billion which caused a dramatic plunge of almost 10 per cent in real GNP from the first quarter of 1937 to the first quarter of 1938. The steep decline in GNP ended when this deficit reduction policy was abandoned in 1938 and increased government spending on public works and the beginnings of rearmament for war revived the economy.

Here then is a useful historical parallel between the economic recovery of Roosevelt's first five years and that of President Reagan's first five years in office. Both Presidents took office in the midst of a massive recession. Both extricated the economy by massive (for their time) increases in the federal deficit. Both initially ignored advice from eminent conservative economic experts who publicly proclaimed that these deficits were courting imminent disaster. In the fifth year of the Roosevelt regime, these claims of forthcoming doom led the President to strongly retrench. The result was to plunge the economy into recession. During Reagan's fifth year, the doomsters' warnings brought on the Gramm–Rudman law which mandated phased-in cuts in government spending until a balanced budget is achieved by 1991. The sluggish performance of the economy in 1986 was related to the *modest* first stage of the Gramm-Rudman reductions in government spending (of 11 billion in March 1986). History therefore suggests that if much larger Gramm-Rudman deficit reductions targets are pursued in 1987–91, the greater the chance that the US economy will experience additional unemployment and a significant drop in GNP.

RONALD REAGAN – THE GREAT KEYNESIAN IN THE WHITE HOUSE

History's greatest deficit spender

Despite all his conservative rhetoric, President Ronald Reagan has been the first President since Roosevelt to embark, in peacetime, on a huge and growing public works programme (military defence). Although government spending has been cut in some areas, overall purchases by the federal government continued to rise (in real terms) throughout the first five years of the Reagan Administration. Simultaneously, in 1982, taxes were slashed creating a rapid rise in after tax-income which encouraged consumer spending to rise by 4.6 per cent in 1983 and another 4.7 per cent in 1984. (Consumer spending had fallen in 1980 and shown only minimal increases in 1981 and 1982.)

Reagan's expansive deficit spending policy combined with a lower interest rate policy since 1982 generated additional profit opportunities. Entrepreneurs were encouraged by the rise in sales not only to hire more workers to meet the growing domestic demand but also to increase net investment spending almost four-fold between 1982 and 1984. The unemployment rate dropped from a high of 10.7 per cent in early 1982 to 6.6 per cent by December 1986. With the onset of Gramm–Rudman spending cuts in 1986, however, further improvement in the unemployment rate due to growth in *domestic* markets slowed domestically.[5]

Professors Bluestone and Havens of Boston College have done a computer simulation study to compare what happened in the Reagan years with what would have happend to the US economy had President Carter been re-elected and had he continued the 'prudent' lower deficits spending priorities he championed in 1977–81.

The comparison is dramatic. The Gross National Product by mid-1985 was 3.1 per cent higher, and an additional 3.4 million additional jobs were created under Reagan than what would have been achieved under the Carter policies to maintain modest deficits. The evidence clearly demonstrates that if we are not constrained by unwarranted fears of deficits, an active government spending policy can rescue the system from continuing stagnation and recession.

There is a value judgement in our society that additional job opportunities should preferably be in the private sector. This can be accomplished by government placing additional orders with private contractors. Expenditures on schools, highways, bridges, hospitals, public libraries, and parks are desirable. Our world today is clearly enhanced by the legacy of public parks, libraries, and other public facilities built by the WPA and the PWA of the New Deal. Even wholly wasteful deficit expenditures by government such an employing workers to dig holes and then fill them up again are useful. Besides providing people with a job and the dignity that goes with being an employed member of society, the income earned will buy more useful products of industry. With tongue in cheek, Keynes once wrote:

Ancient Egypt was doubly fortunate, and doubtless owed its fabled wealth, in that it possessed two activities, namely, pyramid-building as well as the search for precious metals, the fruits of which since they could not serve the needs of man by being consumed, did not stale with abundance. The Middle Ages built cathedrals and sung dirges. Two pyramids, two masses for the dead, are twice as good as one; but not two railways between London and York. Thus we are so sensible, having schooled ourselves to so close a semblance of prudent financiers, taking careful thought before we add to the "financial" burdens of posterity by building them houses to live in, that we have no easy escape from the suffering of unemployment.

To the list of things that do not stale with abundance we may now add military weapons and Ronald Reagan's Star Wars defence initiative financed via government deficits.

The failure of the Reagan prosperity to trickle down

The benefits of the Reagan prosperity, were not distributed to all the members of the community. Bluestone and Havens calculate that the average family disposable income was 7 per cent higher under Reagan than it would have been under Carter. More than 63 per cent of this additional family disposable income went to the richest families in the United States – those in the top 20 per cent of the income distribution. As a direct result of the Reagan expansionist policies between 1982 and 1985, the real income of these richest families increased by 10 per cent over what it would have been under the Carter policies.

On the other hand, families in the lowest fifth of the income distribution – the very poor – actually lost real disposable income under Reagan compared with where they would have been under Carter. Bluestone and Havens notes that

> While 413,000 families who were initially below the official poverty line rose above it by reason of the new tax and spending policies, more than *1 million* previously non-poor families were forced below the poverty line as a direct consequence of the new fiscal policies. This . . . [increased] the proportion of American families in poverty from 13.5 percent to 14.1 percent. Moreover, those families that were originally below the poverty line (and remained below) actually suffered a further 3.4 percent erosion in their already low disposable incomes.

This evidence provides dramatic proof of the failure of the Trickle Down Theory of economic expansion to permeate throughout the society. Deliberate expansionist policies will increase the national income, and hence are a necessary condition for a civilized society to sustain itself in the face of potential stagnation. But a truly civilized society should adopt policies which not only assure a continual tilt towards full employment but also provide avenues of opportunity for sharing the additional income among all members of a society. Only if the goods are widely distributed are the members of society likely to believe the system is working for all. If some lose out while others gain, winners as well as the losers will think that they are in a zero-sum society. The existing polis always tends to be eroded whenever groups in the community are polarized into haves and have-nots.

CONCLUSION ON THE EMPLOYMENT FRONT

For the last half-century, those who have comprehended the analysis of Keynes have understood how to ameliorate the unemployment problem which has consistently plagued *laissez-faire* systems. Government monetary and fiscal policies for expanding demand whenever private spending is otherwise insufficient have always been at our beck and call. Each in his own way, Presidents Roosevelt and Reagan have conclusively demonstrated that job opportunities can be created in the private sector if we have the courage to deficit spend whatever is required whenever unused capacity and un-employed workers are persistent problems. We can control our economic destiny and provide a continuous prosperity for our people, if we do not let the shibboleths of conservative economics regarding the necessity of not running deficits get in the way!

Of course, perfect balancing of aggregate demand to supply is, in a world of uncertainty, not possible. Hence some unemployment can still remain – but the history of the last fifty years clearly demonstrates that in those Administrations where either additional government spending, or additional tax cuts, or both, were actively and vigorously pursued, without letting the size of the deficit limit our expansionary efforts, employment and output rose rapidly and a feeling of prosperity returned. In those years when a reduction of government spending and/or increased taxation were legislated in order to reduce the deficit, unemployment either tended to rise or, at least, did not continue to decline significantly. The facts therefore speak for themselves in justifying Keynsian policies to stimulate aggregate demand at less than full employment.

The reader might ask, if it is so obvious how to eliminate unemployment why has the United States and other developed countries pursued such a full employment policy so sporadically? The answer lies in the fact that normally as our entrepreneurial economy approaches full employment, it develops an inflationary bias. Except for periods of war when the civic (i.e. patriotism) culture is specifically appealed to, modern entrepreneurial systems have not had the institutional framework to eliminate the problem of continuously rising prices in periods when the economy is close to full employment. In the absence of institutions designed to elevate the co-operative civic feelings required to fight inflation, the only alternative programme for limiting price level increases has been the barbaric conservative plan to deliberately create unemployment and slack product markets in order to limit inflationary price and wage increases.

We have not progressed further towards a more civilized way of dealing with inflation in large measure because of the many popular myths regarding the relationship between inflation and the money supply have clouded our vision as to the true basis of the inflation problem. Accordingly, it is to the question of the role of money and its relationship to unemployment (Chapter 6) and inflation (Chapter 7) in a civilized economy system that we turn to in the following pages.

A DIGRESSION ON EMPLOYMENT IN THE PUBLIC SECTOR

In basing our analysis on the view that the private sector is the employer of first resort, we are not implying that there is no aspect of the production of goods and services where public employees can not perform efficiently and effectively. There are many activities where government workers perform as well or better than their private sector counterparts, per dollar spent on such activities. Police, fire protection, the national park service, and air traffic controllers, are some obvious examples.

When government hires workers into activities where there has not been developed a high standard of worker performance and supervisory responsibility, however, the inefficiencies which surface and attract public attention sully all government service reputations. The problem with direct government employment in spheres where it can be demonstrated that performance standards are lower than in the private sector counterpart is that such government make-work projects devalue the reputation of government workers in general. The resulting negative public perceptions ultimately renders the government as employer of last resort policy as untenable. This has been, unfortunately, too often the experience of the United States.

The importance of standards, reputation, pride in one's output, and public perceptions indicates the relevance of internal incentives in any good job creating policy – whether it be in direct job hiring as the employer of last resort, or in the letting of contracts to the private sector to create jobs. If in the letting of contracts, the public perception is one of permissible waste and graft, then the internal incentive that encourages taxpayers' compliance and maintains a pride in citizenship will erode. The challenge facing government is to spend wisely on the goods and services procured for the public, and to ensure that the available resources of the economy are not left idle – but are rewarded via both internal and external incentives.

Notes

1. We should not forget that government can also directly create or destroy jobs, as well as produce desirable goods and services either sold in a marketplace (e.g. electricity from TVA) or distributed to those who need it upon request without charge (e.g. fire-fighting services, public education).
2. For industries that produce primarily 'to contract', statistics are collected on the length of the order books, e.g. machine tool orders, as a leading indicator of current employment and economic activity.
3. This feedback mechanism where an initial change in sales expectations leads to a larger change in actual sales is called the Keynesian multiplier.
4. Other durables called liquid assets can also provide this attribute. Liquid assets other than money are any durables which can be readily resold (for money) in well-organized, markets, e.g., corporate securities or bonds sold in organized stock and bond markets.
5. A further decline in unemployment to 5.9 per cent in 1987 can be primarily attributed to the precipitous drop in the dollar *vis-à-vis* foreign currencies which stimulated export demand and, it is estimated, created almost 300 000 jobs. By encouraging the dollar to fall, the USA deliberately exported a small fraction of its unemployment to Germany and Japan whose unemployment rates consequently attained post-Second World War highs. (For a further discussion of this uncivilized policy of exporting one's unemployment, see Chapter 8.)

6 Unemployment Develops Because Money Doesn't Grow on Trees

A war of words is better than a real war because it inflicts less suffering on society. In economics, however, controversy generated by confusion and the misuse of language can often produce policies which inflict terrible – and needless – cruelties on many unfortunate members of society. Nowhere is this more obvious than when the subjects are money, unemployment, and inflation.

Conservatives insist that any anti-inflation policy must invoke strict – and predetermined – limits on the growth of the money supply even when they admit that this will cause unemployment and business failures in the short run and a permanent class of unemployment in the long run. The fact that the United States has been running an unemployment rate of 6 to 7 per cent or more in the 1980s is not, according to conservatives, a cause for policy concern. Nobel Prize-winning economist Milton Friedman, in his Presidential Address to the American Economics Association tried to justify this barbaric infliction of permanent unemployment by labelling it 'the *natural* rate of unemployment'.

We object to this misuse of language and the attempt to solve the problem of unemployment by the semantic trick of defining it away. The real problem with this conservative approach lies much deeper. In the underlying neoclassical model upon which such definitions are based, money is inappropriately conceived of as something that can grow on trees. Hence any one who wants to work can always get a job harvesting *money trees*. By conceptualizing money as a readily producible commodity similar to oranges or peanuts, conservatives completely misrepresent the role of money in our economy. No wonder such an analytical confusion leads to wrong-headed monetary policies which have barbaric and detrimental effects on our economy.

A conceptualization of a money which does *not* grow on trees will show the root cause of unemployment in the real world and the necessity of expansive liberal policies to eliminate the problem of unemployment. Since a civilized society must always have full

117

employment of its resources as a primary goal, this means that for policy purposes any significant level of unemployment can not be accepted as 'natural'. Policies to reduce unemployment must take priority over policies to limit the national debt or to achieve a balanced budget, or to limit the money supply.

If, as conservatives claim, inflation can be curbed *only* by deliberately creating a planned recession and persistent unemployment, then our economic society will never be a civilized one. Fortunately, however, once a correct conceptualization of money and its role is developed, then it will be obvious that civilized policies to control inflation can be designed without deliberately imposing job losses on groups in our society.

Although more ink has been spilt by economists in discussions of money than on any other topic, most people would be surprised to learn that economists have neither carefully defined money nor do they agree on a single common meaning. The public is most familiar with the Monetarist approach to the theory of money. The flavour of the Monetarist approach is reflected in the simplistic slogan that 'Inflation is always due to too many dollars chasing too few goods'. This dictum argues that if the growth of the money supply accelerates, then inflationary trends will be exacerbated even though the facts, as we previously noted, show that while the growth of the money did accelerate between 1982 and 1986, inflation diminished.

DEFINITIONS AND DIALECT

The Monetarist's definition of money

Monetarists, such as Professor Milton Friedman, have taken the lead in the economics profession in laying down the ground rules as to what is to be discussed in public forums under the rubric of money. They have combined the basic neoclassical model with their own idiosyncratic approach to money.

Monetarists believe that the use of illustrative examples can provide a definition of the money concept. The Monetarist literature abounds with these 'definitions' of money. For example, M_1 is defined as equal to the total (legal tender) currency in circulation plus checkable bank deposits plus travellers checks. M_2 money is equal to M_1 plus some non-checkable bank deposits plus other financial items such as the shares of money market mutual funds, overnight eurodollars and overnight repurchase agreements. Finally, M_3 money is M_2 plus additional items such as large time deposits, institutional money market funds, etc.

If the distinction between these various categories of money seems confusing to the uninitiated reader, let him take heart in knowing that this current Monetarist classification scheme of money is an improvement over earlier published Monetarist 'definitions'. At one time in the late 1970s, the literature teemed with seven of these money categories – from M_1 to M_7. In recent years these seven 'definitions' of money have been collapsed into the three categories mentioned above.

Semantic confusion and conflict rather than clarity

Confusion rather than clarity is due to the fact that these M_1, M_2, M_3 concepts are exemplifications rather than explanations; they do not constitute a *definition* of the money concept.

Imagine the confusion and chaos that would occur if astronomers defined the concept of planets by using the name of specific heavenly bodies. Suppose, P_1 planets are Mercury, Venus and Earth; while P_2 planets are P_1 plus Mars, Saturn, Uranus, Neptune and Jupiter. (How in this scheme would one know what separates a planet from a moon?) Or if some chemists defined molecules in terms of M_1 molecules which consisted solely of inorganic salts, while M_2 molecules which are defined as M_1 plus inorganic acids, and M_3 molecules which is M_2 plus organic compounds, etc.

Such an obviously bizarre classification scheme for 'defining' planets is, however, analogous to the status of the current Monetarist definitions on money. Just because of its conceptual fuzziness, however, the Monetarist approach can be reduced to simplistic rhetoric which makes acceptance easier. Its universal appeal, although inconsistent with the facts, is in its simplicity which permits it to dominate public discussion of the importance of money. Unfortunately, if the concepts used in public discussions are fuzzy, then the resulting conclusions will be muddleheaded and the development of a civilized monetary policy will suffer accordingly.

Whenever a Monetarist is quoted in the financial pages on the rate of growth of the money supply, one is never sure whether the reference should be to M_1, M_2, or M_3. In fact, some Monetarists often switch between these designations depending on which category provides the better statistics to back their particular argument.

Why the conservative Monetarist's approach has been able to dominate public discussions may not be at all obvious – especially if one believes that economists are engaged in 'scientific' research devoid of politics and value judgements. In reality, of course, economics and politics are intimately bound together and what is promoted as science is often nothing more than the political ideology favoured by the economically powerful to conserve their status. Nor is this situation unique to our own time and place. In the 1930s, for example, Keynes explained that the overwhelming consensus of the financial and political community in support of the conservative Monetarist doctrine of his day was due to a

> complex of suitabilities in the doctrine to the environment into which it was projected. . . . That its teaching, translated into practice, was often austere and often unpalatable lent it virtue. That it was adapted to carry a vast and consistent logical super-structure, gave it beauty. That it could explain much social injustice and apparent cruelty as an inevitable incident in the scheme of progress . . . commended it to authority. That it afforded a measure of justification to the free activities of the individual capitalist, attracted to it the dominant social force behind authority.

We suspect that a similar expediency lies behind the mass media's propagation of the Monetarist approach which fundamentally has provided a psuedo-scientific rationalization for the latent anti-labour sentiment that has developed in industrial economies. Years of labour union excesses created sufficient public inconvenience to loosen the social glue that had bound us into a civilized society of workers, managers, and property owners. The growth in the popularity of Monetarism in the last two decades suggests to us how far developed economies have regressed from the civilized stature they had reached in the first two decades after the Second World War.

Since Monetarists have not provided a clear definition of the money concept their analysis of money *vis-à-vis* unemployment and inflation permits a variety of vague interpretations appealing to slogans regarding the chase between money and goods. If civilized reasoning rather than intuition, emotions, and fears is to become the basis for developing our economic policies then we must insist on a clean, clear, and crisp economic dialect which correctly reflects the world we live in. Only then can progress be made towards understanding the relationship between the money supply, the banking and financial systems, and employment and inflation. Thus, in this chapter, we must first develop a clear definition of the money concept. This will permit us to explain (a) why the banking and financial industry plays a crucial role in determining the level of employment, while in Chapter 7, we will discuss why rising prices (inflation) of products are primarily related to rising money wages and other production costs rather than directly related to increases in the quantity of money.[1]

DEFINING MONEY

Defining concepts by essential functions and properties

Communication and progress can occur only when concepts are cast in terms of *functions* and *properties*. That is why scientists define planets not by example but via functions and properties, i.e., a planet is any large heavenly body which shines in reflected sunlight and revolves around the sun. Such a definition involving critical properties which permits one to distinguish between planets and moons, for the latter although they may reflect sunlight, do not directly revolve around the sun.

In developing a precise dialect, anything which possesses the *essential* functions and properties will be an example of the defined concept, no matter how strange they may appear. In the biological dialect, for example, the functional definition of a mammal is anything that gives birth to live offspring and suckles its young. Thus merely looking like a fish, smelling like a fish, and even swimming like a fish is not enough to make a mammalian whale into a fish!

The contractual settlement or claiming function of money

In a civilized society behaviour is governed by well established laws, shared norms, and commonly understood traditions. One of the most fundamental attributes of civilized economic behaviour is the belief that people will honour their contractual commitments under the civil law of contracts. In such a system, the essential function of money – the characteristic that sets it apart from everything else – is that money is that thing, which by delivery, settles a contractual obligation.

Whatever the Community declares is money will possess this

essential function of a means of contractual settlement. In an entrepreneurial system, money and the use of explicit money contracts are fundamental civilizing institutions.

Money as a claim on resources. The resources of any economy are its labour force, its natural resources, and its stock of plant and equipment. One of the basic platitudes of economics is that 'everyone has his/her price!' By this we mean that in an entrepreneurial system, the services or products of any of these ultimate resources can always be purchased via a contract for a specific sum of money – a money price. This money price is the measure of the external incentive which conservative economists argue is the *only* factor necessary to motivate people to perform any economic activity.

Whenever we use money to buy goods, or hire workers, or purchase property, we are exercising or using claims upon the ultimate resources of the system. Just as a hat-check ticket allows one to go to the cloak-room to claim one's hat and coat, so, in an entrepreneurial system, the green ticket we call money is by law and by custom, the universal claim check on the available goods and services in the economy. Money possesses generalized purchasing (claiming) power – but it does so in an economy which utilizes money contracts to organize production and trading activities.

The sources of these claims. There are three ways whereby people come to possess claim tickets that we call money. First is by the earning of money income. The second is by borrowing from others who have earned income and do not wish to spend all they have earned.[2] The third way is borrowing money from the banking system – where the banks can create additional *new* money under the rules of the game. (Other ways such as stealing money or counterfeiting it are both uncivilized and illegitimate methods.)

Liquidity: the time machine function of money

Whenever people plan to save some portion of their currently earned income, it means that they are planning *not* to exercise all of today's earned claims by buying today's products. Instead the saver wants to defer exercising these current claims, and store this claiming power until some future date. These stored money claims provide liquidity, i.e., they provide the ability to meet a contractual obligation when it comes due. If the saver thinks that at some future time, he/she may need to claim a sum of goods and services which exceeds the income that is expected to be earned in that future period, then the saver may want to build up his/her liquidity today. The saver, for example, might be worried that some unforeseen calamity (e.g. unemployment, sickness or severe accident) may occur which either reduces future income or requires significant additional unforeseen expenses or both. To store currently earned claims in order to be available for use at a future date requires a *time machine* to transport purchasing (claiming) power to a future date.

For example, suppose that Ms Jones decides to save $100 out of her January paycheck so that whenever she takes her next holiday she will be able to buy souvenirs. The saved $100 can be stored in the form of either money (in a bank account or as currency hidden in her mattress or safe deposit box), or other liquid assets (e.g. stocks and bonds). Money and/or liquid assets are different stores of value which Ms Jones can use to move today's claiming power to the future. Money is, however, different from all other liquid assets in that only money can be used to settle contracts. If Ms Jones were to use any liquid assets besides money as a store of value, then at some future date she will have to resell this asset in a market (like the New York Stock Exchange) in order to obtain money to pay for her purchases of souvenirs when and if she goes on holiday.

In sum, money is defined as anything that possesses *both* the universal contractual settlement function and the time machine function. Accordingly, currency and checkable bank deposits, including traveller's checks, are money in the current environment for only these can settle contracts. Other liquid assets (e.g. stocks, bonds, non-checkable deposits, etc.) may possess the time machine function but do not have the claiming function of settling contracts and hence they are not money!

MONEY DOES NOT GROW ON TREES

All liquid assets, including money, possess an obvious – but rather peculiar property – they do not grow on trees. This may seem so evident that the reader may wonder why we raise the issue. The reader may be surprised to learn that the model underlying conservative doctrine not only permits, but *requires*, money to be a producible commodity such as wheat, bananas, etc. For the conservative analysis to demonstrate that markets, free from government interference, will automatically generate full employment, the money of the economy must be able to be 'harvested'. (Peanuts – which grow on the roots of bushes if not on trees – are typically used as an example of money as a commodity in many neoclassical textbooks.)

If money is a producible commodity, then there would never be any unemployment. If the money commodity did grow on trees, then unemployed persons, who want to work but are not hired by any firm, can always become self-employed entrepreneurs who can harvest money trees in order to earn income. This 'proves' that in a free market system where people are free to work at whatever they wish, unemployment is impossible. It therefore follows from the logic of defining money as a readily producible commodity that anyone who is unemployed does not want to work for a living. The unemployed can therefore be conceptualized by conservatives as parasites living off government handouts. Hence, it is easy to justify policies, which, in the real world cause unemployment and then treat the unemployed callously.

If only money did grow on trees, recession would be impossible. When people become more worried about the possibility of future 'rainy days' and therefore cut their spending on goods, such as cars, in order to build up liquidity, employment will decline in the car industry. If, however, money is a producible crop, such as peanuts, the resulting increased demand for liquidity will increase the demand for peanuts and hence employment in the peanut industry. In this illustration, where money is peanuts, increased unemployment in Detroit's car factories would be offset by increased employment on Georgia's peanut farms. If money really was peanuts, President Carter might have fared better had he appointed his brother Billy rather than Paul Volker to be chairman of the Federal Reserve.

In our world, on the other hand, an increase in the public's demand for liquidity, at the expense of the public's spending on goods, is not translated into new job opportunities in the private sector. Business firms can not meet the increased demand for liquidity by hiring workers to harvest more liquidity from trees or to print more money!

In an entrepreneurial economy it is the presence of a money that does *not* grow on trees in combination with the public's desire to hold such money (for liquidity purposes) which refutes Say's Law. Whatever income is earned via the production of goods does not assure sufficient demand to sell all the goods produced, as long as people decide to hold money instead of spending it. Whenever the public reduces its total spending on goods in order to try to enhance its liquidity position, sales must decline causing entrepreneurs to lay off workers.

THE ROLE OF THE BANKING SYSTEM

Full employment occurs only when entrepreneurs believe that there are sufficient profit opportunities to justify offering jobs to all who are willing to work. Managers will be willing to provide jobs for all, but only if they expect that they can sell the resulting output at profitable prices. Unemployment develops, therefore, whenever income earners do not spend their entire full employment income to purchase the products of industry.

That portion of current income that people do not spend on consumption is called savings. The gap between what people earn when the economy is at full employment and what people wish to spend on consumption of goods out of this income is called the *full employment savings gap*. If all spending is financed out of income, then this savings gap means that people are not spending enough. Consequently, sales will not be sufficient to induce managers to hire all who want to work. To fill this savings gap another source of spending – one which is not financed out of current income – is required. If large enough this second type of spending can, when added to consumption spending, generate enough sales revenue to encourge managers to produce at full employment.

In a modern monetary economy total spending can be financed (1) either by spending one's own current income or by borrowing other's income, and (2) by borrowing newly created money from the banking system. Whenever borrowers' requests for bank loans to buy goods are increasing, the banking system can provide 'new' finance to buy these goods by creating checkable deposits (money) for borrowers. This bank created credit finance permits spending which is not financed out of current income. It is – as our condominium construction example below will illustrate – primarily associated with private sector investment spending and especially construction loans (sometimes called working capital loans) used to pay for the production of capital goods such as plant and equipment.

Even with new bank financing for investment spending, *total* spending may not be sufficient to completely fill the full employment savings gap if either borrowers can not conceive of enough profitable investment projects or the cost of borrowing is too high. Whenever such an insufficiency of total effective demand occurs, managers whose self-interest is solely related to 'the bottom line' will not hire enough workers to sustain full employment. Consequently, there is a role for government borrowing in order to finance an increase in deficit spending and thereby augment private investment spending sufficiently to make it profitable for managers to hire all workers who want to work.[3] Whether banks create new money to finance additional investment or to finance government spending, the resulting expenditures can fill the full employment savings gap.

Our argument so far has required the reader to accept our claim that the expansion of bank credit to borrowers creates new money. It may be desirable, at this point, to explain in detail why this is so – given our conceptualization of money. To do so it is necessary to discuss the relationship between legal tender currency and bank money (checkable deposits.)

LEGAL TENDER VERSUS BANK MONEY

Legal tender money

Legal tender is defined as that thing which must be legally accepted for goods purchased and for the discharge of all debts, under the law of contracts. Since money is, in our scheme, defined by its contractual settlement feature, then whatever is declared by the State to be legal tender must be money, as long as a national polis has not been eroded to the point where no one has faith in the government's ability to enforce contract performance. In the United States, legal tender currency consists of Federal Reserve Notes (IOU's of the Federal Reserve Banks) and United States Notes (IOU's of the United States Treasury). In mid-1987, these currency notes amounted to $200 billion.

Bank credit money

Other things besides legal tender can be money if they are accepted by law, or by custom, in the discharge of contractual obligations. In fact, most contractual obligations are settled, not with the payment of legal tender currency, but rather with the tendering of a check. Hence, that portion of bank credit which is composed of checkable deposits are part – the major part – of the US monetary system. In mid-1987, checkable deposits equalled $550 billion.

A checkable deposit represents a contractual obligation of a banker to transfer, on demand, money (and if requested, legal tender currency) to whomever the holder of the deposit designates, as long as the amount on deposit equals or exceeds the sum on the cheque. Hence the recipient of the cheque 'knows' that receiving a cheque is as good as receiving legal tender currency. Bank deposits can be considered a 'tap issue' of legal tender notes as bankers provide depositors with an 'instant repurchase' clause in which they guarantee the depositor instant convertibility of cheque-book balances into legal tender. Although bank deposits are liabilities of private corporations, bankers can guarantee that they can convert their customers' checkable deposits into legal tender immediately because of the bankers' special relationship with the Monetary Authority (The Federal Reserve) whose IOU's are the legal tender of the country.

The Federal Reserve Bank (or Fed) assures all bankers that their checkable deposit liabilities can be converted into legal tender at the immediate option of the banker – as long as the banker is operating under the rules and regulations set down by the Fed. The Fed can always provide these legal tender notes to bankers since these notes are merely its printed IOU's. There is no limit – within the law – as to how much legal tender the Central Bank can print and provide to bankers.

No liabilities of any private corporations other than those of bankers' checkable deposit liabilities have this instant convertibility to legal tender guaranteed by the Federal Reserve. Therefore only the checkable deposit liabilities of bankers are 'as good as' legal tender, and checkable bank deposits and/or legal tender are equally acceptable to settle contractual obligations. Since payment by cheque is easier and safer than payment by legal tender, checkable deposits have become better than legal tender and are the major form of money in modern economies.

We live in a bank-credit monetary system. Whenever a banker provides a borrower with a loan, the banker does so by creating either a new checkable deposit account, or creating an additional credit to be added to the borrower's original checkable deposit account. Every time the banking system increases its total checkable deposits by making additional loans to the public or to the government, bank credit and therefore the money supply has increased.

Why do firms borrow from banks?

Firms borrow from banks because they want to buy things which they can not afford to purchase out of current cash inflows. Such purchases create future cash outflows in excess of their expected cash inflows. The bank loan is undertaken in order to make up the expected cash-flow deficiency. The borrower either expects to have sufficient cash inflow at some further future date to repay the loan, or else plans to refinance the loan again, thereby postponing repayment till even some further date in the future.

From an economy wide view, therefore, the use of money contracts and the development of a banking system which can create credit-money have been important institutions for regulating cash-flow circulation for the production system. The availability of bank credit on favourable terms can often encourage sufficient private borrowing to provide the proper volume of circulating 'blood' to an entrepreneurial system striving to promote maximum economic activity. If, on the other hand, monetary policy is too 'tight', then the monetary circulation to vital parts of the production system is diminished or even cut off as private borrowing is discouraged. The resultant loss in spending can cause a loss of vitality (unemployment and lower profits) and even mortality (bankruptcies).

MONEY AND THE USE OF CONTRACTS

The institution and evolution of the use of money and contracts to organize complex production processes has contributed significantly to the development of the industrialized world. Contracts permit managers (a) to control their costs by fixing the price of labour and materials, (b) to know their future cash outflow obligations and, (c) to efficiently organize the proper sequencing of delivery by suppliers.

The Economist (10–16 March 1979 issue, p. 12) noted that Toyota became a leader in the car industry only when it implemented its production control system known as the 'just in time' system. In this system, any manufacturing department manager by using contractual arrangements could

> collect his goods [from his supplier] in the precise quantity and exact time he needs them. The component producer . . . thus has an orderly market and so can adjust its production (using the same approach) accordingly.

An illustration: building a condominium

The importance of contracts for fixing costs, providing the basis for bank financing, *and* the efficient carrying out of a complex, lengthy production process can be illustrated with the following example. Suppose a developer is considering building a condominium apartment tower in mid-Manhattan. To decide whether the project will be profitable, the developer will not only have to estimate demand for the apartments, but he will also need to 'know' the construction costs involved for the two to three years that it takes to complete the building. To get a handle on these costs the developer will request that the competing construction firms provide bids with written contract offers indicating the costs for construction according to the developer's specification.

For managers of construction firms to be willing to commit themselves to a fixed money sales contract, they will demand fixed money contracts from their workers, suppliers, and subcontractors in order to nail down their own production costs. Similarly, the subcontractors will require fixed contractual commitments from their workers and suppliers. The total monetary costs of this complex project can then be contractually fixed in advance *before construction*. This permits the various entrepreneurs involved in this project to get a firm grasp on their costs *and* sales revenue as they produce only when they receive a signed contractual order.

In this simple example, only the condominium developer is willing to sell 'to market'; undertaking a commitment to produce living space before buyers have been lined up to purchase the total output.[4] By fixing cash outflows via contracts for the next two to three years the developer can calculate whether the condo will be a profitable one. The developer must (1) estimate the market prices that can be charged when apartments are ready for sale in order to assure himself that sales revenues will ultimately cover all committed cash outflows, and (2) obtain finance to meet any cash-outflow commitments which will come due before the sales revenue from the apartments is received. The developer typically finances the contractual construction cash outflows required via a construction loan from his banker. Armed with this loan commitment, the developer 'knows' he has the wherewithal to carry the project to completion. He can therefore execute all the construction orders necessary and use the contracts to produce an efficient 'just in time' production process. Clearly, fixed money contracts are an essential instrument for the developer.

Why are the *sellers* of labour and materials willing to enter into contracts fixing their future money income payments? These contractual arrangements assure the workers and subcontractors future cash inflows which they can use to meet their future contractual cash-outflow obligations.

If the various subcontracting firms do not have sufficient liquidity to meet their payrolls before they will receive their sales revenues, they can finance these obligations by borrowing from their bankers. For a fee, their bankers will be glad to provide these subcontractors with sufficient bank loans to meet their payrolls in the interim before they are paid since the revenues necessary to cover these loans are contractually assured. Thus the uncertainties facing the subcontractors and bankers are reduced. Bankers are therefore willing to create credit to finance the necessary costs to keep the production process going.

In sum then, fixed money contracts and a banking system which creates bank money are the best institutions that civilized societies have evolved over the centuries to encourage and permit entrepreneurs to finance and carry out complex, long duration, production. The enforcement of these contracts in terms of fixed money sums protects the cash inflows and incomes of workers, as well as those of the seller-entrepreneurs and their bankers. Simultaneously it limits the liabilities or cash outflows of buyers: thereby protecting both parties to the contract no matter how adversely unpredictable and uninsurable future events may be.

MONEY, BANKS, AND THE PRICE LEVEL

As firms expand production in anticipation of greater future sales, additional production commitments will require an increase in borrowing from the banking system. Only if the total volume of loans is permitted to rise as entrepreneurs desire to expand production can our economy grow. If impediments are placed in the way of the banks responding to entrepreneurial needs, the economy will stagnate and die. As a wise man once noted, bank credits are the paving stones upon which production travels, and if bankers know their business they will always provide stones just as fast as producers wish to travel!

This process of having a banking system responsive to the needs of expanding trade is called the *real bills doctrine* by economists. This doctrine was the conceptual framework underlying the development and passage of the Federal Reserve Act of 1913 which set up the Federal Reserve as the Central Bank of the United States; a monetary authority to specifically provide for an 'elastic currency' to meet the 'needs of trade'.

The money supply increases envisioned under this doctrine are called 'real bills' because it was assumed that all bank loan increases would be used to finance a concurrent growth in the production costs associated with the needs of managers to expand *real* output. In terms of the simplistic motto of the Monetarist cited at the beginning of this chapter, under the real bills doctrine the additional bank money created via expanded bank loan activity would be chasing additional goods. Under the 'real bills' approach, therefore, increases in the money supply would never cause inflation. The Monetarist avoids facing this obvious fact by *assuming* that (a) in the short run there can be no significant increase in production so that an increase in the money supply must be 'chasing too few goods', while (b) in the long run we will always produce the full employment output no matter what the money supply!

Thus, by assertion, assumption, and definition, rather than demonstration, conservatives deny the need for a banking system to discretionarily provide for varying needs of trade as changing conditions warrant.

In contrast, our approach has argued that in a money-using entrepreneurial society there is no natural tendency or invisible hand to guide the system towards the full utilization of all its potential resources. Instead the economy will only perform up to the level of demand expected to be forthcoming from buyers. This demand will be financed either out of current income or from accommodating bank credit. To the extent that purchases financed out of current income are less than current income, then borrowing via additional bank loans is necessary to prevent unemployment from developing.

If private borrowers do not fill the gap, the government must. The size of the government deficit necessary to promote sufficient demand to achieve full employment, and the resulting expansion of the bank credit money supply, should be of secondary importance. It is of no value for a civilized community to have a government that maintains a balanced budget while its citizens are impoverished because of a lack of opportunities due to an insufficiency of private borrowing and spending. It is of great value to a civilized society to have a government that goes as deeply into debt as necessary to provide for the full employment and prosperity of its citizens.

Similarly, it is of no value to restrict the growth of the money supply to some arbitrary value, as Monetarists do, to fight inflation. If the government tries to borrow to expand spending in order to increase demand to generate jobs for all who want to work in a period of unemployment while the money supply is constrained under a Monetarist rule, then, the banks will be unable to accommodate additional government borrowing without having to ration credit and raise interest rates to private sector borrowers. The end result is that entrepreneurial borrowers are 'crowded out' of the loan market, increased government borrowing will reduce private borrowing concomittantly, and no expansion of total demand will be possible. No additional job creation will occur. Monetarist policy, in these circumstances, merely perpetuates unemployment and recession.

CONCLUSION

An accommodating banking system which has the capacity to change the volume of money with the needs of trade is a necessary – but not sufficient – condition for lifting an economy out of an unemployment morass. If a banking system is permitted to flourish and if the government will act as the borrower of last resort to borrow *and* spend whatever is necessary to fill the remaining savings gap, then the entrepreneurial system has both the necessary *and* sufficient conditions to assure its citizens that they will prosper in a full employment economy. Government must always be ready to borrow and spend whenever there is a lack of private sector spending. The Federal Reserve must accept responsibility for keeping the banking system sufficiently accommodating to provide finance at interest rates which encourage as many private sector borrowers as possible as long as a full employment savings gap exists.

Notes

1. If wages and other costs rise, inflation will occur whether the money supply increases or not. Or, if wages and other costs are not rising rapidly, as in the period 1982–6, then inflation will diminish even if the money supply is growing more rapidly.

2. For purposes of this discussion we can treat gifts from other income earners as a loan where there is no requirement of repayment of any sort.
3. Of course, in an open economy, another alternative buying source not financed by current domestic income would be for foreigners to increase their purchase orders from domestic industries. Thus, many countries look towards export-driven growth, rather than increased loan expenditures by government, for their prosperity.
4. Of course, if the developer can get buyers to contractually agree to purchase condo apartments before they are built, then the developer is also assuring his future sales revenues.

7 Controlling Inflation

The analysis in Chapter 6 has brought us to the root of the inflation – unemployment dilemma facing an entrepreneurial economy possessing an accommodating banking system and a government responsible for creating the demand necessary to ensure full employment. A banking system which can provide finance for managers as they expand output, is also capable of providing finance for managers to meet inflating wage and other raw material costs. How does an economy, assured of full employment and a banking system ready to finance rising production costs, prevent managers and workers from raising their prices in their own self-interest?

The conservative answer to this question is that there is only one way consistent with maintaining liberty in a society where people are motivated solely by self-interest. In a 'free' society, workers and entrepreneurs should be free to demand any price for their services, even if such demands are inflationary. As long as there is an obdurate, pre-announced limit to the growth in the money supply, banks will not be able to provide sufficient finance for production and these inflationary demands. If some workers and managers raise their prices, the restraint on bank money creation means there will not be enough claim checks in circulation to buy the things that can be produced at these inflated prices. The resultant weakening of demand – a planned recession – forces managers to lay off some workers. The resulting 'natural rate' of unemployed[1] will threaten the jobs of employed workers, thereby, according to conservative doctrine, curbing future wage demands to non-inflationary levels.

We challenge this conservative view that it is necessary to perpetuate an underclass of unemployed in order to keep demands of the remaining employed at non-inflationary levels. Persistent unemployed workers are not 'natural'. Planned recessions are not worthy of consideration as explicit policy goals for any society claiming to be civilized. To understand the basis of our challenge, it is necessary to examine the relationship between inflation, income, and employment.

INFLATION AND INCOME

Inflation occurs when the prices of things we buy are rising i.e., it takes more dollars to buy the same volume of goods. There are various price indices which attempt to measure inflation. The Consumer Price Index (CPI) is the index most familiar to the general public. It is a measure of changes in the average price of goods that urban consumers buy. The GNP price index is a broader and more comprehensive price statistic measuring changes in the prices of all the products that make up the nation's Gross National Product (GNP).

GNP includes all domestically produced goods; those bought (a) by consumers, (b) by managers for investment purposes, (c) by government, and (d) by foreigners (exports). Since the National Accounting System which is used to measure GNP is based on a system of double-entry bookkeeping, the 'double-entry' offsetting the value of gross national production is the value of the total gross national *income* of the economy. Any increase in the prices associated with GNP must be accounted for by an identical increase in the prices (i.e. wages, rents, interest, profits) paid to income earners. *Every price increase is an increase in someone's income.*

The GNP can be thought of as a huge pie (see Figure 7.1) 'baked' or produced by the combined efforts of workers, property owners, and entrepreneurs. Each contributor to the production of this pie receives, in payment for his/her efforts, a sum of money income. This income gives the recipient a claim to a slice of the GNP pie. The size of the slice claimed depends on the price of the productive services the contributor has provided. Consequently, if the money income people receive increases more rapidly than the size of the GNP pie (the 'real' output), then the GNP price level must rise (inflate) to keep the National Accounts in balance.

Anyone whose services are highly priced earns a claim to a large piece of the pie. Those whose services have a lesser value in the market-place will earn smaller claims. The unemployed earn no claims at all. Individually, or as members of a group (e.g. labour unions, cartels), self-interested people can improve their relative living standard if they can negotiate a higher price for their services compared with the prices paid to others. If, however, the size of the GNP pie does not increase at the same time, then the gain in the slice of pie by any one group raising its price is at the expense of the rest of the community. If money incomes increase faster than the

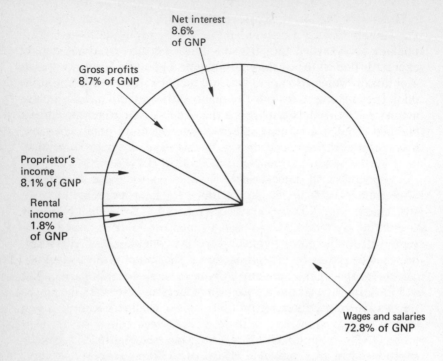

Figure 7.1   Income shares of US GNP (1986)

real pie grows, the accounting result is inflation as measured by the GNP price index.

Inflation is, therefore, a symptom of a struggle over the distribution of income. Whenever individuals or groups try to increase their share of the pie by contriving to raise their price faster than the pie is growing, inflation results. In the struggle to gain at the expense of others, those who receive the largest price increases for the services they sell will be winners able to buy more pie; the price of the services they sell are rising faster than the price of the goods they buy. Those whose prices have not increased (or have increased less than the average) will find that their money incomes fail to keep up with inflation. They will be forced to claim a smaller piece of pie. This struggle over income shares is really what Professor Lester Thurow means when he characterizes the economy as *the zero-sum society*. The winners' inflationary gain is offset by the losers' smaller pie slice – as long as the total size of the pie is unchanged.

Obviously, the losers will be unhappy with the outcome; but even the winners may be disappointed since increases in their income will not buy as many additional goods (more pie) as they might have expected, due to the ensuing rising price of goods. Hence, inflation is politically unpopular among all groups, even the winners who often do not regard their own 'hard earned' and 'deserved' money income increases as causing inflation. To the extent that the authorities use planned recessions to fight inflation, then the 'zero sum' for society becomes a negative one as the size of the pie is reduced.

THE POST-WAR INFLATION AND UNEMPLOYMENT RECORD

In the absence of an explicit polis consensus on an acceptable distribution of income, a fully employed but 'free' economy cannot harmonize the conflicting income demands of people motivated solely by self-interest. Indeed in a world devoid of civic constraints on income demands, conservatives have recognized that the only way to fight inflation requires incomes losses, unemployment, the destruction of profit opportunities, and a resulting reduction in the total size of the pie in order to keep peoples' income demands in their place!

The historical record since 1950 shows that only during the period 1961 to 1968, and again briefly in 1972 to 1973, when the government developed a polis consensus supporting a policy of directly constraining money income growth to the real growth in the GNP pie (so-called 'incomes policies'), the US economy could approach full employment without suffering inflation.

During the Kennedy–Johnson years of 1961 to 1968, prices were held in check by a wage–price 'guideline' policy which urged limits to money wage increases. These guidelines were entirely voluntary – there were no external incentives, no monetary rewards or punishments, to enforce labour to behave! These guidelines relied solely on the internal incentives of the democratic polis for public compliance enhanced by President Kennedy's stirring inaugural motto 'Ask not what the country can do for you, ask what you can do for the country'. For years, the guidelines worked! At the same time, the real GNP pie grew rapidly as the result of increased government deficit spending resulting from a military build-up and a tax cut. With the growth of the unpopular Vietnam war under Johnston, however, the civic cohesion generated by the Kennedy charisma was shattered.

Compliance with the guidelines disappeared in the last year of the Johnson Administration as civic values were degraded and self-interest became dominant.

For the next thirteen years, part of the public agenda was a continuing search for an acceptable incomes policy to replace the 'guidelines' to control inflation and to provide for an equitable sharing of the economic largess of a fully employed society. Except for the 17-month period of Nixon's wage and price controls beginning in August 1971, however, the main tool actually used to fight inflation was planned recessions induced by restrictive monetary policy. Between 1969 and 1980 each tight money episode increased unemployment rates to what were thought to be politically unacceptable levels. With Congressional elections every two years and Presidential elections every four years, most politicians lost the political 'stomach' for the resulting unemployment and deserted the conservative cause. As soon as the inflation problem began to abate, political pressures built-up to re-stimulate the economy. Consequently, the 1970s was a period of on-again off-again restrictive monetary policies stringent enought to raise unemployment but neither strong enough nor long enough to permanently subdue the inflationary struggle over the distribution of income. Until 1979 conservative monetary policy appeared to provide only a temporary respite from inflation.

In August 1971, President Nixon successfully instituted a direct incomes limitation policy via wage and price controls. (This approach was, of course, in direct conflict with the expressed conservative philosophy of his Administration.) This incomes policy, freed the Federal Reserve of responsibility for controlling inflation. The Fed immediately eased monetary policy. The result was a vigorously non-inflationary economy where real GNP grew at a rate in excess of 5 per cent during 1972 and 1973, while inflation dropped from 4.5 per cent to 3.3 per cent. This vigorous recovery with lower inflation contributed to the Nixon landslide victory. After re-election, Nixon removed most of the controls. Prices climbed by 6.2 per cent in 1973 and by 11 per cent in 1974. Inflation was again the principal economic problem on the public agenda.

By 1975, President Ford felt the necessity to hold a 'White House Conference on Inflation' where approximately 700 leading US economists engaged in a two-day discussion of what to do about inflation. The only tangible result from this meeting was President Ford's WIN (Whip Inflation Now) Campaign which tried to emulate Kennedy's example of appealing to civic values. The public saw the WIN campaign as a stunt, not a policy. After the erosion of civic values under Johnson and Nixon, the environment was not sufficient for 'catchy' advertising slogans to whip up public support.[2]

Unemployment increased from 4.9 to 8.2 per cent between 1972 and the planned recession of 1974–5. Inflation dropped to 5.8 per cent by 1976. With a recovery in the early years of the Carter Administration, however, the inflation rate again rose to 6.5 per cent in 1977 and 7.7 per cent in 1978. Inflation was getting out-of-hand. President Carter therefore proposed a direct incomes policy – a 'real wage insurance' scheme – which would use the external incentive of reducing taxes for those who limited wage increases to a socially acceptable level. The Carter proposal, however, was abandoned by the President even before Congress could act.

Thus after Nixon's successful 1971–3 incomes policy, any suggestions for adopting an incomes policy were hesitatingly proposed and quickly abandoned. Restrictive monetary policy became the 'only game in town' to fight inflation. When inflation reached the 11.3 per cent in 1979, the Federal Reserve – under a new chairman, Paul Volker – invoked a brutally restrictive monetary policy. Interest rates were pushed to unprecedently high levels, finance dried up, and loan defaults proliferated.

The result was to create a severe world-wide recession, the worst since the Great Depression of the 1930s. Unemployment soared from 5.8 per cent in 1979 to a peak of 10.8 per cent in 1982. The rate of inflation dropped from 13.5 per cent in 1979 to approximately 4 per cent in the last few months of 1982. In August 1982, the Fed relented, and the economy revived. By 1986, despite a much looser monetary policy, inflation had fallen to less than 2 per cent per annum – but the unemployment rate hovered around 7 per cent,[3] higher than it had been for decades before Monetarism had been officially adopted as Fed policy by Mr Volker.

Inflation had been stilled but only at a great cost in terms of persistent high unemployment and significant unused industrial capacity. Inflation was not eliminated as an affliction of modern economics striving for full employment. In fact, by 1987 the first rumblings of a renewed inflationary era could be heard.

AN ASSESSMENT OF THE MONETARIST EXPERIMENT OF 1979–82 AND THE REAGAN REGIME OF 1981–6

By August 1982, three years of very severe and lengthy Monetarist policy had brought the international and domestic financial systems to near collapse. With the fire of financial panic breathing down his neck, Fed Chairman Volker was forced to abandon this stringent monetary policy.

By 1985 financial reporters regularly announced that the war on inflation had been won. This triumphant war successfully silenced any discussion of a direct incomes policy as an alternative to planned recessions. We did not require civilized direct controls on income as long as society apparently accepts barbaric indirect controls via permanent unemployment.

The Reagan–Volker success has doused the liberal yearning for full employment. Conservative dogma suggesting the need for a permanent underclass of unemployed has become socially acceptable doctrine even among liberal economists eager to share in the conservative success.

Even though there were almost 8 million unemployed workers in the United States, on 1 March 1987 'liberal' economist and Nobel Prize winner Franco Modigliani wrote in the *New York Times* that 'we are now relatively close to the minimum level of unemployment that can be reached and maintained without a serious risk of rekindling inflation'. Modigliani unabashedly claimed that there is broad agreement among (employed) economists that not more than 1 million jobs could be filled by the 8 million unemployed without inflationary repercussions. Apparently 'liberals' are willing to sacrifice the economic lives of the 7 million jobless. Conservative barbarism had become the collective wisdom of most economists.

While it is true that the inflationary battlefield was quieter than it had been in over a decade, the results of the war against inflation waged by the Reagan Administration and the Fed leaves the questions of how it was 'won', at what cost, who has won, and what are the spoils of that victory.

Much of the real credit for the mid-1982–6 recovery is due to the Reagan Administration's policy of reducing taxes while *increasing* expenditures just as the Federal Reserve was relaxing its stringent monetary policy. This success was not in any way related to the supply side promise that the 1981 tax-cuts, which would stimulate so much more additional work and investment, that the cuts would pay for themselves. The huge and continuing federal deficit since 1981 is vivid evidence of the failure of supply-side economics.

Nor should credit for the 1982–5 recovery go to Chairman Paul Volker of the Federal Reserve and the relaxation of the high interest rates he foisted on the US and the result of the world between 1979 and 1982. This 1979–82 Volker tight money policy forced the United States into the second largest economic depression in the twentieth century. Between 1979 and 1985 alone, the loss of real income to Americans from not running a full employment economy has been estimated at almost 3 trillion dollars.

In terms of our GNP pie analysis this means that had the US managed to maintain a full employment economy, the average American would have had a 12 per cent larger slice of the pie *in each and every year since 1979*. This diminution in the relative economic well-being of the American people, owing to the Fed's acceptance of the barbaric belief in the need to maintain a natural rate of unemployment, is truly staggering. Of course had the Fed not relaxed its barbaric Monetarist policies in mid-1982, the resulting economic losses would have been more staggering.

The fuel that has been driving the Reagan recovery since mid-1982 has been the enormous federal deficits. Rather than constituting a new age of Republican economic policy based on 'sound' finance, the 1982–6 recovery of the US economy is primarily attributable to a repackaging of old Keynesian policy prescriptions of stimulating demand via deficit spending plus providing the economy with sufficient liquidity via a less restrictive monetary policy.

Did we really conquer inflation?

Whatever victory against inflation has been achieved in the last half-decade should be put into perspective. Inflation has declined from double-digits of the last year of the Carter Administration to below 4.5 per cent – an inflation rate that may look 'low' compared with recent experience, but one which traumatized President Nixon in 1971 to imposing wage and price controls. Meanwhile unemployment has not fallen below the 1979 level and economic growth since 1979 was only 2 per cent per annum over the entire period – well below the post-war average. Even during the Reagan 'boom' years of 1982 to 1986 growth was only 3.3 per cent – about equal to growth averaged over prosperous times *and* slumps since 1946.

The anti-inflationary policies adopted by the Reagan Administration are different both in degree and in kind from those of his predecessors. First, early in his Administration, President Reagan made union breaking respectable when he demolished the Air Traffic Controllers' Union. Reagan's anti-union stance was legal, but for the prior half-century (since Calvin Coolidge broke the Boston Police

Strike in the 1920s), government officials have been extremely hesitant to use legal measures to bring about the demise of a workers' union. The vigorous anti-union action by President Reagan altered the public perception of the permissible relationship between government and unions, severely weakening the militancy of the entire union movement in the United States. That change, in itself, significantly lowered the pressure for inflationary wage demands by workers.

Secondly, Ronald Reagan unlike most politicians in the 1970s stayed the course with Federal Reserves Chairman Volker's strong Monetarist policy. The result was that, in the first 20 months of the Reagan presidency, the US experienced the worst recession since the 1930s. Any improvement in economic performance was bound to look good after that dreary experience.

THE MONETARIST VIEW – BLEEDING THE ECONOMY TO CURE THE PATIENT

Milton Friedman, the world's foremost Monetarist economist, is usually credited with coining the statement that 'Inflation is always and everywhere a monetary phenomenon'. Friedman asserts that there is a *fixed* long-run relationship between increases in the quantity of money and the rate of inflation. This Monetarist argument is ultimately based on the old homily that inflation is merely 'too many dollars chasing too few goods'.

This 'too many dollars' cliché is usually illustrated by employing a two island parable. Imagine a hypothetical island where the only available goods are 10 apples and the money supply consists of, say, ten $1 dollar bills. If all the dollars are used to purchase the apples, the price per apple will be $1. For comparison assume on a second island there are twenty $1 bills and only 10 apples. All other things being equal, the price will be $2 per apple. *Ergo*, inflation occurs whenever the money supply is excessive relative to the available goods. The inevitable conclusion of this 'beat your wife' paradigm is that had the second island limited its money supply to $10, no inflation of apple prices would have occurred.

In this parable no explanation is given as to why the money supply was greater on the second island. Nor is it admitted that if the increase in money supply is associated with entrepreneurs borrowing 'real bills' from banks to finance an increase in payrolls necessary to harvest, say, 30 additional apples so that the \$20 chases forty apples, then the price will be only \$0.50 per apple. If a case of real bills finance occurs, then an increase in the money supply is not associated with higher prices but with greater output.

A tight money policy operates by raising the costs to bankers of borrowing funds; hence, bankers charge higher interest on loans to entrepreneurs. These higher finance charges increase managers' operating costs thereby reducing profit opportunities. This will reduce entrepreneurs' willingness to borrow to finance additional payrolls which, in turn, means that managers cut back on hiring and/or wage payments. This desire of management to shed labour may be exacerbated if managers interpret the higher interest costs as a warning signal that a recession is on the way.

If the resulting recessionary market environment forces workers to limit or reduce contract demands (so-called 'givebacks') during future labour contract negotiations, then the rise in production costs inflation will begin to slow. In the interim there will be a painful 'stagflation' – a stagnating production of goods with rising prices as some inflationary costs work their way through the system. Thus, the Great Recession of 1979–82 produced stagflation during its early stages, while leaving a legacy of reduced wage demands in the 1983–6 period.

If, on the other hand, the Fed does not develop a restrictive monetary policy when labour is demanding inflationary wage increases, then bankers can expand their loan operations. Accordingly, if a community vigorously pursues a full employment goal, while simultaneously having no societal limitations on people's inflationary income demands, then the economy has a built-in inflationary bias. Since conservatives do not believe that civic forces can affect either people's behaviour or the real economy, this has led them to argue that an anti-inflationary tight monetary policy is the 'only game in town' as governments' pursuit of full employment created continuous incomes inflation pressures.

By creating unemployment, income losses, and weak markets for goods, conservatives expect to make most people too weak economically to fight over the distribution of income. In puritanical terms, Monetarists often suggest that such monetary discipline 'is good for the system' – comparable with the curative blood-letting practices of fifteenth-century physicians. Conservatives acknowledge that recessions may inflict pain and suffering but, they claim, that a stiff dose of monetarist medicine is needed to purge the system of those who would otherwise try to extort inflationary money income demands on the rest of society. In the long run, in true Social Darwinistic philosophy, this monetarist prescription necessarily punishes the lazy and makes industry leaner and more efficient. Once again, conservatism resorts to the barbarism of a Leviathan which governs by inflicting pain on the public.

There is, however, no evidence that after a planned recession the economy will *automatically* snap back to its (assumed) unchanged full employment growth without inflation, rather than languishing in a stagnating state of torpid growth or stagnation. By mid-1986, for example, despite almost four years of 'prosperous recovery' from the planned Monetarist recession of 1979–82, the US economy continued to find itself operating at only 80 per cent of capacity and with 7 per cent of the labour force still unemployed – an obvious waste of potential resources.

The intentional infliction of economic pain, i.e., the use of an external disincentive of a loss in real income to keep inflationary income demands down results in the economic maiming or even death of many innocent companies and people. Conservatives claim that this pain is the inevitable price for fighting inflation. But Monetarist policies that fight inflation via recessions are but one option – a barbaric one. A civilized society should seek more humane ways to limit the income distribution conflict among members of its economic community. This conservative policy of deliberately hurting people should never be a first choice solution for a civilized society. Austere and unpalatable policies are not necessarily virtuous. Planned recessions are the last resort of a failed policy!

CONTRACTUAL PRICES AND INFLATION

It is possible to build on our discussions of the role of money and contracts in Chapter 5 to design direct and civilized policies to fight inflation without throwing people out of work.

In Chapter 5, it was argued that business firms could either produce 'to spot market' or 'to forward contract'. Conceptually, this means that an economy can suffer from (a) spot price inflation, and/or (b) contract price inflation. Accordingly we must develop policies to deal with each kind of inflation.

SPOT PRICE INFLATION

Spot prices require immediate delivery. Since production takes time, only goods which already have been produced and are currently being stored as shelf inventory can literally be sold in spot markets. Any sudden increase in demand for immediate delivery (or decline in shelf-inventory supplies) will cause a *spot or commodity price inflation*. The result will be a windfall change in the income of those possessing the existing commodities. The homily of the two islands, each with a fixed inventory of 10 apples and (sudden) different demands (assumed to be related to differing money supplies), is a simple illustration of such a spot price inflation.

Buffer stocks as a solution for spot price inflation

Since a spot or commodity price inflation occurs whenever there is a sudden and unforseen change in demand or available supply *for immediate delivery*, this type of inflation can easily be avoided if there is some institution which is not motivated by self-interest but which will maintain a 'buffer stock' to prevent unforeseen changes from inducing wild spot price movements. This buffer stock is nothing more than some commodity shelf-inventory which can be moved into and out of the spot market in order to buffer the market from disruptions by offsetting the unforeseen changes in spot demand or supply.

For example, since the oil price shocks of the 1970s, the United States has developed a 'strategic petroleum reserve' stored in underground salt domes on the coast of the Gulf of Mexico. These oil reserves are designed to provide emergency market supplies to buffer the US oil market if it is suddenly cut off from foreign supply sources. In such a situation, the spot prices of oil would not increase as much as it otherwise would; a spot oil price inflation could be avoided as long as the buffer stock remained available. Similarly, if the United States had increased its purchase for the strategic oil reserves during the first half of 1986 when spot oil prices dropped from $20 to almost $10 per barrel as the result of world-wide excessive inventories of crude, the resulting oil price deflation and its devastating impact on the income of domestic oil producers in the oil patch of the southwestern States could have been mitigated.

In the absence of such buffer stocks of commodities, every

unexpected change in spot demand or available supply will produce an immediate change in spot prices. In times of great uncertainty about the future use and/or availability of important commodities, e.g. oil, metals, etc., the spot price can fluctuate dramatically in short periods of time – as they did during brief periods in the 1970s and 1980s.

Rising spot prices signal an inventory shortage and thereby encourage an output expansion. The resulting rebuilt inventories will end the spot price inflation. Falling spot prices signal producers that inventories are excessive. Managers will cut back future production in order to work off the existing inventories, thereby stopping the price decline. Essentially spot price inflation (or deflation), provided it does not induce change in the future costs of production, should subside. To the extent that the spot price of commodities are rising, however, it may take too long for new supplies to come to market. Buyers may not be able to wait for a return to more normal supply–demand conditions, or they may be stampeded by fears of an uncertain future into thinking that the current spot price inflation will permanently affect future costs of production, thereby encouraging producers to raise their supply contract prices.

The policy solution to a spot price inflation that tnreatens to outlive the buyers' patience is as old as the biblical story of Joseph and the Pharaoh's dream of seven fat cows followed by seven lean cows. Joseph – the economic forecaster of his day – interpreted the Pharaoh's dream as portending seven good harvests where production would be much above normal followed by seven lean harvests where annual production would not provide enough food to go around. Joseph's civilized policy proposal was for the government to store up a *buffer stock* of grain during the good years and release the grain to market, without profit, during the bad years. This would maintain a stable price over the fourteen harvests and avoiding inflation in the bad years while protecting farmer's incomes in the good harvest years. The Bible records that this civilized buffer stock policy was a resounding economic success!

Obviously the idea of using buffer stocks to stabilize commodity prices is not new. It was used briefly by the United States during the First World War. It was revived as part of the agricultural policy of the New Deal to maintain farm income.

In the period from the end of the Second World War until the 1970s, an expressed US government policy was to maintain significant buffer stocks of agricultural products and other strategic raw materials to support prices which adequately rewarded producers for efficiently organizing the production process. This US policy helped stabilize commodity prices worldwide even as world demand for foodstuffs and other basic commodities exploded under the stimulus of global economic growth.

The other side of the coin of stable commodity prices was stable incomes for farmers and other commodity producers. The result was (a) prosperity for raw material producers, (b) encouragement of continuing productivity enhancing investment in these areas, and (c) a non-inflationary price trend for the food and basic commodity component of the consumer's budget despite a soaring global population and rapid world-wide economic growth. In fact, from hindsight it is clear that the stability of commodity prices was an essential aspect of the unprecedented prosperous economic growth of the world's economy over a quarter of a century.

The success of this post-Second World War buffer stock programme over several decades, however, was its ultimate undoing. As productivity in food and other primary products increased (encouraged by a guaranteed price), some taxpayers began to object to the cost of carrying the buffer stock. Objections were also raised to the idea that the income of farmers and other commodity producers was being guaranteed at what appeared to be consumers' expense. After all, if the existing surplus buffer stock was dumped onto the market, spot prices would fall, providing the consumer with a 'bargain' – at the expense of producers.

Public attention was not drawn to the fact that the urban taxpayer as a consumer received the benefit of a plentiful food supply at stable non-inflationary prices. And as workers and entrepreneurs in the industrial sector, they had plenty of job opportunities producing the many industrial products that only prosperous raw material producers could demand.

When the Nixon Administration dismantled these buffer stock programmes in order to save warehousing costs and to use these savings to help finance the war in Vietnam, world spot commodity markets were left to the mercy of unforeseen and unforeseeable events. The result was the violent commodity price fluctuations that occurred in the 1970s and 1980s. In the early 1970s – even before the first oil shock – world spot food prices began to soar as a result of some natural disasters that reduced harvests and fishing catches. Since world commodity supplies were no longer buffered, prices swung widely in response to these unforeseen disasters. As the buffer stocks disappeared, cartels or producers had the freedom to raise prices by restricting supplies. Cost-of-living escalator clauses in many wage contracts were triggered by this commodity inflation thereby causing this spot price inflation to spill over into production costs (incomes) inflation for industrial goods. This process was already well under way in 1972 even before the OPEC oil cartel's embargo drove oil prices through the roof, and exacerbated the situation.

As a result, many foreign nations who were net importers of agricultural products and petroleum were especially hard hit by the ongoing world-wide commodity inflation. In the absence of any significant international buffer stock, each nation attempted to become more self-sufficient in these basic commodities rather than pay the 'exhorbitant' prices to the traditional foreign producers. This policy of self-sufficiency meant subsidizing less efficient domestic raw material producers. This self-sufficiency movement was further fanned by the Carter grain embargo in 1979 which signalled to foreign grain importers that for political reasons they could no longer count on United States production to feed their population at any price!

The politically motivated actions by the Nixon and Carter Administrations eliminated the United States as the world's major buffer stock operator who had, for decades, maintained international spot commodity price stability. When the US publicly abandoned the role of the world's non-profit buffer stock operator, commodity producers and consumers were given a clear signal that their future prosperity could no longer be secured on the civilized post-Second World War international institutions. Between 1945 and 1972, the United States acceptance of the role of buffer stock co-ordinator in many internationally traded raw materials had contributed dramatically to the development of an international polis which had guaranteed profitable prices for basic commodity producers and the promise of especially good profits for those who searched out the most efficient production methods. In return the consumer received plentiful supplies without inflation. Under this social regime, the global production and consumption of basic commodities involved a positive-sum game with both producer and consumer groups sharing in the resulting economic gains. When this polis collapsed, producers' prosperity began to depend on their ability to form coalitions against consumers to extract income from them – at best, a zero-sum game.

As the post-war international economic polis broke down, many of the efficiencies of a civilized world were lost. To counter soaring basic commodity prices, many nations subsidized inefficient domestic producers. The result was that the world's production for many basic food commodities expanded and excesses came onto world markets just when the United States and then most of the rest of the industrialized world were plunged into the Great Recession of 1979–82. This led to a startling commodity spot price deflation in the early 1980s. As a result, agricultural and energy prices in the United States and around the world plunged bringing the agricultural and petroleum sector of the US to the brink of disaster.

If we have learned anything from this history of commodity price gyrations, it is that wild commodity spot price swings in free markets create havoc, inefficiencies and misery – sometimes among producers and sometimes among buyers. At any point of time these volatile spot price movements produce some winners and offsetting losers between producer and consumer groups, giving the impression that it is the zero-sum game described by MIT Professor Thurow. But from a longer prospective, the whole world has been a loser as a result of the unbuffering of commodity prices under the Nixon presidency compared with world economic performance from 1945 to 1969 when spot-price stabilization was an explicit policy goal.

INCOMES INFLATION

Changes in wages and material costs in production contracts always involve someone's income. With slavery illegal in civilized societies, the money-wage contract for hiring labour is the most universal of all production prices. Labour costs account for the vast majority of production contract costs in the economy, even for such high-technology products as NASA spacecraft. That is why inflation associated with production prices is usually associated with wage inflation.

Wage contracts specify a certain money wage per unit of time. For example, a secretary may earn $10 per hour. If during the hour, the secretary types 20 letters then the unit labour cost of each letter is $0.50 (20 letters divided by 10). This labour cost plus a profit margin or mark-up to cover material costs, overheads, and profit on the investment becomes the basis for managerial decisions as to the price they must receive on a sales contract in order to make the undertaking worthwhile. If money wages rise relative to the productivity of labour, then the labour costs of producing output must increase. Consequently firms must raise their sales contract price if they are to maintain profitability and viability. When production costs and hence contract prices are rising throughout the economy, we are suffering an *incomes inflation*.

A PROPOSAL FOR A TAX-BASED INCOMES POLICY (TIP)

To prevent an incomes inflation requires some method of limiting money wage rate (and gross profit margin) increases.[4] In 1970, Professor Sidney Weintraub laid out a simple but clever anti-incomes inflation policy which he called TIP or a *Tax-based Incomes Policy*. TIP made use of both civic values and self-interest, although the latter was more prominently displayed in the proposal. TIP is designed to counter inflation by placing a penalty – an external disincentive – on those companies which grant wage increases in excess of a socially acceptable non-inflationary norm based on average labour productivity increases.

The basic philosophy of TIP is that wage increases in excess of productivity growth will harm all members of society – and hence violates a basic civic value. Firms that accede to inflationary wage demands are inflicting a cost on the entire society, similar to what polluters do when they discharge wastes into the air or public waterways. Weintraub's penalty TIP charges enterprises for the 'economic pollution' that granting inflationary wage increases produces.

Entrepreneurs who accept inflationary wage demands at the bargaining table would be punished for their indiscretion. But the punishment differs from the Monetarist policy. TIP involves external disincentives (higher taxes) levied directly on those whose behaviour fosters inflation. To offset the extra tax revenues paid by those penalized under TIP, those firms and workers whose behaviour was not inflationary would receive external incentive rewards in the form of a tax cut. Under Monetarist anti-inflation policy, on the other hand, punishment is inflicted indiscriminately on the entire community; workers are thrown out of jobs whether their specific behaviour was inflationary or not. Tight money bites by reducing the community's income and idling significant resources so that it does not buy as much of the GNP pie as before.

Once instituted, TIP would have to be a permanent policy institution if the inflationary dragon is to be permanently tamed. There must always remain on the books a civic statement of acceptable non-inflationary behaviour as a constant reminder that inflating one's income is always contrary to the governing polis. If a specific future date for the end of TIP was to be announced, its effectiveness would diminish as that date approached. Everyone would be told, in effect, that soon constraints on inflationary income behaviour will disappear. The existing polis would erode as each member of society could no longer rely on the civilized behaviour of others. Self-interest alone would encourage each person to try to increase their own money income *before* others did so first. The struggle over the distribution of income would be re-ignited – and could be dampened only by the dousing waters of a planned recession.

Credibility and compliance with TIP

TIP is based primarily on the external incentive of tax penalties for anti-social behaviour. But it also mixes education and internal incentives in a manner similar to the way road regulations govern driving behaviour on the nation's highways. Speed limits, for example, are permanent but the magnitude of the speed limit can change depending on driving conditions, the need for energy conservation, etc. – factors whose *raison d'être* in achieving society's goals are clear to an educated driving public. Similarly, TIP would be a permanent institution but the magnitude of the allowable wage increase could vary depending on economic conditions. Public education would be necessary to explain the factors affecting the magnitudes involved in TIP.

Speed limits, paying one's taxes, and similar civic behaviour, depend to a considerable extent on voluntary compliance working in tandem with fines levied on those who excessively violate the rules. Governments never reward good drivers for not exceeding the speed limit – nor taxpayers for paying their proper taxes – that is expected social behaviour of all citizens – even if it is not in their own self-interest. Similarly, those whose wage and income increases are non-inflationary would not be rewarded – such social behaviour would be expected.

Civilized governance relies on a co-ordination of enforcement with social norms. Sanctions work best when their primary function is to guarantee that social norms will not be taken lightly. This provides social norms with the credibility to develop, and it prevents the erosion of the norms by those who would ridicule the law.

The institution of TIP would violate the current norms of both unions and business firms who believe in 'free collective bargaining' i.e., wage negotiations without government interference – just as a pollution tax can violate the norms of environmentalists who believe that polluting is an absolute evil and therefore no one should be permitted to pollute the air or waters merely because the polluter can afford the charge. Consequently the implementation of TIP must be accompanied by a strong effort to earn credibility in the eyes of both entrepreneurs and labour. As we discussed in the example of tax compliance in Massachusetts, implementation policies would involve four broad areas.

Framing the issue

(1) Entrepreneurial fears of massive government regulation and additional record keeping requirements must assuaged. Weintraub's TIP proposal was to be applied to only the top 2000 firms in the United States. These firms produce over half of the GNP and are key to the general wage level and profit margins set in the rest of the economy. Managerial control of such large enterprises already requires extensive record keeping. TIP would not add to this burden as compliance could be calculated from existing records and shown on an additional three or four lines on corporate income tax forms. Smaller businesses – and especially new enterprises – on which the vitality of the entrepreneurial system depends would not be affected at all.

(2) The public must be educated to understand that TIP will be inexorably linked to a set of expansionary fiscal policies. Acceptance of TIP, therefore, guarantees maximum production and the highest standard of living possible for the community. It must be carefully explained that the only alternative to a permanent incomes policy is either permanent high unemployment (to limit inflation) or high inflation (which creates turmoil and destroys the economic polis). TIP is the tool which allows the society to unleash its full economic potential without having to fear either of these consequences.

(3) TIP must have credibility. TIP must possess a simple structure so that the public can comprehend what is being implemented. Business, labour, and the general public must be assured that TIP represents a ubiquitous social norm in the sense that:

(a) TIP will not be vulnerable to political manipulation; it will not create a new arena where individuals and groups compete for higher incomes through political pressure or backroom deals.
(b) TIP will not be vulnerable to non-compliance resulting from accounting gimmicks and other misrepresentations which hide excessive wage increases of dishonest firms while penalizing workers and entrepreneurs of honest companies;
(c) TIP will not grossly distort the economy by creating a new set of strange incentives.

(4) TIP must be recognized as a permanent part of the economic landscape.

Transitional problems in installing TIP

Those whose money income status is caught in the transition from the current situation to a TIP relation must be treated fairly. This suggests that it will be easier to institute TIP during a period when inflationary forces are not strong (as in the 1980s). When the ongoing struggle regarding income redistribution is lowered (perhaps as a result of the Great Recession of 1979–82) then it may appear that there is less need for a TIP policy – but if we are to avoid permanent slow growth or stagnation then a direct incomes policy is essential. The US and most of the rest of the industrial world has an especially attractive window of opportunity for instituting TIP during the mid-1980s (as compared with the 1970s when it was clearly needed – but the transition would have been especially difficult).

It is always difficult to transmute human nature – especially as it has developed in our entrepreneurial economy since the early 1960s. Although it is necessary to develop a core of civic values around the need to stop inflationary income demands, it would be foolish to rely solely on civic values. TIP will have to rely heavily on external incentives as well. This is not a fatal problem. Societies often develop institutions which draw significant support for their existence and acceptance from related – but separated – civic values. For example, there is no excellence involved in simply donating money to charity. As Dickens' self-interested entrepreneur, Ebenezer Scrooge, recognized the more one gives to charity the less one has for oneself. Only within a larger framework of a polis which values highly charitable contributions can there be an internal incentive to override self-interests and behave philanthropically.

To promote the civic values which TIP requires to operate effectively, the linkage must be made between TIP and the larger civic virtue of providing an environment in which it is possible to attain a non-inflationary full employment economy.

IMPORTED INFLATION

Until this point, the discussion of inflation has implicitly assumed that inflation is always due to a rise in prices of domestically produced goods. Yet with nations that trade with other nations, rising prices of goods brought from abroad can result in an *imported inflation*. Although a complete discussion of the ramification of international transactions must wait until the next chapter, it is useful at this point to briefly summarize how inflation can be imported.

Imported inflation occurs when the price of imported goods in terms of the domestic currency rises. If there is a fixed exchange rate where the amount of domestic currency paid for a unit of foreign currency does not change, then as inflation occurs in a foreign economy, the cost of imports in terms of money is rising. The rising cost of imports is due to either a foreign commodity and/or incomes inflation.

One of the conservative arguments against a fixed exchange rate system has been that it would therefore transmit inflation across national boundaries. Instead, conservatives insist, that under a flexible exchange rate system (where the amount of domestic currency paid for a unit of foreign currency varies) an inflation in the other country will lead to a *pari passu* drop in the amount of domestic currency paid for a unit of foreign money thereby insulating domestic markets from importing inflation.

This claim of insulation was used by conservatives as a justification for encouraging President Nixon to move to a flexible exchange rate system in 1972. Recent history has shown, however, that a flexible exchange rate system *per se* does not insulate the domestic economy from importing inflation.

Any time there is any reduction in the exchange rate of domestic currency *vis-à-vis* the foreign currency, there can be an imported inflation – even if there is no change in the foreign production costs and foreign prices charged by foreign suppliers.

CONCLUSION ON A CIVILIZED ANTI-INFLATION POLICY

To paraphrase that old-sage Benjamin Franklin, if as a community we do not all hang together to fight inflation, then we will all hang separately via barbarous Monetarist anti-inflationary policy.

Civilized policies to handle inflation rely on us acting as a community. One of the most important functions of government is to educate the public that any on-going income distribution struggle is ultimately costly for all. It is a mug's game – a no-win, everyone loses negative-sum game – although at any point of time there may appear to be some winners.

In the absence of a sensible policy about a civilized resolution to the income distribution question, the result is not a zcro-sum game, but a real loss in total income as governments pursue restrictive monetary and/or fiscal policies which feed back depressionary forces on each other.

ARE DECLINING PRICES A GOOD THING? A PROBLEM FOR THE 1980s

Just as the decade of the 1970s was a period of almost continuous spot and incomes inflation, so the mid-1980s has been a period of modest income inflation partially offset by some noticeable situations of sectoral commodity and incomes deflation – notably in agriculture and oil. After suffering through the pain of inflation and the planned recessions of the 1970s, some economic commentators have looked favourably upon the sectoral price deflations we have experienced. Piqued by the 1970s bumper stickers in the oil producing regions of the US which proclaimed 'Drive at more than 55MPH; and freeze a Yankee', people in the northern energy consuming states in the 1980s might relish in the income deflation suffered in the oil patch region of the USA. Taking pleasure in the economic misery of others is clear evidence of the breakdown of civilized behaviour.

A civilized society must accept the responsibility of not only containing inflationary surges in the income demands of groups in our community at the expense of others, but it must also act to limit *sharp* declines in the income of others. Just as we moderated the real income loss of energy consumers towards domestic energy producers via oil and natural gas price controls and the windfall oil profits taxes in the 1970s, so it should also be the government's responsibility to provide some relief for the loss of income oil producers suffered from the capricious changes in oil prices in the 1980s. One possible policy has already been suggested in the accelerating of purchases of a strategic petroleum reserve as a buffer stock in the period of falling crude oil prices.

More important than specific policies to deal with specific sectoral price changes (all deflationary and inflationary price movements start off as sectoral changes), there is an important civic principle involved. We can not govern a civilized economy by encouraging or even permitting open conflict amongst members of the community. The recent resurgence in the popularity of the idea that it is proper to primarily look out for one's own income without any thought of social responsibility has produced dreadfully detrimental economic effects. Just as civilized people, in this age of advanced technology and massive destructive weapons, have realized that 'war is too important to be left to the generals', so in this age of complex interdependent economies, we should realize that 'income distribution is too important to be left solely to the capricious forces of the market'. If we have not learned this latter principle yet, then the terrible economic costs of the Federal Reserve's planned Great Recession of 1979–82 to fight inflation may have been in vain.

In the past few years, we have been lulled into a false sense of security by the temporary reduction of OPEC's market power and the reduction in militancy of unions. The external incentives which create conflict have been weakened by running the economy at slow throttle. As the pendulum inevitable swings back, the important question is will we be ready.

Fifty years ago, Keynes warned that 'the outstanding faults of the economic society in which we live are its failure to provide full employment and its arbitrary and inequitable distribution of income'. In the last half-century, modern economies have learned how they can avoid the great unemployment problems of the past, but in so doing we may have exacerbated the income distribution faults in our system, first by creating the economic conditions for the inflation of the 1970s without having a civilized incomes policy in position, and then by relying on monetarist's restrictive policies to create the wage and commodity deflation of the 1980s.

Having paid the terrible price to stop inflation, we should use this *temporary* overall-peaceful price level experience of the 1980s to develop incomes policies to protect our civilized system from either continuing seriatim deflation of sector by sector incomes and/or the next surge of inflation.

Notes

1. Marxists would call them the 'industrial reserve army of the unemployed'.
2. President Carter experienced a similar disappointment when he tried to enlist public support for energy conservation by declaring it the 'Moral Equivalent Of War' without any positive leadership actions. The cynical public labelled the Carter moral equivalent policy 'MEOW'.
3. Inflation in Europe had also subsided but unemployment remained at a post-war high.
4. Between the end of the Second World War and the oil and other commodity price shocks in the 1970s, the major inflation problem experienced by the United States was primarily due to money wages increasing at a more rapid rate than productivity increases. From the early 1970s into the 1980s, however, profit margins also rose substantially.

8 Policy for a Civilized Global Economy – Whose International Debt Crisis is it Anyway?

An important requisite of civilized activity is the ability to communicate via a shared dialect. Near the end of the Second World War, economists representing the Allied nations met in Bretton Woods, New Hampshire to plan a post-war international monetary community. Basic to the civilized scheme developed at Bretton Woods was a belief that the nations of the world should be united via a fixed exchange rate system in which the value of one nation's currency in terms of another currency rarely changes. For example, if one could be assured of always being able to exchange one US dollar for 150 Japanese yen, we would have a fixed exchange rate between yen and dollars.

This Bretton Woods fixed rate system lasted approximately a quarter of a century until, in August of 1971, President Nixon unilaterally withdrew the United States. Since then, most of the nations of the world have conducted business with the United States under a system of flexible exchange rates where the amount of foreign currency (be they yen, deutschmarks, lira, francs, etc.) one can obtain for a US dollar varies daily – if not hourly.

It is not an accident that during the period 1945–71, under the Bretton Woods system, global economic growth was unprecedentedly high. From hindsight, the Bretton Woods period was a remarkable crisis-free economic era. Since the breakdown of Bretton Woods, on the other hand, the global economy has stumbled from one economic crisis to another. Economic growth has slowed significantly while the growing global population threatens to reduce standards of living – number of the mouths to be fed are increasing at a faster rate than global GNP. Economics has once more become the dismal science with its Malthusian overtones.

Instead of bringing the Utopian benefits promised by conservative economics, the flexible exchange rate system that replaced the Bretton

158

Woods system has generated an international monetary crisis. In the 5 September 1986 issue of the *New York Times*, reporter Flora Lewis noted that government and business leaders recognize that 'the issues of trade, debt, and currency exchange rates are intertwined'. The world is on a course leading to an economic crisis, yet 'nobody wants to speak out and be accused of setting off a panic . . . the most sober judgment is that the best thing that can be done now is to buy more time for adjustments to head off a crash'. Lewis warns that 'decision makers aren't going to take sensible measures until they are forced to by crisis'. Apparently, no one has the courage to suggest that the conservative philosophy that has governed economic affairs recently is leading us towards economic calamity.

THE INTERNATIONAL DEBT CRISIS

The spectre of two international debt problems haunts the world – one is associated with the liabilities of Less Developed Countries (LDCs) of Latin America, the other is the obligations of the world's largest debtor, the United States. These two debt situations are, in one sense, unrelated in that they developed at different times and for different reasons. The Latin American debts of both oil producing and oil consuming LDCs are essentially the result of the oil price explosions of the 1970s; while the United States debt is due primarily to the Reagan recovery from the Great Recession of 1979–82.

But in a more fundamental sense, these twin debt conditions are inextricably tied together in that (a) they threaten the very viability of the international financial community and (b) their resolution will involve innovative and unorthodox policies.

The Latin debt

The fundamental fact that must be faced is that, in essence, most of the international debt of Latin American nations is in default. The repayment of the debt is not possible in the foreseeable future – and given the magic of compound interest, most of the debt servicing will probably be in default soon, if not, as in the case of Brazil, already. Conventional, conservative analysis has not been able to resolve or even ameliorate the international debt problem. There is therefore, an urgent need for innovative approaches and policies which will (a) permanently remove the threat of default – and the ensuing ramifications on the balance sheets and banking systems of major creditor nations, and (b) prevent future recurrences of these problems.

The United States debt

Between 1982 and 1985, the Reagan government administered the largest peacetime dose of 'Keynesian' deficit spending in history, inducing an economic recovery from the worse recession in half a century. Much of the increased demand for goods that resulted spilled over into a demand for foreign goods and services thereby stimulating additional employment in foreign lands. As a result US purchases of imports have soared relative to exports causing significant annual deficits in payments balances between the US and its trading partners.

Conservatives see this international deficit as indicating that Americans are consuming beyond their means; and they add, with a tone of moral righteousness, that Americans are not saving enough – they are using foreign savings to finance a sinful splurge of wanton consumption! Germany, Japan, South Korea, and other nations have been beneficiaries of this increased US demand for their products. They, however, did not reciprocate by stimulating their own domestic economies or respending all their dollar earnings on additional imports. If they had they would have set up a back flow of orders for US goods, which would have helped redress the imbalance between US imports and exports that have developed since 1982. Instead, these nations enjoyed export-induced economic growth, in contrast to the US where growth was primarily due to the deficit spending – tax reduction policies of the Reagan Administration.

As a direct result of the Reagan Administration's expansionist policies, the United States government debt doubled from $1 trillion in 1981 to $2 trillion by 1986, while the US balance of exports *vis-à-vis* imports dropped from an annual export surplus of $6 billion in 1981 to an annual value of imports over exports (a deficit) of $148 billion by 1986. To finance this huge deficit, United States residents have had to either borrow and/or to sell many assets for foreigners in order to obtain the necessary foreign funds to meet their net import purchase commitments. The Japanese and Germans have been only too happy to oblige. In the four-year period between 1982 and 1986, the US moved from being the world's major creditor nation to being the globe's largest debtor.

THE CONSERVATIVE SOLUTION

It is an economic truism that if a nation is importing more than it is exporting, then other nations must be exporting more than they are importing. The former nation is running an international deficit while the latter are in surplus. Conservative conventional economic doctrine teaches that the deficit nation is 'living beyond its means'. It *must* take drastic action to reduce spending on imports by 'tightening its belt' and adopt some form of deflationary policy. Surplus nations are not required to make any adjustments on their own initiative.

Conservative economists tell the United States and the Latin American nations that there are only three policy choices – of which only the first two are acceptable. The first policy requires the government to increase taxes to reduce consumer spending and to reduce government spending thereby reducing the services provided to its citizens. That such a policy would further aggravate the depressionary tendencies in these nations, and create widespread unemployment and economic hardship, does not matter. Creating income loss, unemployment, and increased poverty is 'the *necessary* price we have to pay' for the nation's prodigal ways, as any high-paid consultant economist will tell policy makers – over his sumptuous expense account dinner!

Warming to his topic, the conservative economist will explain, as he puffs on his cigar over an after-dinner cognac, the second policy which can be used as either an alternative or a supplement to the first is to permit the exchange rate to decline so that an 'impersonal' market force reduces the nation's standard of living by making imports more expensive. It also makes the nation's industries 'more competitive' in both overseas markets and at home. Of course, our conservative economic expert, does not explain that this policy of encouraging a falling dollar (or pesos, or cruzado, etc.) will, if successful, merely export the nation's unemployment to foreign workers whose bosses will find their companies suddenly becoming less competitive.

A third alternative, the introduction of 'protective tariffs' – such as undertaken by the Reagan Administration against the Japanese microchip industry on 17 April 1987 – will not be recommended by conservative economists because tariffs 'interfere' with free markets. Yet tariffs have an effect similar to the second policy in that tariffs make the deficit nation's industry more competitive in the home market and thereby export the deficit nation's unemployment to the surplus nation's industries.

The ultimate effect of these three belt-tightening policies will be to reduce the standard of living of *both* deficit and surplus nations. The deficit nation's living standard declines as its gross national product falls under the first policy. Under the second and third policy options the real income of the deficit nation declines as its people pay a higher price for the goods they buy. The surplus nation's living standard declines as any of the three belt-tightening policies lead to a decline in its export markets and hence it suffers from increasing unemployment.

From a global standpoint, adoption of belt-tightening policies do not improve the world's economy as unemployment and idle capacity is, at best, merely shifted from one nation to another. Global employment and real output will fall if these belt-tightening policies unleash depressionary forces. If these conservative policies are aggressively pursued, then, as the history of the Great Depression demonstrated, the surplus nations will not stand idly by when their industries lose foreign markets. Instead they will retaliate with like policies in an attempt to re-export the unemployment to others. The resulting trade wars can only make all nations worse off!

UNDERSTANDING THE TRADE DEFICIT PROBLEM

There is no universally agreed upon international money which settles contracts between residents of different nations. Crossing national boundaries, traders must agree on which nation's laws and money will govern their contractual agreement. One or both of the parties to an international contract will be using a different currency to settle their domestic transactions than the one required for the international commitment. Either the buyer will have to obtain foreign money to meet the commitment or the seller will receive a foreign currency in payment. In some cases, both buyer and seller may be dealing in foreign money as, for example, when a French refiner buys crude oil for US dollars from the Kuwaiti government.

The monies of other nations are called *foreign exchange* and these various currencies are bought and sold in the *exchange market* at a price called the *exchange rate*. Co-operation between governments is an important factor governing the ease and the terms upon which foreign exchange may be purchased. Depending on the degree of co-operation between the governments, the exchange rate may be either fixed or flexible.

Fixed versus flexible exchange rate systems

In a fixed exchange rate system, the central bank of one (or both) nations acts as a 'market maker' for foreign currencies. In this market maker role the Authorities fix the exchange rate by posting the price that they stand ready to buy and/or sell unlimited quantities of the foreign currency. If the Authorities announce that they will maintain an unchanging exchange rate, and if the 'maker' has sufficient reserves to back this announcement, the exchange rate between the monies will remain fixed!

For example, in 1986, the Central Bank of South Korea maintained an official exchange rate by agreeing to sell 878.50 Korean won for each US $1 offered, or to sell US dollars at the equivalent rate of 0.00114 dollars for each Korean won. In order to back this offer, the Central Bank of Korea had to have an inventory of US dollars (or other liquid assest readily resaleable for US dollars) sufficient to meet all the demands of those who wish to sell won for dollars. This inventory of dollar assets is called the *foreign exchange reserve of Korea*.

Under a fixed exchange rate system, bankers, who deal directly with the public, can be assured of a fixed price for buying or selling various foreign monies. A small service charge is added to this price whenever a banker buys foreign monies from, or sells to, the public. In turn the public is thereby assured of a fixed price for any foreign currency it has to buy or sell.

In a flexible exchange rate system, on the other hand, there is no 'market maker' institution which guarantees an unchanging price for foreign money. Hence, if people increase their demands for a foreign currency, then the price of that money will rise. If the demand for the currency declines, the exchange rate will fall. Although the Monetary Authority may still 'intervene' in the foreign exchange market to affect the price by buying or selling currencies in the foreign exchange market, this intervention is usually limited to preventing the market from becoming what the Authorities call 'disorderly'. By 'disorderly' the Authorities mean that the 'free market' exchange rate is moving, in their judgement, too rapidly in either an upward or downward direction.

For example, the Federal Reserve Bank of New York announced on 4 September 1986 that to limit the fall of the US dollar, 'foreign central banks intervened to slow the decline in the dollar by making sizeable purchases of the currency between May and the end of July, but the Federal Reserve Bank stayed out of the currency markets'. The foreign Authorities intervened to prevent the dollar exchange market from becoming disorderly, but they did not try to fix the dollar exchange rate at any specific level. Despite this intervention the dollar fell by 9 per cent against the Japanese yen and 5 per cent against the German mark during this period.

Those engaged in international trade are continually entering into contracts calling for future payments or receipts in terms of foreign currencies. To reduce uncertainties about the costs of these future commitments, traders need some assurance of the meaning of these future values. A fixed exchange rate system provides the international production and trading community with a Rosetta Stone for precisely translating values from one national money to another over the life of the contract. As such it forms the basis of a common or shared dialect of worth – of financial values – which is an essential element in avoiding inefficient economic activity. In effect, a fixed exchange rate system reduces all the world's various monies to a single common denominator. Everyone can then understand the value of the sums involved in any contract whether they be denominated in dollars, yen, marks, won, or pesos.

A stable civilized system with interacting groups, each with its own language, requires that the dialect of one group possesses a clear correspondence with the dialects of the others so that all of the separate dialects form a compatible whole. A fixed exchange rate system, by ensuring a precise translation of values over time, strengthens the foundations of the international polis. The unprecedented growth of the world's economy under the fixed exchange rate system of Bretton Woods is clear evidence of the tremendous payoff that can be obtained from such a civilized trading system.

In a flexible exchange rate system, on the other hand, the common value dialect among traders is either defective or absent. Good decisions can yield bad results if exchange rate changes are unforeseen. For example, in 1983 when the dollar equalled approximately 250 yen, the management of a large US firm decided it would be very profitable to build a factory in Japan to produce goods for the American market. Managers estimated that the dollar cost of hiring Japanese workers when the plant became operational would be significantly less than hiring US workers to operate a similar 'state of the arts' plant in America. When this Japanese factory came on stream, however, the dollar equalled 140 yen. Management found that this new efficiently engineered plant was economically inefficient and could be operated only at a terrible dollar loss.

Whenever changes in the exchange rate occur (or are expected), the value of an international commitment in terms of domestic money at the time of the agreement can differ in an unpredictable way from the value at the date of settlement. Flexible exchange rates, therefore, inherently engenders more uncertainty about the meaning of international values.

The more uncertain the economic future appears to be, the more managers will hesitate to make commitments and the greater will be their desire to stay liquid in order to be able to meet any unforeseen economic contingency. Under a flexible exchange rate system, therefore, the lack of a common dialect of economic values will mean that the demand for liquidity will be greater than with a fixed exchange rate system. Since, as we noted earlier, any increase in demand for liquidity reduces the total demand for producible goods, *a flexible exchange rate system is an additional recession-provoking force in the global economy.*

A CONCEPTUAL ILLUSTRATION

People's eyes often glaze over when economists try to explain the international deficit problem. Complications multiply when the participants are located in different countries.

In what follows we hope to provide a stimulating, but simple, illustration comparing international financial transactions with interregional ones within a single country, for the latter, with its use of single currency, is easier to comprehend.

An international payments deficit is merely a special case of unbalanced trade between two geographical regions (A and B) where the value of A's exports to region B is less than the value of A's imports from region B. In these circumstances, region A is running a trade deficit with region B. A is therefore under pressure to raise sufficient money to settle this payments imbalance by either borrowing funds or selling assets. Region B's residents are not under any immediate economic pressure. They can accumulate money or future claims against the residents of deficit area A (e.g. by making loans to residents of A) or they can stop selling to region A as the latter experiences difficulties in meeting its payments.

If regions A and B are in separate nations, conservative economists insist that the only permanent remedy for the trade imbalance is for exchange rates to change so that A's money is worth less in terms of B's currency. The competitiveness of A's industries to buyer's in B is improved and hence A will sell more to B. Simultaneously, B's goods become more expensive to residents of A. The latter will reduce their imports until the export–import imbalance disappears.

If, however A and B are regions within the United States, then, as we will demonstrate, government fiscal policy rather than an exchange rate change provides the proper relief. (In fact, as long as the regions are in the same nation, there is never a question of a change in the exchange rate between the money used in region A *vis-à-vis* the money used in region B, nor would any conservative economists recommend such a policy.)

Why does the fact that regions A and B are within the same national boundary make a difference? This can best be explained by conceiving of what would happen if various regions in the United States were in separate nations.

Envision the United States divided up into 12 separate nations – one for each Federal Reserve Bank District.[1] In each District there is a Central Bank which issues its own legal tender. (This is, in fact, the situation in the United States.[2]) Yet the exchange rate between a dollar Federal Reserve Note issued by the San Francisco Federal Reserve Bank and one issued by any of the other 11 banks is always fixed, e.g., $1 San Francisco = $1 Boston.[3]

During a period when no trade imbalance exists between the San Francisco region and the Boston region, for example, payments for each region's imports are offsetting; the demand for money by New Englanders to pay Californians equals the demand for money by the latter to pay the former. If, however, Bostonians suddenly decide to import more Californian oranges, there will be a net flow of dollars west to pay for the additional oranges. As checks clear through the banking system to pay for these oranges, banks in the Boston area will experience an outflow of dollars and reserves while banks in California will see their depositors' dollar balances grow.

The conservative economist would use the law of supply and demand to argue that this trade payments imbalance should result in Californian dollars rising in terms of Bostonian dollars. In fact, however, we never experience such an exchange rate change occurring within the US, because (1) the Federal Reserve System maintairs a fixed exchange rate by acting as the clearing house to ensure that San Francisco and Boston dollars always exchange at a rate of one for one, while (2) the federal government's regional taxation and spending policy acts as a longer-term transfer device to induce a reverse flow of dollars.

As income increases in California, government's tax revenues will rise. The government can draw off these additional tax revenue dollars from California and spend the dollars (and more) in Boston, where income and liquidity is being lost (and therefore recessionary pressures are building up). The result of this policy will be to set off a net flow of bank clearings from California to Boston – a reverse direction compared with the original regional export–import spending pattern in the private sector. The government is, in essence, helping to finance Boston's continuing orange imports.

Post-war *non-conservative* governments, recognizing that the regional trade imbalance will depress the deficit region's economy, have used such fiscal policy to shore up employment. The civilized result of this enlightened policy is that *both* regions benefit. In our example, Californians continue to earn higher incomes via a strong continuing demand for orange exports and New Englanders, with the help of a sufficient government spending, can still earn sufficient income to maintain their standard of living including buying California oranges.

In the absence of such regional fiscal policies, Californians would end up losing their additional income earned from the increased sale of oranges as Bostonians run out of funds to buy oranges. Boston's economy would become more depressed as its banks, losing funds to California's banks, can no longer finance local entrepreneurs even to the extent of maintaining payroll and employment levels.

The moral of this story is that in the absence of an active government policy to offset this cash-flow problem both regions would ultimately be worse off. In a world of *laissez-faire*, the Californians would find their Bostonian customers becoming so impoverished that they would not be able to buy oranges unless the Californians either (a) continually 'lend' them funds to maintain purchases or (b) bought more products from Bostonians so they could afford to buy the additional oranges. It is unlikely that the Californians would be so accommodating. The result will be detrimental to all in the private sector of both regions!

In the case of international trade deficits there does not exist a global taxing and spending authority, or any other institutional arrangement to redress persistent trade imbalances which occur and which can unleash global recessionary forces. Yet the benefits of such an arrangement to residents of both deficit *and* surplus nations should be obvious from our illustration!

Our analysis is not merely an interesting hypothetical illustration. Rather its message is supported by the facts of the Marshall Plan where both deficit and surplus nations benefited because a large trade surplus nation actively worked to prevent the build up of its claims on foreigners.

THE MARSHALL PLAN: AN HISTORICAL ILLUSTRATION

In the immediate post-Second World War period, only the United States had sufficient productive capacity to supply the food and machinery desperately needed in Western Europe and Asia. As a result of the war, however, it was impossible for Europe and Asia to produce enough goods to export to the US to pay for their imports from America. Nor did they have sufficient assets to sell to the US to finance a trade imbalance on the scale required to put their devastated economies back together.

If the United States had left the deficit nations to adjust to the vast looming trade imbalance by reducing imports, then (a) the standard of living of Europeans and Asian residents would have been substantially lower *and* (b) the United States would have slipped into a great recession as there would have been too little international demand for the products of her industrial capacity.

Instead, the United States instituted the Marshall Plan and large scale foreign military and economic aid programmes. These *gave* foreigners large sums of American dollars – *as a gift* – so that they could buy American products. The result was that

(1) Huge benefits accrued to both the foreigners who used these gifts to buy the American goods necessary to rebuilt their economies and to feed their people, and to Americans who obtained jobs and earned incomes by selling exports to these foreigners;
(2) By its generosity the United States invigorated, enriched and strengthened the international polis among Western Europe, North America, and Japan to the immense economic gain of all nations outside the Iron Curtain.

This civilized historical episode in enhancing a post-war free world polis can be compared with the barbaric policy and the resulting fragmented international system that followed the First World War. At that earlier time, the victorious Allies imposed a harsh settlement on the defeated nations. Massive reparations were imposed on Germany as the European Allies attempted to obtain compensation for the general costs of the war that they had incurred.

Perhaps those European nations whose citizens had suffered through years of war can not be blamed for mistrusting either the civilized economic arguments against reparations presented by John Maynard Keynes in his best-selling book *The Economic Consequences of the Peace* or the political ideals of President Woodrow Wilson. The evils of waging war may have eroded civilized values of the European Allies to the point where they felt compelled to demand a barbaric financial retribution.

The result of this barbarism might have been initially satisfying to the warlike passion for revenge by humiliating a former enemy. But barbaric treatment can breed more barbarism, as the evils imposed by the oppressor shape the polis of the oppressed. Although the primary responsibility for Nazi Germany does not lie with the British and French economic policies after the War, to the extent that they helped to shape the German polis of the 1920s and 1930s, the harsh Allied terms for peace did have a significant role in shaping the outcome which occurred in the 1930s and 1940s in Europe.

Moreover, this economic barbarism did not help the economies of the victorious European Allies. The United States, the only victorious nation pursuing a relatively civilized policy not claiming reparations and also developing a plan (the Dawes Plan) for aiding the Germans to meet the Allied claims, enjoyed an economic boom in the 1920s. The European victors, even with the boost of war reparations, experienced much tougher economic times.

ARE DEFICIT NATIONS LIVING BEYOND THEIR MEANS?

When conservatives state that a trade deficit nation is living beyond its means, the implicit 'means' test being employed is the income earned by selling goods and services to foreigners. Employing this specific means test implies, *by definition*, that anytime a nation runs a trade deficit it must be living beyond its means!

The fallacy in this 'living beyond one's means' argument involves the belief that a nation's means is the *actual* export income it earns. A nation's 'means' is not its actual export earnings; rather it is the income the nation would have earned if it had operated with the full employment of all its resources. Using this full employment concept of 'means', is it true that the United States (or even most of the LDCs) is really living beyond its means?

The US case

In 1985 and again in 1986 the annual US trade deficit was equal to approximately 3 per cent of the nation's GNP. If we had put our unemployed workers and idle capacity to work, the United States could have produced a GNP which was at least 5 per cent larger than it was in those years. Thus, had foreigners used their surplus income (earned from selling more to the US than they brought from us) to buy additional goods produced in the USA, we clearly had the resources to meet this foreign demand for additional goods and services. The problem then was not that we did not have the resources (the means) to earn more income – we did not have the opportunity to earn income because nations such as Germany and Japan refused *to live up to their means*!

What about the LDCs?

LDCs appear to be particularly susceptible to developing trade deficits and the resulting balance-of-payments problems. There are only two reasons why any LDC will have a persistent international deficit: either (a) the resources of the LDC are fully employed but the LDC faces unfavourable terms of trade, or (b) the LDC suffers from unemployment because there is an insufficient international demand for their products.

If the problem is the lack of international effective demand for the things a nation produces, the solution – as Keynes proved a half-century ago – is to increase demand for the products of the nation's industry, not, as conservatives would have it, to reduce demand. A civilized solution to a payments deficit of a nation which has significant unemployed resources, therefore, would be to develop international policies which encourage additional foreign purchases in order to give the country the opportunity to earn more!

Only if the deficit LDC is already at full employment, can it be said that the nation is living beyond its full employment means and hence restrictive demand management may be, in some sense, justifiable. But even in this case, the problem, from a global perspective, is that this fully employed 'poor' nation is poor because the market value of its output is so low. (A low value for the products that a nation sells is called an 'unfavourable terms of trade' by economists.)

The poor nation is therefore analogous to a working poor family within a nation such as the United States. A family that is still in poverty, although it is working to its capacity, can not support itself on the market value of its labour services that it sells. To ask the fully employed poor to tighten their belt because they are too low income earners is simply an uncivilized attitude. It does not make good political, or economic, sense to require 'belt tightening' from either the working poor families within a country or the family of working poor nations in the global community. A policy of forcing belt tightening by the 'working poor' will ultimately foment political unrest among the industrious poor who despite their best efforts earn so little that they have very little they can lose.

Belt tightening by deficit nations can not be in the self-interest of the surplus nations for it means less export demand for the industries of these rich countries. To foster global deflationary policies on the deficit nations will merely unleash global recessionary forces making both creditor and deficit nations worse off. The best customers of any nation are rich customers. For example, the developed nations of the world buy two-thirds of what the United States exports. If wealthy nations can make the poor nations richer it will be good business!

If we are to create a truly civilized international system, then the creditor surplus nations must accept the responsibility to initiate policies to reduce trade imbalances. The payments surplus that the creditor nation can earn provides the wherewithal for a painless adjustment. Creditor nations have the ability to pay – they can always buy more imports and/or give grants to LDCs to pay for the LDCs' import demands. Because they are earning high incomes, creditor nations have a greater global responsibility to perpetuate global prosperity.

Whenever surplus nations build up (hoard) international reserves and foreigners' debts – as the Japanese and Germans have been doing in recent years – this excessive demand for international liquidity on the part of surplus nations not only depresses global economic activity but it also creates a future commitment by debtor nations to pay interest and principal (what economists call 'servicing the debt') which the debtor is unlikely to be able to meet, except in the most optimistic of all future circumstances. If the best case scenario does not work out, as the current plight of the Latin American nations and their bankers demonstrate, the contractual debt servicing requirements can create devastation not only for the debtor but for the creditor nation's banking system. If the debtor defaults then standard accounting practice requires the banks to write off the loan thereby reducing the banks' net worth and threatening their viability.

Hence, there is the obligation and responsibility, in its own self-interest, for each creditor nation to make adjustments – within an expansionary global economic context, to avoid such troubled situations. And if the threat of default already exists, the creditor should avoid at all costs either calling in the loan or even cutting off of further credits!

IS FREE TRADE AND A LOWER DOLLAR, OR ARE TARIFFS, THE RIGHT POLICY FOR MAKING US INDUSTRIES COMPETITIVE?

During the Carter Administration, except for the last few months in 1980 when the USA was slipping into a planned Great Recession, unemployment never exceeded 6.3 per cent. During the Reagan Administration, on the other hand, only after four and a half years of a 'vigorous' economic recovery, did the unemployment rate slip slightly below this 6.3 per cent level. The persistent high unemployment rates of the Reagan era combined with huge international payments deficits have led to Congressional demand for 'protective' tariffs in the hopes of restoring jobs in American factories and reducing the trade deficit.

Conservatives, on the other hand, argue that US industries are not 'competitive' because the dollar is overvalued so that foreign goods appear to be cheaper in terms to Americans and American goods appear to be expensive to foreigners. According to this conservative philosophy, what is required is to make American industries competitive. This can be accomplished via a (slow) reduction in the dollar to a lower permanent value (sometimes called a 'soft landing').

Talking down the dollar: an alternative to protective tariffs

'Protectionist' tariffs (i.e. taxes levied on imports) interfere with the conservative principle of free trade. To head off the growing Congressional sentiment for tariffs, Treasury Secretary Baker, in September 1985, embarked on the alternative conservative policy of 'talking down' the value of the dollar in the foreign exchange market. A similar experiment was tried a decade earlier by Treasury Secretary Blumenthal during the Carter Administration.

An intended result is to make imports more expensive for Americans and American goods cheaper for foreigners. The effect will be to lower the standard of living for the average American, even if more jobs are created in the US *at the expense of destroying job opportunities in foreign lands*. In the 1930s such uncivilized policies were known as 'exporting your unemployment' and were justifiably condemned. Today they are recommended by conventional economic wisdom!

Between September 1985 and 1986 the decline in the dollar's value by some 30 per cent did not create many new jobs in the US (while it did create an increase in unemployment in Japan). A further dollar decline of approximately 20 per cent in 1987 expanded US export demand somewhat and therefore finally provided some improvement in the US employment picture. Nevertheless, even after almost halving the value of the dollar over a two-year period, the huge trade deficit and high unemployment rates remained. (Moreover, the fall in the value of the dollar meant a decline in the real income of the American workers as the prices of imports (and domestically produced goods) began to rise faster than money wages.)

Obviously, a much larger plunge for the dollar is required if the US payments deficit is ever to be eliminated. But since every exchange rate devaluation lowers the purchasing power of the domestic currency in terms of foreign products, the effect will be to further reduce the standard of living of Americans.

Those who argue for a further devaluation of the dollar to make US goods more competitive, are demanding that, in the absence of any dramatic increase in productivity, American workers accept a much lower living standard. If we are to become truly competitive merely by talking down the dollar, then the average American worker's standard of living will have to be reduced to the living standard of workers in competitive industries in Asiatic countries such as Korea or Hong Kong. The conservative argument for a lower dollar to improve the 'competitiveness' of American industry, amounts to a hidden agenda to lower the real income of the American worker.

In the modern industrial world there are not significant differences in the productive capabilities of workers in the US as compared with Japan, Korea, Brazil, etc. The 'real' productivity of workers employed in the industrial and service sectors of the economy will not differ significantly among nations, if the workers have the same tools to work with.[4] In this age of multinational corporations, the international transfer of technology and tools to the nations with the lowest paid workers is quite rapid – ensuring, even in the short run, similar worker productivities among nations.

Competitive cost advantages will therefore always lie with those industries located in nations where workers are paid the lowest wage per hour of work effort. When worker productivity does not significantly differ among nations, a public policy to improve competitiveness requires lowering workers' wages. Although the case for 'free trade' is often rationalized by the argument that there are (unmeasured) real gains from trade as compared with protectionism, support for free trade *in the absence of full employment* is merely a way of forcing down the income of workers in the 'competitive' sectors while exporting your unemployment.

Only for those products where wild differences in climate and geographic distribution of natural resources (e.g. agricultural products, crude oil, etc.) significantly affects productivity can a respectable argument for free trade based on a 'real' competitive cost advantage be made. Unfortunately, these primary products are often sold in international markets that are affected, if not dominated by, cartels and marketing boards. Consequently, in these markets, the competitive real costs of production among nations are not reflected in international market prices. Typically, cartel arrangements, multinational agreements, and government income support policies, rather than competitiveness, determine the prices and incomes earned in the production of primary products.

RECENT US PAYMENTS HISTORY

Since the first oil price shock of 1973 dramatically increased the value of commodity imports, the US has experienced a merchandise trade deficit in every year except the recession year of 1975. Nevertheless, the US net export payments balance for both merchandise *and* services tended to be in surplus – at least till 1982. It was only the strong 1982–5 recovery – the result of Reagan's tax cuts plus an increased government spending programme – which increased import demand sufficiently to push the US goods plus services balance into deficit. The magnitude of this foreign deficit grew dramatically as the US recovered from recession.

It was, therefore, not an overvalued dollar *in the 1980s* which, by itself, created the US import gap. The US had already experienced significant merchandise trade deficits almost every year since the ending of the Bretton Woods fixed exchange rate. Since 1972, the value of the dollar has undergone large upward and downward swings without significantly altering either the merchandise trade deficit or the available jobs in US industries.

In 1977–8, for example, despite the fact that the dollar dropped by over 10 per cent as a result of the Carter Administration's policy of 'talking down the dollar', there was no improvement in the trade balance and no creation of new jobs in the US.[5] As a result of the 1977–8 policy of talking down the dollar, the foreign exchange markets were more than disorderly, they became chaotic. The Carter Administration had to reverse its policy, and in co-operation with other major trading nations, intervened with an historically large infusion of funds to buoy up the dollar.[6] The dollar remained at a depressed level until the election of Ronald Reagan and the intro-duction of his proposal for expansionary fiscal policies.

By mid–1982 the dollar was 20 per cent higher than in 1973; nevertheless the goods plus service payment account of the US was still in surplus. Thus while the dollar value gyrated up and down over 30 per cent between 1973 and 1982, the US maintained an international payments surplus during that period.

The dollar continued to climb as the Reagan prosperity made the US economy an attractive investment in foreign eyes. The dollar peaked in March 1985 as the Administration and Congress discussed and later passed the Gramm–Rudman legislation which promised to reduce government deficits – and hence slow down the Reagan prosperity. Between March 1985 and October 1986, the dollar declined by 30 per cent to approximately its 1978 level. By February 1987, it had declined by almost another 10 per cent.

The continuous US international payments deficits experienced since 1983, are due to the recovery and relative prosperity of these years under Reagan's Keynesian policy, not due to an 'overvalued' dollar. Treasury Secretary Baker's 1985 initiative to lower the dollar reduced the importance of the US as the engine of growth for the world economy without significantly denting the US international deficit.

The volume of America's exports fell by 1.6 per cent in 1985; the volume of its imports rose by 9 per cent. In 1986, despite the Baker initiative, the trend was not significantly better. Exports did rise but less than 2 per cent, imports grew 11 per cent. In 1987, economists expect US exports to rise by 10 per cent and imports by only 6 per cent. Because of the drastic decline in the dollar, however, the value of the trade deficit in 1987 is expected to shrink by only approximately $3 billion to $145 billion. Such an improvement hardly suggests a dramatic reversal in the continuing US trade deficits – yet the real costs of the dollar devaluation in terms of potentially reigniting inflation in the US via higher import prices, plus the loss of real income for unemployed Japanese and German workers makes the whole exercise questionable.

In September 1986 it was already clear that the economic improvement promised from a 'soft landing' of the dollar would not occur. Secretary Baker than tried a new tack by requesting an *ad hoc* mix of international co-operation to 'encourage' the dollar to fall further while Japan and Germany stimulated their own economies via lower interest rates and government spending to induce some portion of this stimulus to leak into increase demand for imports from the United States. This 1986 phase of the Baker plan was too little and too late, since for every one percentage point increase in German and Japanese economic growth, the US annual trade deficit will decline by only $12 billion. The economies of Germany and Japan would have to increase economic growth by more than 10 percentage points – an unobtainable amount – to eliminate the US payments deficit. Consequently, the Baker Plan, *circa* 1986, does little to resolve the international payments problem.

In the latter half of 1987, Secretary Baker apparently recognized the impotence of his 1986 proposal and again reversed direction by again trying to talk down the dollar. Only a few days later, on Black Monday, 19 October 1987, stock markets around the world crashed. The immediate cause of this dramatic end of the 1982–7 bull market could, in large part, be attributed to Secretary Baker's latest switch in his policy statements regarding the value of the dollar.

WHY THE POLICY OF DELIBERATE REDUCTION IN THE VALUE OF THE DOLLAR IS WRONG[7]

Those who, in September 1985, recommended a 'soft landing' devaluation of the US dollar – the so-called Baker initiative – did not realize that any reasonable decline in the dollar's value would neither eliminate the payments imbalance, nor significantly alter the merchandise trade imbalance which has been in deficit for fifteen years. This soft-landing approach is based on the false premise that given world aggregate demand, a reduction in the value of the dollar will encourage foreigners to buy sufficiently more US goods and for US residents to buy fewer imports eliminating the multi-billion dollar deficit.

In 1985, oil imports accounted for $55 billion of the trade deficit. Since oil prices are fixed in terms of dollars, a dollar devaluation can not *per se* reduce the cost of these imports. Secondly, $22 billion of our merchandise trade deficit is with non-OPEC nations (e.g. Korea, Canada) whose exchange rate either is fixed to the dollar or is falling relative to the dollar. Hence a 'lower dollar' in terms of the yen and the Deutschmark does not increase the dollar price of imports from these other nations and will not increase the competitiveness of US industries *vis-à-vis* those in countries such as Korea or Canada.

The major gain for the US from the dollar devaluation might be expected to occur in increased agricultural exports such as grain, where international markets are relatively free from cartels. Since the US grain embargo of 1979–80 disrupted international grain markets, however, former importers of US grains (e.g. India, China, Saudi Arabia), decided not to be left to the mercy of such political whims, and have subsidized their farmers to produce grain. (By 1985, Saudi Arabia was a grain exporter!) It is therefore very unlikely that these countries will increase the dollar value of their grain imports even if the dollar is devalued in terms of their own currency.

In sum, between $70 and $90 billion of the US import surplus will not be significantly affected by any reasonable reduction in the value of the dollar.

What of the remaining trade imbalances – involving industrial products such as Japanese TV sets, Japanese and German cars, etc.? The evidence since the Baker initiative in September 1985, is not particularly encouraging. By early 1987, the trade deficit in these 'competitive' foreign industries had been only minimally affected by the dramatic 40 per cent decline of the dollar against the yen and the

Deutschmark. Manufacturers in Japan and Germany experienced huge windfall profits and increased their market shares dramatically between 1982 and 1985 when the dollar was rising. With dollar devaluation, these manufacturers could afford to significantly reduce yen and mark prices to maintain a competitive dollar price and US market share.

For the Japanese manufacturers especially, the internal incentive involving the entrepreneur's 'position in the society of industry' is very important. As Rodney Clark points out in his book *The Japanese Company*, the Japanese community's vision of status ranks companies and therefore their entrepreneurs by the business they are in, their size, and their market share among other values. The external incentive of profits is not ignored but profits are not the sole focus motivating Japanese entrepreneurs. For Japanese firms, the maintenance of market shares is an objective that is highly valued in the Japanese culture and hence is vigorously pursued even if it means not increasing their dollar prices as rapidly as the yen value increase since September 1985.

In the longer run, as Japanese entrepreneurs attempt to maintain market share by reducing yen prices, profit opportunities in the United States are squeezed. This forces Japanese managers to either lower the money income of workers (to reduce costs) – or to lay off workers. Despite the highly touted implicit social contract between Japanese firms and their workers ensuring lifetime employment, unemployment in Japan rose to an historic high of 3 per cent in January 1987 as managers laid off workers. Persistent higher Japanese unemployment will foster either demands for protectionism in Japan so they can export some of their unemployment, or the acceptance of a lower standard of living for Japanese workers towards the lowest common denominator of wages of industrial workers in Korea, Hong Kong, Brazil, etc. If the Japanese workers resist the lowering of their living standards, then the result will be even more undesirable – as the political and economic stability of Japan will be threatened.

Without either a very stiff tariff or a significant further steep decline in the dollar, US manufacturers will still find Japanese and German prices too competitive *to eliminate*, or even substantially reduce, the trade payments imbalance. Even as there is a significant reduction in Japanese or German imports due to further dollar devaluation, however, the lost German and Japanese shares of the US market are more likely to be scooped up by the Koreans (who peg their currency to the US dollar) rather than being recouped by US industries.[8]

The magnitude of a fall in the dollar that would be necessary to eliminate the US payments deficit is probably so large as to threaten the stability of the economies of the free world. Any 'reasonable' further reduction in the dollar's value will mainly force a savage reduction on the real income of America's industrial workers, and in the longer run, spill over into a reduction in the real income of our Japanese and German trading partners. Reducing the import imbalance while simultaneously increasing global real income and living standards requires a more innovative approach.

WHAT CAN BE DONE?

What is required are measures which get the major surplus nations such as Germany and Japan to accept their *global* responsibilities by directly *spending* their export surplus on either more imports, and/or direct new foreign investment, and/or grants to less developed nations (foreign aid). In the best interests of international civilization, Japan and Germany must not be permitted to simply continue to build up liquid claims against the rest of the world.[9]

Conservative economic analysis has, unfortunately, provided a rationalization for the barbaric trade surplus policies that Japan and Germany have been pursuing in the 1980s in that it asserts the entire fault of an international trade imbalance can be blamed on the deficit nation. One hopes that, in the longer run, public discussion of civilized economic policies will educate the decision-makers to the error of these conservative ways and surplus nations will recognize that in the self-interest of the *global* community, excessive accumulation of such surpluses is undesirable.

A civilized, co-operative, international policy of limiting trade surplus accumulations will foster a global expansionary bias towards improvements in the economic well-being of all nations. It will stabilize the political basis for modern capitalist development around the world. The conservative approach, on the other hand, will promote only dissension and political unrest, as 'free' economies fail to deliver all the goods they are capable of producing. The Japanese and Germans should be reminded of the old Ben Franklin homily – which is especially true in this age of global economic interdependence – 'we must indeed all hang together, or, most assuredly, we shall all hang separately'.

The civilized example of the Marshall Plan should be held up as an example to encourage surplus nations to meet the challenges of our global economy. Our allies should co-operate not because we threaten them, but because they, like us, value a civilized global economy.

As the previously cited *New York Times* article by Flora Lewis indicates, current government and business leaders, although they recognize that we are heading for an economic crisis, are frozen into inaction. These leaders will not take action unless forced to by a crisis. Reform by crisis is better than no reform at all, but there is still time to avoid the crisis and to abandon the barbaric path that conservative policy has forced us on. We can steer a more civilized course if the United States is willing to take on a courageous leadership role.

Although it looks as though the US economy is caught between a rock and a hard place, there are some actions that the US can take to improve its trade payments position and simultaneously promote world economic growth.

First, although the US oil trade deficit was reduced somewhat by the dramatic fall in international oil prices in 1986, there will be a tendency for oil prices to increase again as the Organization of Petroleum Exporting Countries (OPEC) regains its cartel control of the world's oil market. This is in large part due to higher cost non-OPEC crude oil producers being forced into bankruptcy by the fall of the dollar price of oil engineered by Saudi Arabia in 1986. The United States should do everything it can to prevent the regaining of power by OPEC – for much of the world's inflationary ills in the 1970s were initiated by OPEC's exercise of cartel power during that decade. That unhappy episode will be repeated if conditions permit a resurgence of OPEC power.

Consequently, the US can improve its trade position and simultaneously deal a blow to OPEC by levying a large, say $10-a-barrel tariff on crude oil or petroleum products imported from any OPEC source. Canada, Mexico, Britain, Norway, and any other oil producing nation that cuts its ties to OPEC would be excluded from this tax. This discriminatory tariff against OPEC, which we have recommended in hearings before numerous Congressional Committees since 1974, can drive a wedge between cartel and non-cartel members. It can also create an external incentive for some OPEC members to cheat on the cartel's price by transhipping crude oil to third parties for export to the United States. Such cheating will accelerate the disintegration of the cartel – thereby benefiting the rest of the global community. Moreover, this discriminatory tax can, by keeping some domestic oil producers in business, play a significant role in reducing the US trade deficit.

More important, however, is to design a general policy that develops an international polis which encourages trade surplus nations to initiate adjustment policies to reduce surpluses by either increasing spending on imports, making direct investments abroad, and/or making gifts and grants to deficit nations to offset the latter's deficits. Internal incentives should be fostered which encourage the co-operation of nations in the spirit of the Marshall Plan for improving global well-being and, simultaneously, external incentives should be developed to make it costly not to co-operate. Because the US is still the world's strongest economy, it can take the lead in fostering such a civilized approach.

For example, in September 1985, Senator Lloyd Bentsen of Texas introduced a prototype policy to encourage surplus nations to actively reduce their surplus and liquidity build-up. The Bentsen proposal, the *Trade Emergency and Export Promotion Act*, relied primarily on the threat of external incentives to induce surplus nations to act. This legislation threatened to impose stand-by import duties against nations possessing large trade surpluses against both the United States *and* the rest of the world. Nations who had 'excessive trade surpluses', i.e., whose exports to the United States exceeded imports by 65 per cent and whose exports to the rest of the world exceeded its imports by 50 per cent, would be informed that unless they reduced these surpluses by a significant amount each year (say 15 per cent), they would become subject to large and increasing import duties to force a substantial reduction in their share of the US market. To avoid the tariff and possible market share loss, the foreign nation would have to adopt policies which result in an actual reduction of its export surplus.[10]

Although one might quibble with the actual magnitudes used in the act to define the 'excessive trade surpluses' the pragmatic approach of this suggested legislation is excellent.

Countries that are continually running large trade surpluses are acting as drags on the economic growth of the rest of the world as well as constraining the standard of living of their own citizens below what their citizens have earned! They should have a strong incentive to live *up to their means*!

CAN WE UTILIZE INTERNAL INCENTIVES AS WELL?

Currently there is no strong international polis which can generate internal incentives for surplus nations to accept the obligation of initiating adjustments to persistent payments imbalances. Since deficit nations tend to be poor ones (the United States, in recent years, being an exception to this rule), the onus for adjustment is barbarically placed on the poor members of the global community, those least likely to be able to afford it.

Earlier, we noted that post-war non-conservative governments have recognized the desirability of having a fiscal policy which stimulates demand and recycles income and money from trade surplus to trade deficit regions. The result promotes the well-being of citizens in both areas.

There is no existing international organization which can generate a similar policy which effectively reduces international payments imbalances. The development of such an international organization would be highly desirable. But, we recognize that this is, in the current conservative environment, an unlikely development. It must wait until our civilization develops further. What is feasible and what can be done, at a minimum, is to awaken a public awareness that everyone in the global community could, on average, benefit when surplus nations take positive actions to prevent a build-up of their international liquid surpluses. Raising the public consciousness on this matter can encourage a surplus nation to increase imports and/or provide financial aid to deficit nations. The self-esteem of trade surplus nations will be increased once it is widely perceived that providing aid or buying more imports not only improves the economic lot of all in a globally interdependent economy – but it is the civilized solution to a global problem.

At any point of time, there will be the incentive for surplus nations to co-operate with the deficit nations in working out the adjustment processes utilized, if the former are aware of the existence of an international polis which encourages similar co-operative measures in the future should the tables be turned. One reason that many nations currently hoard their surpluses instead of spending them is that they fear that the trade pattern may change against them in the future, as it has in the past. Under the current conservative philosophy, the only protection against such an adverse event is to use current trade surpluses to build up the nation's liquidity reserves.[11]

A co-operative international economic community to promote

expansionary tendencies can result in increased productivity and greater economic well-being for all. The resulting mixed capitalistic system, where the community encourage the conditions for an overall expansionary growth environment while permitting private production and marketing decisions can only reinvigorate the tremendous potential of the existing resources.

If we can get a global co-operative system initiated which uses a mix of internal and external incentives to discourage nations from building up persistent large surpluses, there still remains the pressing current question of how to remedy the problem being created by the existing international debt of Third World borrowers to creditor banks. The potential for default on the part of the Third World debtors threatens the very existence of any civilized global trading community.

AVOIDING DEFAULT OF THE EXISTING DEBT

Keynes once noted that when a man owes his banker 5 pounds it is the man's problem but when he owes the banker 500 pounds it is the bank's problem. The major Latin American debtors together are equivalent to the 500 pound debtor in Keynes's analogy. The outstanding Latin American debt is truly the international bankers' problem.

When Mexico defaulted on its international debt payments in August 1982, many bankers and other financial advisers were surprised.[12] Had the Mexican default been permitted to remain, the Western world would have suffered through an international banking crisis as the outstanding international loans were written of the balance sheets of major banks thereby reducing the banks' net worth.[13] Emergency measures for rolling over and stretching out the debt were instituted with the organization and co-operation of the Federal Reserve and other Central Bankers. These arrangements preserved the net worth of the lending banks by converting a potential huge capital loss into an actual income gain, while reducing the initial cash drain on the debtor. The hope – and it was only a hope – was that this accounting sleight-of-hand would buy sufficient time for the debtor nation to develop a trade surplus which would grow sufficiently (as a result of inflating dollar values?) to permit the debtor to continue to meet stretched out debt service obligations. Similar arrangements were then pursued with other Third World Debtors.

With the decrease in the global rate of inflation experienced since

1982, and the deterioration of the terms of trade for primary producers, any reasonable hope for such muddling through on the Third World Debt problem should have disappeared. When the next major recession hits the United States, if not before, all the Latin American (and other Third World) debtors will find their dollar export earnings insufficient to service their debts and provide for economic growth. If the overhanging debt problem has not been remedied before then, global financial collapse is very possible.

In February 1987, Brazil defaulted on more than half of its debt service payments obligations to the major banks. The Brazilian default taken by itself may, in the short run, be absorbed at a significant, but bearable, cost by the banking community. Citibank's decision, in May 1987, to write down the value of its $14 billion portfolio of developing country loans by about 20 per cent as the result of the Brazilian default, followed by similar actions by most of the remaining US banks, resulted in the US banking industry posting a record loss[14] of more than $10 billion in the second quarter of 1987.

Any further large reduction in the book value of their international loan portfolio could seriously jeopardize the net worth of the major international banks. The pressure is, therefore, on the bankers to induce the Brazilians to resume all their debt servicing payments, before the other debtors voluntarily, or are forced by poor net export earnings, to follow Brazil's lead.

Both the debtors and creditors have a common interest in resolving the debt problem while there is time – and without the emergency of a potential crescendo of bank failures. If these debts can not be repaid in the foreseeable future, then the value of the loan portfolio must ultimately be written off. Will the world wait for a global default crisis before writing down these assets to their 'true' (near zero) worth and therefore jeopardize the viability of the banks and the ability of countries to get credit for the necessary financing of increased foreign trade? Or can we devise some civilized scheme which removes these contractual liabilities from the backs of the debtor nations while saving face (and the net worth) of the creditor banks and avoids putting the global economy through the wringer of a major depression and decline in trade?

Why not try to muddle through?

The first question one might raise, is why not wait? A crisis may not occur. Some have argued that the proposal of US Treasury Secretary

James Baker to have the bankers extend additional credits to Third World debtors will buy sufficient time to muddle through. This Baker finance scheme would *increase* total outstanding Latin American debt through the rest of this century as the debtors would be borrowing to pay a significant portion of the annual interest payments on the already existing debt. But given sufficiently optimistic forecasts of economic growth in these debtor nations (and no adverse change in the terms of trade), their dollar denominated debt–income ratios could fall over time. Consequently, *if* a constant proportion of this sanguine rate of growth in the debtors' national income is committed to servicing the debt, then, by the turn of the century, the debtors might begin to amortize the debt.

For example, in an article in the 27 June 1987 issue of *The Economist*, Harvard Professor Martin Feldstein projects that by 1998 Brazil will begin to amortize its accumulated debt (which Feldstein estimates will have risen from $111 billion to $137 billion in the interim). In 1998, Brazil will be able to amortize half of 1 per cent of its debt. This 'optimistic' forecast is not based on any facts. It results strictly from the mathematical outcome of assuming that the annual debt service payments will grow geometrically at 3.5 per annum while Brazil's needs for external credit grows arithmetically at $4 billion per year into the indefinite future. Similar thinking and hopeful projections underlay the 'solution' adopted in 1982. The facts since 1982 have not borne out these earlier sanguine projections.

Some conservative economists might argue that if a crisis did occur, such an outcome would be harsh (barbaric) but desirable. For those who believe in a free market philosophy of survival of the fittest, the death of some banks is a necessary Darwinistic requirement to promote efficiency in banking. The bankers who made, from hindsight, 'bad loans' would be punished by the 'invisible hand'. The remaining bankers, if any, would avoid such bad loans in the future. Of course, a banking collapse would involve the mortality of some of the free world's mightiest financial institutions as their net worth disappeared, while the debtor nations can not go bankrupt.[15]

If a banking crisis does occur, however, it will be systemic to the banking industry and not episodic to individual bankers who have made mistakes. A systemic crisis can bring the whole financial system down. Any cumulative Latin American debt default could just about wipe out the international banking industry just as an earlier biological crisis removed the dinosaurs from the face of the earth leaving only their small reptile cousins to carry on. Man could survive and even thrive without the presence of dinosaurs. Economic man, as we know him, can not survive without a viable international banking community.

A civilized society can not permit the private sector international banking system to crash merely to 'improve its efficiency'. To do so, would be equivalent to optimizing the position of the deck-chairs on the *Titanic* as it experiences its unfortunate encounter with an iceberg!

When it is recognized that an international debt crisis is not in anyone's interest, the only question is how to remedy the problem. Two basic ways are:

(1) Debt for equity swaps, or
(2) Debt forgiveness.

Debt-equity swaps

Under a typical debt-equity swap, the banks would sell at a loss, in secondary markets, whatever portion of their Third World loan portfolio they wish. The price in these secondary markets would, of course, be a fraction of the amount of the loan.[16] The non-bank entities who purchase these debt obligations could then present these obligations to the central bank of the debtor nation in exchange for domestic currency (at the going rate of exchange) equal to the face amount of the loan. This currency would then be used to buy either existing equity securities and/or new issues of either private sector firms or denationalized enterprises *in the debtor country*.

For the debtors, the net effect of such a debt for equity swap would be that they would never have to amortize their existing obligations. Foreign investors, however, would expect to obtain a perpetual stream of dividends.[17] The debtor nation would therefore be accepting the obligation to pay dividends in perpetuity equal to the dollar value at the current obligation for interest payments.

This relief from amortization, however, may be more imaginary than real. Using the previously cited Feldstein projection for Brazil as illustrative, it is obvious that, even in this best case scenario, the Latin American debt is likely to continue to rise until the end of this century. Accordingly, no significant permanent amortization of the total external Latin American debt can be expected in the foreseeable future. Aggregate external debt amortization by the Latin American countries is consequently irrelevant – except perhaps in the long run when we will all be dead!

In return for the release from an irrelevant contractual amortization obligation, the debtor nations would, in essence, implicitly be agreeing to a perpetual drain of income to foreign investors – unless the enterprises fail to earn any profits and management did not bleed the enterprise by repatriating funds even if profits can not sustain such payments.

The debtor nations recognize that following a debt-for-equity swap of any major magnitude, future international bank loans would be all but impossible to obtain under reasonable credit terms. No prudent banker would make reasonable commercial loans to a debtor who was unable to pay back an earlier loan and who essentially forced the banker to take (directly or indirectly) an equity position in lieu of debt repayment. Once burned by this international debtor, the prudent banker, if he could survive the loss in net worth, would not make additional loans without significant guarantees from his government and central banker. Accordingly, a debt-for-equity swap should not be a very attractive alternative for the debtor nations *vis-à-vis* the current situation where, because the outstanding debt is the bankers' problem, debtor nations find they can negotiate further credits merely by rolling over the debt and thereby promising to pay in the further distant future.

Nor would the bankers really benefit under a typical debt-equity scheme. The bankers would have to accept a capital loss, based on the secondary market's evaluation of the outstanding debt in exchange for liquefying an otherwise unproductive loan obligation. The severity of the impact of the resulting loss on the banks' net worth would depend on how deeply the secondary market discounted the outstanding debt obligation.

To avoid this bookkeeping loss from damaging net worth, Citibank and some other major bankers want a debt-equity swap where the bank would *buy and hold*, for some time, equity investments for their own portfolios. This would permit the bankers to exchange (at face value) non-performing loans for equity securities valued (at least initially) at the same dollar value. Hence the bankers could, in principle, avoid accounting for the capital loss (or at least postpone it for a significant length of time). Hopefully, the bankers could sell these equities in the distant future at less of a loss than the secondary market's current discount of Latin American debt.

In sum then, the typical debt-for-equity swap would recognize the weakened net worth position of the bankers without offering any real benefits for the debtor nations *vis-à-vis* the current situation. For the bankers, a debt-for-equity swap is preferable to a cumulative debtor default crisis.

For the global trading community, any solution which does not restore the full liquidity of the international banks and simultaneously relieve the burden of perpetual income repatriation payments from the backs of the Latin American nations is likely to hold back global economic expansion and prosperity. Thus, a debt-for-equity swapping plan is far from the most desirable permanent remedy for the existing external debt problem, especially when compared with a civilized policy based on debt forgiveness.

Debt forgiveness

Double-entry bookkeeping is the way we keep score in the game of 'economics'. Unfortunately, the rules for keeping score can adversely affect how the game is played – and nowhere is that more obvious than in the question of how can we extricate the international bankers from scoring such large capital losses on their financial statement scoreboard that they are no longer able to play the game! For it is a fundamental requirement of the entrepreneurial economy in which we live that the production and international trading of economic goods necessarily requires a viable, vigorous international banking system that is able to provide credit as quickly as entrepreneurs can increase global production and trade.

Under conventional accounting practices, the existing international debt situation will not permit either a vigorous international banking system to persist or the LDC debtor nations to show marked economic improvement. It is of little value to retrace history to see who is to blame for arriving at this situation and to 'punish' them. The purpose of policy should be to remedy the situation in the most productive way possible, not to assess and attribute blame.

What is required is some creative accounting which lifts the yoke of the inevitable non-performing international loans from necks of the bankers *and* simultaneously reduce the obligations of LDCs to what their export earnings can afford. A sufficient portion of the export earnings of these Latin American debtor nations must be free to buy enough imports to sustain a rate of economic growth which exceeds their population growth.

Debt forgiveness is the obvious solution.[18] It permits the debtor countries to more fully use their export earnings to increase economic growth and raise the consumption standard of their people. Unfortunately, the managers of the major banks are legally unable to provide such forgiveness for it would jeopardize the net worth of their enterprises and thereby make the managers legally liable for the resulting damages to the stockholders. Hence no matter how obvious it is to the bankers that the current situation is intolerable and debt forgiveness is inevitable they can not publicly admit it. Consequently, the responsibility falls on the major Central Bankers to provide the foresight, leadership, and creative accounting practices to readily resolve the problem without any real costs to the global economy.

A modest proposal to remedy the situation at no real costs to the global economy is for the Central Bankers, in co-operation with government leaders of the various nations which regulate the creditor banks, to stand willing to accept a significant portion of the bankers' portfolio of international loans in exchange for stock in the Central Bank. This would relieve the bankers of any threat of capital loss, by providing them with earning assets. The Central Bank would in turn sell these loan securities to its government in exchange for government bonds. The government would in turn negotiate a forgiveness ratio with each debtor nation.[19]

In essence this proposal would provide that the developed nations would be co-operating in a sort of Marshall Plan where the government grants (forgiveness) are used to retire a portion of the debtor countries' external debts and free up their export earnings for more productive purposes than debt service payments. One would desire, in line with our earlier argument that nations showing a persistent current account balance be especially generous in their forgiveness ratios.

The amount of international debt the central banks should stand willing to purchase from the international bankers (and at what penalty if any), and the forgiveness ratio each country should try to negotiate is beyond the scope of this book. What is required is some international conference of creditor bankers, central bankers, and debtor nations where these aspects could be thrashed out and negotiated in a spirit of achieving a civilized remedy for what otherwise might be the worst global financial crisis of the twentieth century.

Notes

1. This regional division is the result of regional fears that existed when the Federal Reserve System was set up in 1913. The country was divided into 12 Federal Reserve Districts with a separate Federal Reserve Bank in each district (e.g. Boston, New York, Philadelphia, Cleveland, Richmond, Atlanta, Chicago, St Louis, Minneapolis, Kansas City, Dallas, San Francisco).

2. If the reader doubts this, he/she should look at the US currency in one's pocket. To the left of the portrait on the face of each bill there is a seal indicating which of the 12 Federal Reserve Banks issued that particular piece of currency. Most people will find they have currency from more than one of the District Banks – but that they treat each Bank's issue interchangeable – because the exchange rate between the currencies is always fixed! Yet it was not too many years ago, that each District Federal Reserve Bank would send currency issued by other District Banks found circulating in its region back to the issuing bank for redemption.

3. Just as the Authorities always ensure that the exchange rate between dimes and dollars are ten to one.

4. Yet those conservatives who proclaim the need to make US industries competitive are not developing policies which stimulate improvements in technology to make workers more productive.

5. For comparison it should be noted that in the first twelve months following Secretary Baker's talking down of the dollar, the dollar fell 32.5 per cent from its February 1985 high and just under 30 per cent from its September 1985 level – with little or no gain in US job opportunities.

6. In September 1986, major foreign governments – except the United States – met in Gleneagles, Scotland to institute a similar co-operative effort to reduce the chaotic activity in the foreign exchange market caused by the fall in the dollar. Without the active co-operation of the United States, however, this meeting was doomed to failure.

7. The analysis of the following section is not based solely on hindsight. The arguments presented were provided in written testimony to the Joint Economic Committee on 18 September 1985 – one week before the Baker initiative – by Paul Davidson.

8. With the further fall in the value of the dollar between February and December 1987, German and Japanese imports into the US showed some signs of turning down, but much of this slackening off was offset by (a) an increase in motor-car imports from other nations such as Korea whose exchange rate has been tied to the dollar, and (b) rising oil imports whose international price is quoted in dollars.

9. In the latter part of 1987 Japan showed some signs of moving to reduce its desire to hoard additional international reserves. West Germany, on the other hand, apparently was still adamantly striving to increase its foreign reserves.

10. In April 1987, Congress passed the Gephardt amendment to a trade bill which would force nations with large trade surpluses with the US *achieved*

through 'unfair trade practices' to reduce those imbalances by 10 per cent per annum or face retaliation. This requires the surplus to be due to 'unfair trade practices' – which presents an incorrect focus by implying that in a free market persistent surpluses and deficits could not occur. The problem is the surplus *per se*, not whether it was due to unfair practices or not. The amendment is not given much chance of becoming law.

11. For example, after the first oil price shock of 1973, Japan ran huge payments deficits. No nation came to assist her. Only by running down previously built-up foreign reserves was Japan able to weather the storm of the mid-1970s.

12. Most bankers believed that oil prices would continue to rise – perhaps reaching $100 per barrel by the end of the century. (Hence, the Mexican loans were thought to be well secured by Mexico's large oil reserves.) This belief in an annual rate of increase in crude oil prices was rationalized by conservative economists who predicted, using their traditional model of market pricing for optimally allocating a depleting resource over time, that the price of oil would continue to rise geometrically. When oil prices peaked in 1980, the Mexican loans were in trouble.

13. Since the size of the loans to Mexico (and other debtors who might follow Mexico's default action) involved could potentially equal or exceed the net worth of major creditor banks, a complete write-off of such loans would reduce the financial net worth of the banks to zero or negative, thereby bankrupting the most important international bankers, for example, Citibank, Chase Manhattan, Bank of America, etc.

14. The industry's previously worst performance was during the Great Depression – when for all of 1934, the loss was $600 million – equivalent to about $4 billion in 1987 dollars.

15. In the case of a debtor default crisis, the debtor nations may find it impossible, in the short run, to obtain any additional credit. Accordingly it would be in their best interest to preserve their international reserves in a form (of gold or other assets) whose market value would not be completely wiped out in the ensuing banking system collapse. Hence if debtor nations expect to default, they may try to build up their gold reserves.

16. According to the 18 July 1987 issue of *The Economist*, the secondary market evaluates the face value of the Latin American Debt as follows: Brazil 58 per cent of face value, Argentina 48 per cent, Mexico 53 per cent, Venezuela 68 per cent, Chile 67 per cent, Bolivia 10 per cent, Peru 10 per cent, Ecuador 42 per cent, and Colombia 82 per cent.

17. If the dividend stream is not to be perpetual, then foreign investors will want the debtor nation to pay full compensation at some future date in order to repurchase the equity position.

18. The major argument against international debt forgiveness is that it will merely encourage 'profligate' governments to again build up huge debts, thereby recreating the problem. If, however, the proposal suggested in the 'What Can Be Done' section is adopted, such future debt build-ups would be impossible.

19. This scheme has advantages compared with the case where the government directly purchases the non-performing loans by issuing government bonds to the banks. In the latter case, (a) the banks could sell the bonds thereby either pushing up interest rates or forcing the Central Bank to 'monetize' the foreign debt, and (b) the interest payments on the additional government bonds initially issued to the banks are an additional burden on the taxpayers. Under our modest proposal, (a) is impossible, while the interest of (b) is earned by the Central Bank which, as for example in the case of the Federal Reserve, would be 'excessive' income and therefore would be returned to the Treasury account, thereby avoiding any significant additional burden on the taxpayers.

9 A Final Summing Up

A civilized society combines self-interest and civic values so that its citizens may enjoy the benefits of each. In the public debate of the last twenty years, *self-interest* and *civic values* have been offered as alternative guiding principles for the government of America. Conservatives have pursued prosperity through the free market, while liberals have sought justice in community. One camp strives for competitiveness, while the other focuses on excellence. The tragedy is that self-interest and civic values are both part of our national character.

The pursuit of conservative policies which we have witnessed in recent years perpetuates a barbaric role for government, and barbaric treatment of the weak in society. Even honest and well-meaning attempts to devise public policy in accordance with conservative economics will lead us in the direction of barbarism. When an attempt is made to construct a policy agenda around the conservative philosophy, the civic values which support effective government will inevitably erode. In the extreme case, the pursuit of conservative economic policies shape a world where self-interest *is* the only motivation, and consequently the rules of conservative economics *do* explain all behaviour. Unfortunately, the price to be paid for this simplicity would be the loss of our civilization.

The effects of years of conservative policies which motivate through fear and appetite have been witnessed across the USA. For example, in order to collect taxes, the government has tried both bribing taxpayers (particularly the wealthier ones) by cutting their tax rates, and at the same time encouraging an aggressive IRS to create terror in the hearts of all citizens. To resolve any trade imbalance between nations, conservatives have argued that the weaker of the two nations should be the one to make adjustments by 'tightening their belts', i.e., lowering the living standards of its people. Unsurprisingly, over time the people who have suffered under the rule of these policies have learned to hate and despise the IRS and agencies such as the International Monetary Fund. And still the basic problems these policies were intended to address remain unsolved.

Since 1973, American economic history has been shaped by the barbaric conservative policy of planned recession; to fight inflation, the government has on several occasions intentionally depressed the economy so that workers will be so fearful of losing their jobs that they will not demand inflationary wage increases. Despite a wealth of complex analytical studies of so-called 'disciplinary fiscal policy', the premise is simple (although usually the greed of the workers and the absence of any other alternatives is emphasized). This barbaric policy was employed by Presidents Nixon, Carter, and Reagan.

Since 1976, those who follow the conservative philosophy have been dominant in both major political parties, and it is in opposition to their conservative attitudes that we largely direct this book. As the pendulum swings back from the extremes of the Reagan era, we face the danger that we may simply reverse our wasteful habits and discard the beneficial attributes of self-interest even as we rediscover our civic values. A swing to one extreme, as we have experienced with conservatism, tends to be followed by a rapid reversal built upon its excesses. We want to modify the picture presented by the conservative cult of the entrepreneur, but there are better and worse ways to make this change. To abandon the fuel of self-interest which drives us towards entrepreneurial excellence would be an incredible waste. Instead, we must work quickly to develop an ideology and a set of policies which will enable us to enjoy the benefits of both self-interest and civic values.

WHERE DO WE START?

Our understanding of economics can drastically alter the world in which we live, as demonstrated by the story of Arthur Laffer and his supply-side economics napkin. The power of the people to discuss and debate the real issues which America faces is all to often underestimated. People discuss economics all of the time; on the shop floor, in the board-room, in the cafeteria, at the bar, on the softball field, and in the kitchen. Since economics, as we see it, is built not only on the self-interest of the people, but also on their civic values, then national economic debates must necessarily take place in part among the people who will be governed (and will govern themselves!) in accordance with national economic policy.

The use of an impenetrable analytical dialect by economic experts can sometimes be a little overwhelming, but the secret behind the jargon is that the basic issues are normally quite simple. Although we want the excellence of experts in implementing our economic policies, it is our duty as citizens to formulate the goals America should pursue. This duty is combined with self-interest through the institution known as democracy – the election process enlists the self-interest of the candidates to listen to the citizens and to address their concerns. Even if one vote seems small in a nation of millions, to cast a vote properly, after using one's judgement and consideration, is to achieve the civic excellence which the Founding Fathers had hoped for in the American people.

Our understanding of economics must also be shaped in the forum of debate in our academic institutions. Unfortunately, despite a steady stream of critiques, the intellectual fortress of conservative economics has weathered all attacks. In order to look towards harvesting our resources of civic values as well as those of self-interest, we must establish a common language of analysis in which to discuss both of these forces. It is necessary to place the generalized sentiments of civic values into a more analytically rigorous structure, and at the same time, the rigid technical analysis of self-interest provided by conservative economics must be unwound, so that we can examine the general philosophical premises upon which it is built.

We have identified the force behind civic values in terms of internal incentives, which motivate behaviour 'for its own sake' in accordance with a set of ideals established within a community. This is in contrast to the external incentives of self-interest in conservative economics, which motivate only by fear or appetite.

We saw how a society based solely on self-interest would eventually lose the institutions which support civilized behaviour. We also showed how a careless combination of internal and external incentives could render one or both useless in motivating desirable economic behaviour. By carefully utilizing existing institutions of family, community, and nation, we can safely combine self-interest and civic values to achieve civilized outcomes.

Since we were presenting a view quite at odds with the picture given in conventional economics, we turned to the obvious question of what is wrong with economists? In general, the answer is that the profession of economics has bound itself inexorably to an analytic structure known as the neo-classical model. This model focuses solely on self-interest, and thus not only blinds most economists to the influences and importance of civic values in motivating behaviour; but it also reveals an incomplete and unrealistic view of the role of self-interest itself. Consequently, even complicated and sophisticated computer simulations based on the neoclassical model retain these basic flaws and hence are faulty in both their ability to explain and to predict behaviour. Thus, even an economist with civilized intentions is left facing the same problem as a pacifist who works in a gun shop – he cannot use his professional skills to pursue his ethical principles.

We have developed four major concepts which are essential to a civilized economic analysis but which are absent from conservative economics:

Civic values are not the same as the conservative concept of individual preferences. When conservatives refer to preferences for love, duty, honour, justice, and excellence, they can, at most, be describing deteriorated forms of civic values. In a healthy polis, civic values can not be exchanged for money, nor do they exhibit the other aspects of self-interest which conservatives attribute to all goods. On the other hand, these civic values can provide a positive-sum for society, delivering benefits without a compensating cost being inflicted elsewhere.

Civic values come from the polis. Ideals and standards exist only within a community. People develop their individuality and sense of self *from* their membership in one or more communities. A polis provides internal incentives to its members, and as the polis evolves, so do those internal incentives.

Civilized Government is the process by which we combine self-interest and civic values into institutions. These institutions, when properly designed, protect civic values from the corrosive effects of self-interest. At the same time, institutions make use of productive forms of self-interest, enabling people to enjoy the products of both. Effective government must change with the times, adapting old principles and institutions to emerging conditions.

Civic values can be enjoyed only when there is civic virtue. Self-interest is relatively straightforward; effort and cleverness are all that are needed for individuals to reap its rewards by following its dictates. Civic values are equally important, but more complex. For people to enjoy civic values, they must be constantly vigilant in order to protect and maintain the institutions of their civilization from the erosion of barbaric self-interest.

Civic virtue is necessary for society to enjoy the benefits of civilization. This virtue *can not* be pursued solely by each person calculating his own self-interest in terms of costs and benefits. Thus for those who subscribe to a conservative philosophy, the rewards associated with civilization must seem unattainable.

CIVILIZED ECONOMIC POLICIES

Our argument has shown that civilized economic policies require an effort to create a shared dialect of purpose and responsibilities in establishing any new economic institution to meet the evolving economic changes. Civic values provided an additional resource to strengthen civilized economic policies. If government is to make use of internal incentives, then the civic values of the public are of critical importance. This places our economic debate back where all the important national debates should be held: in the forum of concepts and ideals which make up the nation.

In this book we have discussed a number of major initiatives which can make beneficial use of the unique role government must play in a modern economy. Not only does government have the capacity to combine both internal and external incentives in strengthening our interdependent economy, but the government's vantage as a major economic actor not driven by the concerns of individual business permits government to take actions on behalf of the economy as a whole.

Our conclusions regarding specific civilized economic policies can be summarized as follows.

Reviving the post-Second World War international polis. We must create a more civilized approach to international debt and balance-of-payments problems so that the world's trade surplus nations recognize that it is not only in their self-interest, but also their global civic responsibility to avoid excess surplus by living up to their means. Such a change in international attitudes would benefit all nations. It would be best to create institutions which operate similarly to the civilized institutions that we urge for controlling domestic money and inflation problems. We have, however, momentarily lost the opportunity to build on the sound foundation laid at Bretton Woods, an international monetary authority similar to a civilized Central Bank.

Under President Nixon we permitted the potential foundations for an international civilized economic system to begin to erode. The erosion has continued under Ford, Carter, and Reagan. The United States is now the world's largest debtor and hence no longer has the economic power to unilaterally create a civilized international economic order as we did at Bretton Woods, and with the Marshall Plan later in the 1940s. The virtue of our earlier actions, however, cannot be erased from the history books of the free nations of the

West. So while the actions of the Nixon Administration (compounded by Ford, Carter, and Reagan) have wasted much of the goodwill created by Nixon's four predecessors, some credibility can still reside in our words and actions. The United States did commit its economic resources to a civilized economic order when we had the opportunity – now others share that pleasant vantage, and its accompanying responsibilities. But the United States can help by word and deed to design such a civilized system.

Tax-based Incomes Policy (TIP). TIP provides an external disincentive to those whose self-interest contribute to inflation, but unlike the conservative policy of planned recessions to fight inflation, TIP's effects are directed solely at those whose behaviour generates inflation – not at the economy as a whole including innocent bystanders. TIP is built upon external incentives, but will also require the establishment of civic norms which place TIP in the context of an economic system which promotes excellence in entrepreneurialism and full employment.

Commodity buffer stocks. Buffer stocks allow government to pre-empt volatile (and unproductive) swings in commodity prices, such as those experienced with oil, grains, etc. in the 1970s and 1980s. Government buffer stocks can be released to fill the shortfall when natural calamities occur, and furthermore, the existence of these buffer stocks will deter the economic aggression of foreign and domestic suppliers which induce artificial shortages (as did OPEC).

Such a buffer stock policy, if properly designed, will help stabilize the income of commodity producers at a level which encourages the rapid growth in productivity of these essential basic commodities.

Fiscal stabilization of the business cycle. In an entrepreneurial economy, the independent decisions of millions of independent enterprises will sometimes move the economy towards recession. By increasing its purchases from the private sector, government can ensure full utilization of America's productive capacity. This not only makes it possible to provide better government services, but also generates income into the hands of businessmen and households who will spend it elsewhere in the economy.

Tax reform. Civilized tax reform can enlist the voluntary compliance which is necessary to reap the $100 billion per year in taxes which are never collected. More importantly, tax reform is needed to re-establish the civilized relationship between taxpayers and their nation. When we choose as a nation to require citizens to pay taxes, we take on the responsibility to create (and maintain) the civic context which supports such activity. In a healthy civilization where civic values and self-interest flourish, the citizens must be willing to both die for their country and to pay for it. The design of our current tax system does not support the virtue of tax-paying.

We have identified here a number of civilized alternatives to the way we govern. If we try to enlist both self-interest and civic virtues, we may be able to muster all of our resources to address whatever new challenges emerge. However, a civilized perspective is not enough. While sincere efforts are a necessary beginning, there may not be enough virtue in sincerity to govern our nation. We must be as wise and shrewd as possible, so that we can see justice through the haze of circumstances that surrounds our complex public issues, and so that we can out-think those whose self-interest would otherwise take advantage – and pervert – our government of laws.

THE EVOLVING ECONOMY

In his *Tales of a New America* Harvard Professor Robert Reich suggests that the evolution of our economic system is reducing the applicability of the conservative economic vision. Economic conditions which once may have provided some support for the conservative myth have continued to evolve. This conservative view envisaged business as a small, single factory firm led by a single, profit-driven entrepreneur. In the last half-century, however, the evolution of our enterprise economy has accelerated. Today, a typical business must co-ordinate hundreds of factories and other facilities to efficiently provide the thousands of diverse products and services that make up the current American standard of living. As production has become more complex and interdependent, co-ordination and finance of these complex production processes has emerged as a major entrepreneurial problem. This evolutionary trend increases the value of co-operative patterns of behaviour as compared with the individualistic competition of the conservative philosophy.

The failures of liberal practices in the 1970s made the conservative picture *seem* attractive once again. But the nature of the development of our economic environment has not reverted back to this earlier era of the individualistic entrepreneur – only our economic philosophy has. And it is this regression towards nineteenth-century Social Darwinism which threatens the viability of our twentieth-century economic polis.

REVITALIZING THE NATIONAL POLIS

> We will ever strive for the ideals and the sacred things of the polis,
> both alone and with the many.
> We will unceasingly seek to quicken the sense of public duty.
> We will revere and obey the laws of the polis.
> We will transmit this polis not only not less, but greater, better
> and more beautiful than it was transmitted to us.
>
> Oath of the Athenian City State

By this oath the ancient Athenians committed themselves to the
pursuit of excellence in the practice of citizenship – an excellence
demonstrated by how well the people govern themselves and their
nation. We practice our citizenship by actively participating in our
national institutions – by which we mean customs and traditions as
well as more formal structures. We are all participating in the real
government of our nation in the way we lead our lives, whether it be
by apathy or activism, by cheating 'the system' or living up to
our commitments. The ultimate responsibility for maintaining our
civilization is in the same hands that have created it – We the People.
If we strive for our national ideals, seek to 'quicken the sense of
public duty', and voluntarily comply with the rules necessary to
govern society, we will be able to transmit to the next generation an
American Civilization of which we can be rightly proud.

The pivotal word in the Oath of Athens is 'transmit' – the Athenians
understood that time brought change to all institutions, and that the
duty of each generation was to overcome the challenges that history
brought in order to bestow to their children a better world. The
United States Constitution echoes this spirit in proclaiming that we
are 'to secure the blessings of liberty to ourselves and our posterity'.
A society thrives when its members can sustain the integrity and
strength of the values of its civilization across history. This practice
of civic excellence requires that we adapt our social institutions to
changing economic and political conditions. It is not enough to create
a set of civilized institutions at one moment in time. As a changing
world leads to the erosion of the old understandings, we must be
prepared to recreate our institutions; to reaffirm the meaning of 'We
the People'. It is our hope that this volume will help our society
rediscover the way towards a civilized economy as we attempt to
resolve the economic problems of the last decades of the twentieth
century.

Sources and References

Preface

William Stanley Jevons, *The Theory of Political Economy* (New York: Augustus M. Kelley Bookseller, Reprints of Economics Classics, 1965).

1 In Pursuit of Civilization

Thomas J. Peters and Robert H. Waterman, *In Search of Excellence* (New York: Harper & Row, Warner Books, 1984).

Gary Wills, *Reagan's America: Innocents at Home* (Garden City, New York: Doubleday, 1987).

Milton Friedman, *Capitalism and Freedom* (Chicago: University of Chicago Press, 1962).

George F. Will, *Statecraft as Soulcraft* (New York: Simon & Schuster, Touchstone Books, 1984).

Adam Smith, *An Inquiry into the Nature and Causes of the Wealth of Nations* (New York: Random House, The Modern Library, 1937).

John Maynard Keynes, *The General Theory of Employment, Interest, and Money* (New York: Harcourt Brace Jovanovich, 1936).

Thomas Hobbes, *Leviathan* (Indianapolis: Bobbs-Merrill, Library of Liberal Arts, 1958).

Jeremy Bentham, 'Principles of Morals and Legislation' in *The World's Greatest Books vol. XIV* (New York: McKinlay, Stone & Mackenzie, 1910).

The example of goal displacement comes to us from Gary R. Orren, Professor of Public Policy at Harvard's Kennedy School of Government.

Robert B. Reich, *The Next American Frontier* (New York: Times Books, 1983).

William Safire, 'The Crisis of Institutional Loyalty' in *The New York Times*, 18 August 1986.

Robert N. Bellah, Richard Madsen, William M. Sullivan, Ann Swidler, and Steven M. Tipton, *Habits of the Heart: Individualism and Commitment in American Life* (New York: Harper & Row, Perennial Library, 1985). The Madison quotation is from Theodore Draper, 'Hume and Madison: The Secrets of Federalist Paper No. 10', *Encounter 58*, February 1982.

Niccolo Machiavelli, *Discourses*, as translated by Peter Bondanella and Mark Musa, *The Portable Machiavelli* (New York: Penguin Books, 1979).

Niccolo Machiavelli, *The Prince*, in Bondanella and Musa, *The Portable Machiavelli*.

David A. Stockman, *The Triumph of Politics: How the Reagan Revolution Failed* (New York: Harper & Row, 1985).
Lester C. Thurow, *The Zero-Sum Society* (New York: Basic Books, 1980).
George Gilder, *Wealth and Poverty* (New York: Bantam Books, 1982).
Wystan Hugh Auden, *Selected Poems*, 'The Shield of Achilles' (New York: Vintage Books, 1979).
Niccolo Machiavelli, *Discourses* in Bondanella and Musa, *The Portable Machiavelli*.
Edith Stokey and Richard Zeckhauser, *A Primer for Policy Analysis* (New York: W. W. Norton, 1978).
Aristotle, *Politics*, Book III, as translated by Ernest Barker, *The Politics of Aristotle* (New York: Oxford University Press, 1981).

2 The Political Economy of Civilization

Christopher Lasch, *The Culture of Narcissism: American Life in an Age of Diminishing Expectations* (New York, W. W. Norton, 1978). *The Politics of Aristotle*, ed. E. Barker.
Mancur Olson, *The Logic of Collective Action: Public Goods and the Theory of Groups* (Cambridge, Mass: Harvard University Press, 1965).
Thomas J. Peters and Robert H. Waterman, *In Search of Excellence*.
Lee Iacocca with William Novak, *Iacocca: An Autobiography* (New York: Bantam Books, 1980).
John T. Dunlop, *Dispute Resolution* (Dover, Mass.: Auburn House Publishing Co., 1984).
Steven Kelman, *What Price Incentives? Economists and the Environment* (Dover, Mass.: Auburn House Publishing Co., 1981).
Robert Bellah *et al.*, *Habits of the Heart*.
Nation's Business, April 1968.
Barry Schwartz, 'Reinforcement-Induce Behavioral Stereotypy: How not to teach people to discover rules', *Journal of Experimental Psychology*, vol. *111*, No. 1, 1982.
Thomas C. Schelling, *Macromotives and Microbehavior* (New York: W. W. Norton, 1978).
Benjamin Barber, 'A New Language for the Left: Translating the Conservative Discourse', *Harper's Magazine*, XX, November 1986.

3 What's Wrong with Economists?

Robert B. Reich, *The Next American Frontier* (New York: Times Books, 1983).
Walter Bagehot quotation as given by John Maynard Keynes in his *Treatise on Money*, vol. II (Macmillan, London, 1930).
Paul A. Samuelson, 'Classical and Neoclassical Theory' in *Monetary Theory*, edited by R. W. Clower (London: Penguin, 1969).
John Maynard Keynes, *The General Theory of Employment, Interest and Money*.

4 Why Taxpayers Pay their Taxes

Jude Wanniski, *The Way the World Works* (New York: Basic Books, 1978).

David A. Stockman, *The Triumph of Politics*.

George Gilder, *Wealth and Poverty*.

Forbes, 'Good amnesty or poor enforcement', 4 June 1984.

Trend Analysis and Related Statistics: 1986 Update, Department of the Treasury, Internal Revenue Service, Document 6011.

Income Tax Compliance Research, US Treasury Department, Internal Revenue Service, 1983.

Reducing the Deficit: Spending and Revenue Options, Congressional Budget Office, February 1984.

Taxpayer Attitude Study, Final Report, prepared for the IRS by Yankelovich, Skelly, and White, Inc., December 1984.

Burkhard Strumpel, 'Contribution in Survey Research' in A. Peacock (ed.), *Quantitative Analysis in Public Finance* (New York: Praeger, 1969).

M. W. Spicer and S. B. Lundstedt, 'Understanding Tax Evasion', *Public Finance*, 31 (1976).

Joachim Vogel, 'Taxation and Public Opinion in Sweden: An Interpretation of Recent Survey Data', *National Tax Journal*, vol. 27, no. 4, 1974.

Robert Mason and Helen M. Lowry, *An Estimate of Income Tax Evasion in Oregon*, Survey Research Center, Oregon State University, Corvalis, Oregon, January 1981.

Y. Song and T. E. Yarbrough, 'Tax Ethics and Taxpayer Attitudes', *Public Administration Review*, 38 (1978).

Mancur Olson, *The Logic of Collective Action*.

Jerome Kurtz testifying as head of the IRS, US Ways and Means Committee, Second Session on HR 6300, 'Bill to Improve Compliance with IRS Laws', 9 May 1982.

Mark H. Moore, 'On the Office of Taxpayer and the Social Process of Taxpaying', prepared for the International Conference on Tax Compliance, Reston, Virginia, 16–19 March 1983.

Clara Penniman, *State Taxation Policy* (Baltimore: Johns Hopkins Press, 1980).

Fair Share: A Program to Increase Taxpayer Compliance in California, State of California Franchise Tax Board.

Niccolo Machiavelli, *Discourses*, in Bondanella and Musa, *The Portable Machiavelli*.

'Workshop on Increasing Tax Collections through New Enforcement Methods', National Association of Tax Administrators, National Workshop No. 4, 25–28 July 1982, Chicago, Illinois.

An interview with Harry Durning, Director of Pubic Affairs, Massachusetts Department of Revenue, 28 February 1985.

Remarks by Ira A. Jackson, Commissioner of the Massachusetts Department of Revenue at the National Conference of State Legislature, 26 July 1984.

William M. Parle and Mike W. Hirlinger, 'Evaluating the Use of Tax

204   *Sources and References*

Amnesty by State Governments', *Public Administration Review*, May/June 1986.
Hobart Rowan, *Washington Post*, 'Tax Amnesty: Mischievous Nonsense', March 1986.
Thomas K. McCraw, 'With the Consent of the Governed: SEC's Formative Years', *Journal of Policy Analysis and Management*, vol. 1, no. 3, 1982.
Niccolo Machiavelli, *The Prince*, in Bondanella and Musa, *The Portable Machiavelli*.

5   The Basic Problem of an Entrepreneurial System – Unemployment

Alfred Malabre, *Beyond Our Means* (New York: Random House, 1986).
J. M. Keynes, *The General Theory*.
Barry Bluestone and John Havens, 'The Microeconomic Impact of Macroeconomic Policy', *Journal of Post Keynesian Economics*, 8, 1986.

6   Unemployment Develops Because Money Doesn't Grow on Trees

Milton Friedman, 'The Role of Monetary Policy', *American Economic Review*, LVIII, 1968.
J. M. Keynes, *The General Theory*.

7   Controlling Inflation

Sidney Weintraub, 'An Incomes Policy to Stop Inflation', *Lloyds Bank Review*, 1970.
Henry Wallich and Sidney Weintraub, 'A Tax Based Incomes Policy', *Journal of Economic Issues*, 1971.
J. M. Keynes, *The General Theory*.

8   Policy for a Civilized Global Economy

John Maynard Keynes, *The Economic Consequences of the Peace* (London: Macmillan, 1919).
Rodney Clark, *The Japanese Company* (New Haven: Yale University Press, 1979).

9   A Final Summing Up

Robert B. Reich, *Tales of a New America* (New York: Times Books, 1987).

Index